FEMINISM, FOUCAULT, AND EMBODIED SUBJECTIVITY

SUNY series in Contemporary Continental Philosophy
Dennis J. Schmidt, editor

FEMINISM, FOUCAULT, AND EMBODIED SUBJECTIVITY

Margaret A. McLaren

State University of New York Press

Published by
State University of New York Press, Albany

Printed in the United States of America

For information, address State University of New York Press,
90 State Street, Suite 700, Albany, NY 12207

Production by Judith Block
Marketing by Anne Valentine

Library of Congress Cataloging-in-Publication Data

McLaren, Margaret A., 1960–
    Feminism, Foucault, and embodied subjectivity / Margaret A. McLaren.
       p. cm.—(SUNY series in contemporary continental philosophy)
    Includes bibliographical references and index.
    ISBN 0-7914-5513-0 (alk. paper)—ISBN 0-7914-5514-9 (pbk. : alk. paper)
       1. Foucault, Michel.   2. Feminist theory.   3. Subjectivity.   I. Title.
    II. Series.

HQ1190 .M387   2002
305.42—dc21
                                                                2002021087

10 9 8 7 6 5 4 3 2 1

▶●◀

CONTENTS

▶●◀

ACKNOWLEDGMENTS

This project has been informed, sustained and supported by a number of individuals, institutions and communities, and I am happy to have a chance to acknowledge some of them here. Amy Allen, Allison Leigh Brown and Kathryn Norsworthy read drafts of the entire manuscript. I appreciate the time and energy they spent reading my work and their criticisms and comments undoubtedly improved the final product. Sandra Lee Bartky, Ladelle McWhorter, Jana Sawicki, and Ed Royce read drafts of some of the chapters and provided much needed feedback, criticism and support. I also wish to thank Jane Bunker at State University of New York Press for her early interest in and support of this project, and Judith Block for her role in completing the process. Thanks also to Dennis Schmidt for including *Feminism, Foucault and Embodied Subjectivity* in his series on Contemporary Continental Philosophy.

Much of the research for this book was done in the Foucault archives in Paris during the summers of 1997, 1998, and 2000. This research was supported by Jack B. Critchfield faculty research grants awarded by Rollins College. Research for chapter six, also supported by a Critchfield grant, was done in Northwestern University's special collection on women, "Femina." I acknowledge with thanks the curator of Special Collections at Northwestern University Library, R. Russell Maylone, for allowing me access to the Femina collection. My research in Paris depended on the expertise and generosity of a number of individuals. I am very grateful to Madame Isabelle Seruzier, Bibliothécaire, and Father Michel Albaric, op., Directeur, of the Bibliothèque du Saulchoir for allowing me access to the Foucault archives under special circumstances in the summer of 1997. The Foucault archives have since moved to the Institut Mémoires de l'Édition Contemporaine, and I thank Madame Martine Ollion and the staff of the institute for their friendly and professional help. I also want to thank the French journalist, Frederic Joignot, for sharing stories of his personal acquaintance with Foucault through their work on the journal *Libération* and their involvement in political activism.

I had the opportunity to present several chapters of the book, in earlier and shorter versions, as conference papers. An earlier and shorter draft of chapter two was presented at the "History, Technology and Identity: After Foucault" conference. An earlier version of chapter four was presented at the Pacific APA, and I wish to thank my respondent, Eduardo Mendieta, for his comments and feedback on my paper. Parts of chapter five were presented at the Eastern Society for Women in Philosophy, the Pacific APA, the Central APA, SOFPHIA, the Philosophy, Interpretation and Culture conference, and the Truth, Translation and Interpretation conference in Perugia, Italy, and I thank the participants of those conferences for their comments and questions. I had the opportunity to present a much earlier version of chapter three at the Society for Phenomenology and Existential Philosophy, the Central APA, the Midwest Society for Women in Philosophy, the Eastern Society for Women in Philosophy, and the Mid-south Philosophy conference. I appreciate the encouragement and suggestions on this paper provided by: Ellen Armour, Sandra Lee Bartky, Harland Bloland, Susan Bordo, Ellen Feder, Marilyn Frye, Tamsin Lorraine, Ladelle McWhorter and Jana Sawicki. Chapter three is in part based on my article, "Foucault and the Subject of Feminism" in *Social Theory and Practice* 23, no. 1 (Spring 1997) and I would like to thank the editors of *Social Theory and Practice* for allowing me to reprint some of this material here. During the initial stages of this project I participated in a summer seminar on Foucault led by Thomas Flynn at the National Humanities Center (supported by a Jessie Ball du Pont grant). I learned a great deal, and I deeply appreciate Tom Flynn's encouragement and intellectual generosity. I also wish to thank the other seminar participants for the intellectual camaraderie and helpful discussions.

I have been fortunate over the years to belong to a number of feminist communities, both academic and non-academic. The Midwest Society for Women in Philosophy provided intellectual stimulation and support during my years as a graduate student at Northwestern University from the mid-1980s until the early 1990s. More recently, the community of SOFPHIA (Socialist Feminist Philosophers in Action) feeds my intellectual appetite and supports my political inclinations; it is a privilege to be a part of a group of philosophers who recognize the connection between theory and practice and are committed to social justice. I owe a huge debt to my feminist foremothers for the inspiration of their work and for their encouragement and support. Sandra Bartky, Nancy Fraser, Ann Ferguson, Marilyn Frye, Alison Jaggar, Maria Lugones, Sarah Hoagland, Marilyn Friedman, Claudia Card, Susan Bordo, Linda Alcoff, Jana Sawicki, Jane Mansbridge, Ladelle McWhorter, Diana Meyers, Iris Young and Linda Singer have all influenced and encouraged me in significant ways. I especially want to thank Sandra Bartky; her encouragement, support and friendship over the years have meant more to me than I can say.

I gratefully acknowledge the support of the administration of Rollins College and my departmental colleagues who allowed me to extend my sabbatical to complete this project. I have had the opportunity to present some of the ideas in this book at our departmental discussion group, and I thank my colleagues, Tom Cook, Hoyt Edge, Scott Rubarth, Yudit Greenberg, Clarence Hardy, Arnold Wettstein, and Karl Peters for their willingness to engage in conversation. Our departmental administrative assistant, Doris Lynn, expertly prepared the bibliography for me. I am grateful for her willingness to do so and for her unfailing good humor. Thanks also to Ann Steinecke for her expert preparation of the index.

I thank my friend Tanja Softić for generously allowing her artwork to be reproduced for the cover of this book. Kathryn Norsworthy, Chuck Weise, Susan Alterman, Stephen Kellert and Annette Fair reminded me to laugh and offered crucial emotional and moral support during the writing process. Marlene, Nutmeg and Mustafa provided unconditional love and constant companionship. Finally, I am enormously grateful to my partner, Chuck Weise, for his continual faith in my ability to complete this project and for his understanding, patience and support while I did so.

I dedicate this book to Julie Rolston (1960–1996) for the gift of her friendship and the inspiration of her life.

Chapter 1

▶•◀

THE FEMINISM AND FOUCAULT DEBATE: STAKES, ISSUES, POSITIONS

Feminists disagree about the usefulness of Foucault's work for feminist theory and practice. Some feminists advocate a Foucauldian feminism, while others argue that the underlying assumptions of feminism are antithetical to Foucault's theoretical framework.[1] The question about whether or not Foucault's work is useful for feminism is situated within the larger debate about the compatibility of a postmodern approach with an emancipatory, progressive politics.[2] Proponents of postmodernism see it as essential to a progressive politics. They claim that traditional notions of political unity, rights, and freedom carry normative implications that foreclose certain questions about who is included in the political process and that this foreclosure may result in systematic exclusion. Proponents of progressive politics, on the other hand, claim that postmodernism undermines the very possibility of a progressive, emancipatory politics mainly because of its rejection of normative concepts.[3] In an article entitled, "Why Poststructuralism is a Dead End for Progressive Thought," Barbara Epstein claims, "the underlying assumptions of poststructuralism conflict with the assumptions that are necessary for radical politics."[4] Epstein is particularly concerned with feminist poststructuralism, which she claims is amoral and "is a campaign against the basic structures of thought and language."[5] She is not alone in her condemnation of poststructuralism. Many feminists share her concern that postmodernist and poststructuralist approaches are at odds with progressive politics in general and feminist politics in particular. Somer Brodribb says, "Postmodernism exults female oblivion and disconnection; it has no model for the acquisition of knowledge, for making connections, for communication, or for becoming global, which feminism has done and will continue to do."[6] Most feminist attacks on

1

postmodernism include the work of Michel Foucault and some single him out as the prime representative of postmodern thought.

Feminists warn against using Foucault in no uncertain terms. Toril Moi, for instance, says, "the price for giving into his [Foucault's] powerful discourse is nothing less than the depoliticisation of feminism."[7] Likewise Nancy Hartsock says, "poststructuralist theories such as those put forward by Michel Foucault fail to provide a theory of power for women."[8] And Linda Alcoff cautions that "a wholesale appropriation of Foucault by feminist theorists is unwise."[9] Just what is so dangerous for feminists about appropriating Foucault's theories, one might ask. In general, feminist critics of Foucault fear that his rejection of norms undermines the possibility for feminism as an emancipatory political movement. His rejection of norms, combined with his view that truth and knowledge are always produced within a network of power relations, leads many to accuse Foucault of relativism and nihilism. They also worry that Foucault's account of subjectivity does not allow for agency and resistance. Critics think his rejection of a unified subject and his view that subjectivity is produced within power relations results in a concept of the subject wholly determined by social forces. A subject incapable of moral or political agency can only result in quietism, critics say. And finally some feminists specifically criticize Foucault's conception of power.[10] They claim that his conception of "power as everywhere" leaves no way to distinguish the difference in power between the dominators and the dominated. A conception of power that can account for the asymmetry of gendered power relations is essential for feminism. Given this set of reservations about Foucault's work, why should feminists be interested in Foucault at all?[11]

Ironically, those who argue that Foucault's ideas may be useful for feminism focus on many of the same issues as feminist critics of Foucault, such as his rejection of metanarratives and a normative framework, his notion of power, and his critique of traditional philosophical models of subjectivity. In their introduction to the anthology *Feminism and Foucault*, Irene Diamond and Lee Quinby identify four convergences between the theoretical projects of feminism and Foucault; both identify the body as a site of power, both view power as local, both emphasize discourse, and both criticize Western humanism's privileging of the masculine and its proclamation of universals.[12] Some feminist supporters of Foucault see his anti-humanism, his rejection of metanarratives and universal norms, and his challenge to the notion of a unified subjectivity as necessary steps toward a politics of diversity and inclusion. And many feminists find Foucault's conception of power as a network, and as operating through discourses, institutions, and practices beneficial for understanding the ways that power operates locally, on the body, and through particular practices.[13]

I shall argue that Foucault's ideas about the body, power, and subjectivity can provide important theoretical resources for feminists. I focus on the contribution that Foucault's notion of subjectivity as embodied and historically constituted can make to feminist theory. I address feminist criticisms of Foucault's ideas about norms, subjectivity, the body, identity, and power and demonstrate that useful ideas about social criticism, political practice, and subjectivity can be culled from Foucault's work. Feminist criticisms of Foucault have focused on his genealogical work. I offer a reading of Foucault that addresses these feminist criticisms of his genealogical work and I explore the relationship between his genealogical work and his later work. Feminists have paid relatively little attention to his later work. To remedy this, I pay special attention to Foucault's last books, *The Use of Pleasure: The History of Sexuality Volume Two* and *The Care of the Self: The History of Sexuality Volume Three*, as well as some essays and interviews. However, unlike other feminist interpretations of Foucault, I see this later work not as a departure from his earlier work or a return to Enlightenment values, but as a continuation of his earlier project to think through a new conception of subjectivity that is embodied and manifests itself through practices. These practices both enable and constrain, and freedom is conceptualized as situated within material, institutional, and disciplinary matrices. I conclude by showing that his idea of practices of the self can be applied to contemporary feminist practices.

At this point it may be helpful to provide a brief overview of Foucault's work. Foucault's work is usually divided into three phases: archaeological, genealogical, and ethical. These three approaches roughly correspond to a chronological order of early (archaeological), middle (genealogical), and late (ethical).[14] His archaeologies include *The Birth of the Clinic, The Order of Things,* and *The Archaeology of Knowledge*. Archaeology refers to the method employed by Foucault in these early works. The archaeological method attempts to reveal the unconscious limits of thought and knowledge; it investigates the structures that underlie thought and make particular types of knowledge possible at specific historical moments. These structures that underlie thought are discursive formations that govern what can be said. Foucault calls these discursive formations "epistemes." Archaeology examines how new disciplines emerge and how shifts in understanding occur. For instance, in *The Birth of the Clinic* Foucault traces the shift in the medical understanding of diseases from nosological, which relied on categories and essences, to pathological anatomy, which relied on specific, local signs and visible effects of the disease on the body. Archaeology as a method is static because it seeks simply to uncover the structures of rationality that make such shifts in understanding or the emergence of new disciplines possible. The primary object of analysis in the archaeologies is knowledge. Foucault's genealogical works are *Discipline and Punish* and *The History of Sexuality Volume One*. The genealogical method differs from the archaeological method in several ways; it is dynamic, rather than static; it is oriented toward practices as well as discourses; and it introduces a dimension of power. Genealogies are local and specific histories. But unlike traditional histories, genealogies focus on discontinuities and ruptures, rather than continuities. Because of this focus on discontinuity, Foucault's genealogies challenge the notion of progress. Foucault's genealogies reveal the contingency involved in the development of practices and institutions. For instance, in *Discipline and Punish* Foucault focuses on the changes in the way that criminals are punished; he traces the shift from execution to incarceration. The genealogical method raises questions about how current practices, institutions, and categories came to be the way they are. It is primarily in his genealogical work that Foucault develops his conception of power. His conception of power, which I discuss in detail in chapter two, departs significantly from a traditional notion of power. For Foucault, power is not unilateral; it is not negative; and it is not possessed by an individual or group of individuals. Power can be productive and positive; it is a relationship, not a thing. Although Foucault's genealogies trace the history of specific practices and institutions, many Foucault scholars think that power is the primary theme in the genealogies. As we shall see, Foucault's new conception of power has drawn criticism from some feminists, yet has been useful for other feminist analyses. Most feminist engagement with Foucault focuses on his genealogical, chronologically his middle, work.

Before his untimely death, Foucault's attention turned to ethical issues. Thus, the third phase of his work is usually referred to as his ethical work or his later work. The ethical work includes the second and third volumes of *The History of Sexuality* series, respectively, *The Use of Pleasure* and *The Care of the Self,* as well as some significant essays and interviews, notably "On the Genealogy of Ethics: An Overview of a Work in Progress," "The Subject and Power," "The Ethic of Care for the Self as a Practice of Freedom," and "Technologies of the Self."[15] It is widely acknowledged that Foucault's ethical work deals with subjectivity; specifically, it is in this later work that Foucault explores the active constitution of the subject, or what he calls the self's work on the self. Volumes two and three of *The History of Sexuality* examine ancient Greek and Roman sexual ethics and social practices. Foucault notes that the principle of the care of the self played a significant role in ancient Greek culture. Care of the self aimed at producing self-mastery and was achieved through a variety of social practices, including meditation, writing, physical activity, truth-telling, and self-examination. Foucault argues that it is through these practices or techniques of the self that ethical subjectivity was constituted in Antiquity. In his later work he also elaborates on his notion of power, making some helpful distinctions between power and domination. Some readers of Foucault believe that the three phases of Foucault's work that I have sketched above reveal inconsistencies in Foucault's ideas. Indeed, the three phases are not only chronologically distinct, but each is marked by a different method: archaeological, genealogical, and ethical and ostensibly a different object: knowledge, power, and the subject. Although Foucault himself cared little for consistency, believing that one should be transformed through writing, he offers some clues in later interviews about how to interpret his work. He suggests that his work deals with questions about knowledge, power, and the subject not sequentially, but simultaneously. He is, in fact, interested in the relation among them. Moreover, in spite of the different methods used, and the shifts in emphasis from knowledge, to power, to subject, subjectivity is the underlying theme in Foucault's work. His archaeological works challenge the subject of humanism. He shows that the rational unified subject cannot be presupposed, but that instead this idea of subjectivity is a result of particular linguistic practices and discursive formations. Foucault's genealogical works develop his notion of power in relation to subjectivity. He articulates the way that power operates on individuals through social norms, practices, and institutions. And in Foucault's ethical works his preoccupation with subjectivity is quite explicit; there he is concerned with the self's active self-constitution. Foucault himself states that the theme of subjectivity runs throughout his work, and that therefore his work ought not be seen as discontinuous or inconsistent. "My objective, instead, has been to create a history of the different modes by which, in our culture, human beings are made subjects. My work has dealt with three modes of objectification which transform human beings into subjects. . . . Thus it is not power, but the subject, which is the general theme of my research."[16] In this book I follow Foucault's suggestion, and I provide a reading of his work that focuses on the contributions that he makes to rethinking subjectivity.

So far I have been using the terms feminism and feminist in a very general way, divided only into feminist critics of Foucault and feminist advocates of Foucault. But as anyone familiar with feminism knows, feminism is a theoretical orientation that includes a wide range of positions and views. Moreover, there are a variety of ways to categorize different feminist approaches. Nonetheless, all feminist theories are political. One author puts it this way: "feminist theory is not one, but many, theories or perspectives and each feminist theory or perspective attempts to describe women's oppression, to explain its causes and consequences, and to prescribe strategies for women's liberation."[17] All feminist theories, then, begin with women's oppression or subordination, and all aim to liberate women from their subordination. Because most feminists who criticize Foucault do so on the basis of what they see as the political implications of his theory, my focus here is on explicitly political feminist theories. A second reason for this focus is that I am interested in the reception of Foucault by North American feminists. Part of what is at stake in debates about the usefulness of Foucault or postmodernism more generally for feminist theory is the direction of feminist theory itself. Some feminists claim that postmodern approaches are merely solipsistic academic exercises in elitist language that divorce theory from practice and have little to do with women's everyday struggles in the real world. Part of what I hope to do in this book is to demonstrate some overlaps in the concerns and approaches of feminists and Foucault and to show that there are practical applications of Foucault's ideas that promote feminist aims. In order to help sort out the issues and stakes in the Foucault/feminism debate I begin by laying out some important feminist positions. I briefly explicate the assumptions and main points of liberal feminism, radical feminism, Marxist feminism, socialist feminism, multicultural feminism, and global feminism.[18] I also briefly discuss the feminist critical social theory approach and the postmodern feminist approach.

Liberal feminism is characterized by its focus on equality. Men and women are thought to have the same rational capacities. On the basis of this, liberal feminists argue that men and women should be treated equally. If women are given the same educational, occupational, and political opportunities as men, the argument goes, they will realize their true potential and no longer be subordinate to men. Associated with Mary Wollstonecraft in the eighteenth century and John Stuart Mill and Harriet Taylor Mill in the nineteenth century, liberal feminism has a long history. Liberal feminism places great importance on rationality, autonomy, and choice. Liberal feminists view reason or rationality as the quintessential characteristic that is fundamental for moral and political autonomy. Women's exclusion from the public sphere, however, may inhibit their capacity to fully develop and exercise their rationality. So, liberal feminists advocate full political participation and legal equality for women. They believe that women's full inclusion in public life will result in equality between men and women. Like traditional liberal political theory, liberal feminism relies on the notion of rights. Liberal feminists advocate working within existing legal, political, and economic institutions. In order to achieve parity for women they appeal to notions such as autonomy, rights, freedom, justice, and equality. One contemporary proponent of liberal feminism is Martha Nussbaum. She explicitly contrasts the liberal feminist position with a view she attributes to Foucault.[19] Nussbaum criticizes French intellectuals for their anemic politics, blaming them for the idea that seditious speech equals political resistance. She contrasts their view to the liberal feminist view that large-scale political and social change will be achieved through the law and mass political movements. She claims that interpretations of Foucault's ideas have led to "the fatalistic idea that we are prisoners of an all-enveloping structure of power, and that real-life reform movements usually end up serving power in new and insidious ways."[20] Nussbaum attacks Judith Butler's Foucauldian feminism; she claims that young North American feminists influenced by Butler retreat from politics into quietism. She worries that the ideas of French intellectuals undermine what she calls "old style feminist politics" and its concern with material reality. She thinks that the view of resistance held by French intellectuals is personal and private, and does not promote legal, institutional, or material change. She faults Butler, and by extension Foucault, for holding a "narrow vision of the possibilities for change."[21] Nussbaum believes this narrow vision results in pessimism and passivity. Like other feminist critics, she focuses on Foucault's view of power, his notion of the subject, and his rejection of norms.

It is not surprising given Foucault's criticism of the humanistic values that liberalism embodies that liberal feminists would find his work antithetical to their project. Foucault's rejection of universal norms, his suspicion about teleological conceptions of history that imply progress, his rejection of a notion of subjectivity as unified consciousness, and his rejection of the traditional liberal conception of power contradict fundamental tenets of liberalism. In spite of his indictment of humanism and liberalism Foucault recognizes the need for a variety of political practices and strategies, including appeals to human rights and freedom. As I shall demonstrate, Foucault advocates political engagement aimed at decreasing domination and increasing freedom and he endorses a variety of political strategies.

Radical feminism focuses on women's difference from men. Radical feminists note that there are significant and irreducible biological differences between men and women.[22] First and foremost is the difference in reproductive capacity; women can bear children, whereas men cannot. While early radical feminists see women's capacity to bear children as a possible impediment to their full liberation, later radical feminists celebrate women's reproductive capacity.[23] Radical feminists associate women's difference from men with more than simply the capacity to bear children; radical feminists focus on the body and issues of sexuality, violence against women, and women's health, as well as reproduction. Radical feminists advocate the development of institutions that meet the needs of women. It was largely due to the influence of radical feminism in the United States in the late 1960s and early 1970s that institutions such as rape crisis centers, battered women's shelters, and women's health centers were founded. Additionally, radical feminists began educational campaigns and protest movements, for instance, against pornography.[24] Unlike liberal feminists, radical feminists think that existing institutions must be drastically altered, and that new institutions need to be developed as well, in order for women to overcome their subordination.

In addition to their focus on the body, radical feminists emphasize the importance of language. Of course, nonsexist language goes some way toward promoting parity between women and men, as even liberal feminists would agree. But radical feminists go further; they examine the limits of language for articulating women's experience. Some claim that language itself is phallocentric, a male-constructed system representing men's experience. Thus, to represent women's experience, new words, and perhaps a whole new language, are necessary. Through new words and language women can name their experience. Naming identifies and makes concrete experiences that were not represented in mainstream culture.[25] Radical feminists recognize the power of language, and urge feminists to reclaim and revalue words that have derogatory connotations and devalue women, such as spinster, witch, and hag.[26] They believe that language not only describes, but also creates, reality. Words and images are potent transmitters of social and cultural values. Radical feminists believe that all existing institutions, political, legal, economic, social, cultural, and medical, need to be radically transformed. They think that advocating equality between men and women on the basis of sameness will continue to systematically disadvantage women because there are fundamental differences between men and women.[27] Radical feminists think that patriarchal power is not merely located in political and legal institutions. Some have written herstories showing how men have usurped women's power, for instance, through the medicalization of birth.[28] Men's power over women is not confined to the sphere of politics, law, and the economy, but permeates every aspect of life, including knowledge construction. Patriarchy, the systematic domination of women by men, is the fundamental characteristic of social organization for radical feminism. Radical feminists do believe, like liberal feminists, that women need to have equal access to resources and opportunities in order to overcome their subordination. However, equal access is not enough; the institutions themselves must be changed to account for women's perspectives and experiences. And institutions that specifically serve women's needs must be developed and maintained. For radical feminists the sex/gender system is the fundamental cause of women's oppression.

Radical feminists, too, see their concerns and goals as opposed to a postmodern, poststructuralist, or deconstructionist approach. Again the reasons for this are multiple; postmodern attempts to deconstruct categories conflict with the radical feminist dependence upon sex and gender as fundamental categories of oppression. And postmodern challenges to identity and unity threaten to undermine the concept of woman upon which radical feminism relies. This deconstructive approach fails to provide any direction for the positive changes that radical feminists seek. Finally, radical feminists see postmodern approaches as theoretical abstractions removed from the real-life, everyday struggles of women. According to Somer Brodribb, who offers an extended critique of postmodernism from a radical feminist position, "Foucault's theories of discourse and his theories of power both originate in a notion of self-constructing structures and a conception of the social which has no notion of the individual."[29] In spite of radical feminist criticisms of postmodernism, I show that there is some overlap between the concerns of radical feminists and Foucault. Specifically, both reject traditional liberal conceptions of power, both endorse an expanded definition of the political, both focus on material institutions and practices, and both recognize the power of language and representation to shape reality.

Marxist feminists view capitalism rather than patriarchy as the fundamental cause of women's oppression. Adopting the traditional Marxist view that society is structured as a class system, some Marxist feminists view women as a "sex-class." However, there is disagreement within this tradition about how to understand women's position. Because women are distributed throughout economic and social classes (often by virtue of their connection to men), some have argued that it is inaccurate to characterize women as a class and that women are better thought of as an oppressed sex.[30] Marxist feminists also question the patriarchal system of marriage that views women as male property. Traditional Marxists associate women's oppression with the capitalist system, increasing industrialization, and the rise of private property. Marxist feminists agree with radical feminists that women are subordinate to men. But they attribute this to the capitalist system of private property, rather than to the sex/gender system itself. For Marxist feminists class oppression is the primary form of oppression; "sexism, like racism, has its roots in the private property system."[31]

Feminist standpoint theory emerged out of Marxist feminism. Nancy Hartsock developed this view in her classic article, "Feminist Standpoint Theory."[32] Feminist standpoint theory draws on Marx's notion that the oppressed class functions both within the rules of the oppressor class and within the parameters of the oppressed class and therefore develops a heightened consciousness. Because the oppressed class understands their situation as oppressed, and understands the system as exploitative, they are in a privileged position with respect to knowing the reality of the situation. This epistemic privilege accrues to the oppressed class or marginalized group by virtue of their oppression. Nancy Hartsock adapts this idea of epistemic privilege to women as an oppressed group, and develops the idea of a feminist standpoint. She says, "like the lives of the proletarians according to Marxian theory, women's lives make available a particular and privileged vantage point on male supremacy, a vantage point which can ground a powerful critique of the phallocratic institutions and ideology which constitute the capitalist form of patriarchy."[33] Using Marx's category of labor and basing the oppression of women on the sexual division of labor, Hartsock provides a compelling argument for feminist standpoint theory. However, it is precisely this notion of a unified standpoint and women as a unified group that postmodern feminism challenges.

Marxist feminism predominated in the United States in the late 1960s. Like radical feminists, Marxist feminists believed that traditional institutions needed to be radically restructured. The institution most in need of change was, of course, the economy. In addition to the issue of transforming the economy in general, Marxist feminists spearheaded the "Housework for Wages" campaign, highlighting the fact that the economy depends upon women's unpaid domestic labor.

Marxist feminism subsumes questions about women and sexual oppression under a critique of capitalism and economic oppression.

Foucault explicitly criticizes Marxism for its singular focus on the economy. Moreover, he rejects the notion of historical progress underlying Marx's theory. Marxist feminists see Foucault's focus on the local, specific, and concrete as inadequate for explaining class oppression and the subordination of women. Hartsock criticizes Foucault's notion of power as unable to account for pervasive, systematic asymmetries of power. But there are some points of overlap between the concerns of Marxist feminists and Foucault. In spite of Foucault's criticisms of Marxism, he integrates issues of class and economic concerns into his historical analyses. I argue that his notion of power can account for systematic asymmetry, and consequently structural oppression. And Foucault's commitment to anti-domination and social change are apparent in his genealogical work; this commitment is shared by Marxist feminists.

Socialist feminists integrate the Marxist feminist focus on the economy with the radical feminist focus on sex.[34] They do not subsume sex oppression under capitalism like Marxist feminists do. Nor do socialist feminists privilege sex and gender to the exclusion of economic concerns. Socialist feminists believe that both Marxist and feminist analyses are necessary to overcome women's oppression. In Heidi Hartmann's classic article, "The Unhappy Marriage of Marxism and Feminism: Towards A More Progressive Union," she says, ". . . the categories of Marxism are sex-blind. Only a specifically feminist analysis reveals the systemic character of relations between men and women. Yet feminist analysis by itself is inadequate because it has been blind to history and insufficiently materialist."[35] Socialist feminists focus on the material base of social relations and the ways that it creates and maintains patriarchy. Like radical feminists, socialist feminists are concerned with issues of sexuality and the body, such as reproductive issues and issues regarding violence against women. But they see these issues, and patriarchy itself, entwined with economic issues. Furthermore, socialist feminists claim that women's liberation is an unrealizable goal in a capitalist society because capitalism is structured around maintaining specific sex roles, a traditional definition of the family, and women's unpaid domestic and reproductive labor. Socialist feminists think that traditional economic and social institutions need to be transformed, e.g., the family and the capitalist economic system. They view these economic and social institutions as the basis for the patriarchal system. In fact, socialist feminists view the sexual division of labor as helping to create and maintain gender, by perpetuating a gendered division of labor. As Hartmann says, "The strict division of labor by sex, a social invention common to all known societies, creates two very separate genders and a need for men and women to get together for economic reasons."[36] The sexual division of labor takes place both within the home and in the public sector. In the domestic sphere the sexual division of labor includes reproductive work such as bearing and rearing children and other household tasks, such as shopping, cooking, and cleaning. In the public sphere, the sexual division of labor includes divisions along traditional gender lines, such as more men in manual labor jobs that require heavy lifting, and more women in the service sector and in secretarial office work, so-called pink collar jobs. The sexual division of labor creates and reinforces gender differences. These gender differences are perpetuated through a multitude of social relations—heterosexual marriage; traditional family arrangements, including women as primary caretakers of children; women's economic dependence on men; and the state. Socialist feminism calls for a change in the sexual division of labor and the social relations supported by such a division. They urge feminists to engage in a double assault on both capitalism and patriarchy.[37] Socialist feminism's integrative approach improves upon the singular focus of both radical feminism and Marxist feminism. However, insufficient attention is paid to other systematic oppressions, such as those based on ethnicity, culture, race, and sexual orientation.[38]

Socialist feminists echo the concerns of Marxist feminists with respect to Foucault's ideas. They argue that his focus on local institutions inhibits large-scale structural analysis. Socialist feminists are also concerned that Foucault's notion of power does not account for systematic inequalities, such as class inequality or gender inequality. And they claim that Foucault's conception of the subject does not allow for agency or resistance. I draw out the connection between structural change and individual change that is implicit in Foucault's work. I demonstrate that far from being in opposition, large-scale social change and individual transformation rely on one another. Thus, rather than undermining socialist feminism Foucault's ideas can complement and enhance a socialist feminist position.

A feminist critical theory approach has some similarities to a socialist feminist approach; they both rely on a Marxist, historical materialist framework. Critical social theory extends and adapts Marxist theory to account for cultural and technological innovations. The best-known contemporary proponent of critical social theory is Jürgen Habermas. Like Habermas, feminist critical social theorists examine a wide range of social institutions including, but not limited to, economic institutions. Economic, political, legal, educational, and other social institutions structure our individual and collective lives. Feminist critical social theorists add a gender analysis to critical social theory, raising questions about women's place in these social institutions. Issues of women's status, as well as the sexual division of labor, and issues of family structure and responsibilities for child care are highlighted by feminist critical theorists. They focus on institutional change and reform, appealing to notions of justice, freedom, and rights. Similarly to the other feminist positions discussed thus far, feminist critical social theorists view the postmodern position as a threat to feminism. Seyla Benhabib, a contemporary feminist critical social theorist, warns, "The postmodernist position(s) thought through to their conclusions may eliminate not only the specificity of feminist theory but place in question the very emancipatory ideals of the women's movements altogether."[39] Benhabib credits postmodernism for focusing on the excluded and marginal, noting that Foucault's genealogies are histories of the disenfranchised. She also notes that Foucault's notions of surveillance and discipline illuminate some unsavory aspects of contemporary political life. However, Benhabib shares the view of other feminist critics of Foucault that his work leaves little room for agency and resistance. She says, "for Michel Foucault there is no history of the victims but only a history of the construction of victimization . . . for Foucault every act of resistance is but another manifestation of an omnipresent discourse–power complex. . . ."[40] Although feminist critical social theorists acknowledge that Foucault's concepts of power, discipline, and surveillance aptly describe some aspects of contemporary society, they are hesitant to endorse postmodernism or to embrace Foucault's ideas more fully.

Multicultural feminism attempts to address the neglect of race, ethnicity, and culture evident in previous feminist approaches. Although some of these other approaches can accommodate these issues, multicultural feminism focuses on issues of race, culture and ethnicity. Like socialist feminism, multicultural feminism is an integrative approach that analyzes the ways in which oppression is interactive and specific, rather than additive. Gender identity is formed within the context of specific racial, cultural, and ethnic identities. Multicultural feminists point out the ways that by ignoring or minimizing the question of race other feminist approaches assume a white perspective. Multicultural feminists urge white feminists to recognize the bias in mainstream feminist theorizing, and to prioritize issues of race, ethnicity, and culture. Arguing that oppressions are interlocking and interactive rather than separate and discrete, multicultural feminists articulate the ways that gender, sexual orientation, and class are mediated by race, ethnicity, and culture. The approach of multicultural feminists takes into account various forms of oppression and the specificity of women's experience. Multicultural feminism examines the structural aspect of oppressions and the particularity of identity; it challenges the implicit norms and monistic models of identity implicit in earlier feminist theories.

Some multicultural feminists find postmodern theory useful for challenging universal norms and applaud it for its focus on difference rather than sameness. They find that the emphasis on local practices and subjugated knowledges gives voice to the marginalized and less powerful. This encourages attention to the experiences and lives of women of color who have been marginalized not only in mainstream society, but also within feminism itself. Yet some feminists concerned with issues of race question the relevance of postmodern theory and its ability to deal with the concrete, material realities of race and sex oppression. In her classic article, "The Race for Theory," Barbara Christian expresses her reservations about postmodern literary criticism. "My fear is that when theory is not rooted in practice, it becomes prescriptive, exclusive, elitist."[41] Wary of theory that universalizes and overlooks particularity, multicultural feminists believe that theory must be rooted in practice and should account for the diverse experiences of women of different racial, ethnic, cultural, and class backgrounds.

Global feminism extends feminist analyses beyond their often limited focus on industrialized countries in the Western world. Global feminism aims to include the issues of women worldwide. A global feminist perspective includes an analysis of the structural oppressions based on class, gender, sexual orientation, race, and ethnicity mentioned earlier, but recognizes the historical and social realities of colonialism and imperialism. A postcolonial or imperialist perspective examines the impact of transnational capital and its effect on both the economy and culture, especially on so-called "developing countries."[42] The broader perspective of global feminism includes issues such as religion and nationality. A global feminist view takes into account both interconnections and the diversity of women's subordination. Within global feminism there are divergent approaches to analyzing women's subordination. Some global feminists who explore issues of transnational capital, cultural imperialism, representation, and identity have found postmodern theory useful. Other global feminists who take an empirical approach or who are concerned with universal rights object to the relativistic stance associated with postmodernism.

Each of the feminist approaches discussed so far has an explicitly political orientation. The primary concern is to overcome women's subordination. In spite of the various, and sometimes conflicting, assumptions of the feminist positions I have discussed, there are commonalities among them. First, because feminism is a social and political movement devoted to overcoming women's subordination, feminist theory should provide resources for social and political change. These resources can include tools for critical analysis, and positive programs for change. Implicit in this first commitment are two other important feminist commitments; that there should be a relationship between theory and practice and that theory needs to be relevant to experience. Both of these criteria are necessary for feminist theory to effect social and political change; it must be relevant to the actual, concrete lives of real women. It should be able both to inform and reflect our experience. Correlatively, feminist theory should arise from practice rather than being imposed on it. When feminist theory fails to take into account material practices and the concrete lives of women, it risks becoming an empty exercise in elitist language. Finally, feminism is committed to inclusiveness, equality, and democracy.

Thus, feminist theory should be accessible to as many women as possible. Although there are important differences among the liberal, radical, Marxist, socialist, critical social theorist, multicultural, and global feminist positions, all recognize the structural aspect of oppression, and each successive approach integrates additional axes of oppression resulting in a complex and variegated approach for understanding the impact of oppression on women's lives in all their diversity and complexity. The last two approaches, multicultural and global feminism, challenge some implicit normative assumptions about who is included in the scope of feminist theorizing.

Postmodern feminism raises similar issues about the normative function of a singular, unified concept of identity, and who is included in the scope of feminist theorizing.[43] Although often criticized for being apolitical, some postmodern feminists claim that an approach that challenges traditional norms and unified models of identity is essential for a progressive politics. The schism between postmodern feminists, many of whom draw extensively on the work of Michel Foucault, and the explicitly political feminist approaches sketched out above is the issue that underlies the rest of this book. Feminist critics of Foucault staunchly deny that his work can be useful for emancipatory politics, including feminist politics. Despite this dismissal, some feminists who use or apply Foucault for feminist purposes find that his work can be politically useful. My aim is to explore these tensions among feminists, and between feminists and Foucault. I argue that Foucault's work provides resources to articulate a notion of subjectivity that is embodied, and constituted historically and through social relations; and that this embodied, social self is capable of moral and political agency.[44] I pay particular attention to Foucault's genealogical works and his later work on ethics and the self. The rest of this chapter provides an overview of the feminist debate about Foucault.

There is no agreement among feminists about the usefulness of Foucault's work for feminist theory and practice. I will divide feminist engagement with Foucault into roughly four groups: staunch critics; moderate critics; those who use, extend or apply aspects of Foucault's project but with serious reservations about his overall project; and Foucauldian feminists who take up central aspects of Foucault's work or apply a Foucauldian framework with only minor reservations or criticisms.[45] Staunch critics take Foucault to task on at least one aspect of his work, for instance, his conception of power, his notion of subjectivity, or his lack of a normative framework. They argue that Foucault and feminism are antithetical and caution feminists against using Foucault. Moderate critics think that one or more aspects of Foucault's work may be useful for feminism, but that other aspects are at odds with the aims of feminism. Extenders draw on Foucault's work and apply it to women's experience. This has been especially useful to illuminate bodily aspects of women's oppression using Foucault's concepts of disciplines, biopower,

power, and social norms. Finally, feminist Foucauldians adopt Foucault's major ideas for feminist purposes or to apply to feminist issues.

Feminist critics of Foucault, both staunch and moderate, tend to focus on his conception of the subject, his rejection of norms, and his notion of power. I discuss feminist objections to Foucault's lack of a normative framework in chapter 2, and explicate his notion of power in order to try to remedy a widespread mis-reading of it. In chapter 3, I address feminist concerns with Foucault's notion of the subject. Some feminists accuse Foucault of abolishing the subject, while oth-ers charge that he offers only a passive, overdetermined subject incapable of moral or political agency. I demonstrate that Foucault rejects a specific notion of the sub-ject, that of Modern philosophy and that he offers instead an understanding of the subject as socially and historically constituted and embodied. I counter critics' claims that the subject in Foucault's later works is individualistic and merely aes-thetic. I argue that the social, relational, embodied subject embedded in specific cultural and institutional practices found in Foucault's work is compatible with feminist aims.

In chapter 4, I explicate Foucault's notion of the body. Feminists have ac-cused Foucault of androcentrism because he pays no attention to gender-specific disciplinary practices or the impact sexual difference might have on formulating a theory of the body. In spite of Foucault's androcentrism, feminists have success-fully extended Foucault's work to illuminate specifically feminine disciplinary practices. I also address the criticism that Foucault implicitly relies on a natural body. I argue that Foucault's notion of the body is multilayered. He does not deny the materiality of the body. But neither does the body's materiality exist outside a disciplinary framework—in terms of both knowledge and practices. The under-standings of our bodies available to us are shaped by these disciplinary grids and interpretative frameworks. Moreover, as embodied selves we are situated in the world in relation to a variety of social practices that shape not only our under-standings of our bodies, but the materiality of our bodies.

In chapter 5, I demonstrate how normative categories can operate in ways that limit and exclude. First, I discuss this with respect to the identity politics de-bate in feminism. Then I demonstrate how normative categories operate at the level of the body by examining historical and contemporary treatment of inter-sexed persons. Finally, I examine the issue of bisexuality to show how normative categories are maintained by a system of social norms that regulate sex and sexual orientation. In chapter 6, I discuss Foucault's ethical works focusing on the tech-niques of the self. These techniques of the self aim at maintaining and transform-ing identity. For Foucault, practices of the self are characterized by an articulation, either through writing, speech, or bodily practices. Practices of the self are always done with reference to a particular goal. I suggest that consciousness-raising can be viewed as a feminist practice of the self. I discuss the way that consciousness-raising as a practice of the self promotes both individual and collective transformation. I suggest that Foucault's conception of social norms articulates an important mediating structure between individual identity and social, political, and legal institutions. This link between individual identity and social institutions means that self-transformation is not simply an individual personal goal, but must involve structural social and political change. This overlap of the ethical and the political and the conception of the self as embodied and socially constituted are, I believe, important theoretical resources for contemporary feminism.

At the time of this writing, there are three anthologies that deal with the relationship between feminism and Foucault.[46] No single male philosopher since Marx has gained this much attention from feminists. There was no question about the political usefulness of Marx, although feminists worried about the subordination of the woman question to the issue of class. The stakes for feminist engagement with Foucault are even higher. The central question for feminists is whether Foucault undermines the possibility of an emancipatory politics altogether. Feminist passions run deep about both the promises and the perils of Foucault's work. The anthologies that explore the relationship between feminism and Foucault provide a mapping of the terrain of this debate. Although all three explore the relationship between Foucault and feminism, the subtitles are revealing. The earliest collection, *Feminism and Foucault: Reflections on Resistance,* is the most positive about the contribution that Foucault's work can make to feminist theory. *Up Against Foucault: Explorations of Some Tensions Between Foucault and Feminism* emphasizes the tensions between the two. The third collection, *Feminist Interpretations of Michel Foucault,* is split between negative and positive evaluations. It begins with two influential critiques of Foucault, by Nancy Hartsock and Nancy Fraser. While these critiques set the tone for much of the feminist reception of Foucault, the rest of the essays explore some of the positive contributions that Foucault can make to feminist theory, as well as the limitations of applying Foucault's ideas to feminism. Each volume as a whole provides a different perspective on the question of the relationship between Foucault's work and feminism.

Sorting out the relationship between feminism and Foucault is no easy task. Feminists have revolutionized traditional philosophical conceptions of knowledge and the self. Moreover, they have challenged long-standing distinctions between mind/body, culture/nature, and public/private. Foucault, too, challenges many traditional philosophical ideas, especially his idea of power-knowledge, his conception of the self, and his challenge to universal norms. In spite of their common challenge to many of the central ideas in traditional philosophy, Foucault and feminism exist in uneasy tension at best. While some aspects of feminism challenge traditional philosophical ideas, other aspects of feminism or different feminist approaches adopt traditional philosophical ideas. Thus, Foucault serves as a challenge to these feminist positions.[47] Caroline Ramazanoglu notes this complex relationship between feminism and Foucault: "Foucault's ideas on power, knowledge, the self and sexuality, for example, are not compatible with feminist ideas in any simple way, and suggest considerable problems in feminist uses of these terms." Nonetheless, she continues, "Feminism cannot afford to ignore Foucault, because the problems he addresses and the criticisms he makes of existing theories and their political consequences identify problems in and for feminism."[48] Indeed, Foucault's work has implications for a range of topics important to feminists, including issues of methodology, methods of historical investigation, and conceptions of the body, knowledge, power, identity, sexuality, subjectivity, ethics, and politics. Echoing Ramazanoglu's claim that feminists cannot afford to ignore Foucault, Susan Hekman says, "Neither his detractors nor his defenders question that Foucault's perspective provides a challenge for feminism."[49]

Not only does Foucault present a challenge for feminism in terms of redefining central philosophical ideas, but feminism presents a challenge for Foucault. His almost total neglect of gender, women's issues, feminism, and sexual specificity leads some to question the relevance of his work for feminists. Feminists accuse Foucault of being gender-blind and androcentric. Surprisingly, for all his talk about sexuality, Foucault neglects the issue of sexual difference. He is charged with gender-blindness because even in his discussion of bodies he does not make distinctions between male and female bodies or between feminine and masculine disciplinary practices. He is accused of androcentrism because when he does get specific about sexual difference, for instance, in his discussion of the formation of the ethical subject, he focuses on the male subject. In spite of his undeniable androcentrism, I argue that Foucault's work provides important theoretical resources for feminism.

One way to judge whether or not a theory or theorist is useful for feminism is to assess it in terms of feminism's core commitments discussed earlier: (1) resources for political and social change to end the subordination of women, (2) relationship between theory and practice, (3) relevance to experience, and (4) accessibility. In the following pages I hope to provide an accessible account of Foucault's work, and to demonstrate its practical relevance. I contend that Foucault provides a notion of the subject that is useful to feminists, and that his account of social norms provides an important link between individual experience and social change.

Chapter 2

▶•◀

FOUCAULT, FEMINISM, AND NORMS

Foucault has been famously criticized for his lack of a normative framework, and thus his lack of any grounding for an emancipatory or liberatory politics.[1] Yet in Foucault's work, notions of freedom, or at the very least antidomination, figure prominently. What are we to make of this? Is it simply conceptual incoherence as some have claimed? Does Foucault rely on Enlightenment ideals such as unified subjectivity, autonomy, and freedom in spite of his explicit rejection of these ideals? Or should Foucault's concern with antidomination prompt closer scrutiny?

Foucault's apparent lack of a normative framework has been particularly problematic for feminists, who are committed to the emancipatory political project of ending women's oppression.[2] As we have seen in chapter 1, there is no agreement among feminists about the usefulness of Foucault's work. This is particularly true with regard to its potential for politics. There are a variety of feminist positions, but all agree that women have been subordinate to men, and that the primary aim of feminism is to overcome this subordination. Additionally, there is widespread agreement that feminism is committed to overcoming oppression based on class, race, ethnicity, sexual orientation, and ability, as well as gender. Feminism is an emancipatory political movement. Thus, feminist theorists have a particular stake in supporting theories that can contribute to the emancipation of women and challenging those that do not. The emancipatory struggle for women's liberation shares some features with other contemporary social justice movements, such as the effort to abolish racial discrimination, and the struggle to achieve civil rights for lesbians and gays; all invoke notions of freedom, rights, autonomy, justice, and truth. These struggles for social justice appeal to normative ideals based on the idea that all human beings deserve respect, freedom, and fair and equal treatment. Critics of Foucault claim that his ideas about power, truth, and subjectivity undermine the possibility of appealing to normative ideals. Hence, they claim that Foucault's work is not merely politically useless, but that it is downright dangerous. It is not only feminist critics who advise that Foucault's work cannot provide a grounding for emancipatory politics because of its lack of a normative framework. The debate about the necessity of normative notions to ground social and political critique is situated within the broader question about the political utility of a postmodern perspective.

POSTMODERNISM AND POLITICS

Postmodernism challenges many of the Enlightenment ideals associated with modernity. These Enlightenment ideals include a belief in the ability of rational scientific thought to discover truth, the conception of a unified, rational subject aware of his own thought processes, and the idea that freedom requires subjects to be governed by reason and to be free from external constraints. Related to these central ideals are the belief in progress, the idea of human rights, and the notion of autonomy. Enlightenment ideals provided an alternative to religious superstition, unchecked irrationality, tyrannical sovereigns, and provincial traditionalism. At the time they emerged, Enlightenment ideals clearly represented an advance beyond traditional understandings. Humanism took the place of the notions of a divinely ordered cosmos, the divine right of kings, and religious values. For humanism, man is the measure of all things and the importance of religion was eclipsed by rational, scientific inquiry. The values implicit in humanism that emerged during the Enlightenment seemed necessary and positive. After all, recognizing the centrality of humanity helped to undermine social and political hierarchy and foster equality among human beings. But it is this idea of man and the attendant conceptions of rationality, rights, freedom, and equality that postmodernists question. "Who is excluded from this idea of the rational man?" they ask, "And how does this affect the correlative notions of autonomy, rights, freedom, and equality?" Postmodern theorists claim that the Enlightenment humanist ideal of the rational man is based on the exclusion of those who are not viewed as rational, for instance, madmen or, as feminists have duly noted, women. Foucault's *Madness and Civilization* looks at historical changes in the treatment of the mad, and the way that madness and irrationality became increasingly stigmatized and defined as other. Postmodern theorists argue that because the ideal of Enlightenment rationality is constituted through the systematic exclusion of otherness, it is hopelessly flawed as a universal ideal.

The ideal of rationality serves as a basis for equality because human beings are thought to be equal and deserving of respect insofar as they are rational. Notions of equality, rights, freedom, and autonomy are predicated on rationality in the Enlightenment view. Lurking in the background is the assumption that these ideas are supported by a value-neutral framework of objective truths about human nature. Feminist theorist Jane Flax identifies the following ideas as derived from the Enlightenment: the belief in a stable, coherent self; the belief that reason is transcendental and universal and can provide an objective, reliable, and universal foundation for knowledge and that this knowledge will be true.[3] Flax points out that there are complex connections among reason, autonomy, and freedom, as well as among truth, knowledge, and power. As I have noted above, the notion of reason or rationality grounds the ideas of equality, rights, freedom, and autonomy because human beings are considered free and autonomous insofar as their choices and actions are governed by reason. Furthermore, it is assumed that reason legitimates truth and knowledge claims, and that truth and knowledge are neutral, that is, independent of power. Thus, the critique of rationality as substantively flawed because of its constitutive exclusion of otherness extends to ideas of equality, rights, freedom, autonomy, and truth. These Enlightenment notions are generally associated with humanism. But while Foucault explicitly rejects humanism, his relationship to the Enlightenment is ambivalent. Foucault rejects what he calls "anthropological universals," that is, truth claims about man or human nature that are ahistorical or claim universality. Ahistorical, universal claims are typical in both humanism and Enlightenment thinking. But in his later work, Foucault identified a second aspect of Enlightenment thinking that he calls critique; he endorses this critical impulse of the Enlightenment. Most critics, however, focus on Foucault's critique of humanism and the ideals it shares with the Enlightenment. Contemporary social and political theorists such as Jürgen Habermas, Charles Taylor, and Michael Walzer agree with feminist critics of Foucault who claim that Foucault's work undermines politics and inhibits the possibility of social and political change.[4] Their criticisms converge around the issue of a lack of a normative framework in Foucault's work, and his rejection of such normative ideals as freedom, justice, and autonomy. As mentioned earlier, these normative ideals are grounded in a conception of value-neutral objective truth. If there is no truth of the matter, how can we tell right from wrong; how can we tell if things are getting better or worse? Typically, the ideas of objective truth and knowledge serve as the ground for value judgments of right and wrong. Foucault's well-known concept of power-knowledge challenges this normative framework of objective truth. In contrast to the Enlightenment idea that truth and knowledge stand outside of power and political and social relations, Foucault insists that truth is produced by individuals occupying specific social positions. According to Foucault, "truth isn't outside power, or lacking in power . . . [t]ruth is a thing of this world . . . [e]ach society has its regime of truth."[5] The relationship between truth and power is circular; truth is produced and sustained by power, and in turn, truth produces and extends effects of power. Foucault's genealogies demonstrate this circular relationship between truth and power. He claims that knowledge and power relations are inseparable; "power produces knowledge . . . power and knowledge directly imply one another . . . there is no power relation without the correlative constitution of a field of knowledge, nor any knowledge that does not presuppose and constitute at the same time power relations."[6] He shows how social scientific knowledge about sexuality or rehabilitation are both produced by, and result in, new forms of power. The connection between knowledge and power is exemplified in the increased medical and psychological knowledge about sexuality and the corresponding increase in the social control of sexuality. Foucault's concept of power-knowledge anchors the production of truth within specific social and political relations. According to his critics, locating truth and knowledge within power relations undermines the possibility of objective knowledge or any truth outside power relations. Thus, they claim, Foucault's concept of power-knowledge has done away with the possibility of a normative framework. Without a normative framework, they say, critique is impossible.

An important aspect of this criticism rests on the assumption that social criticism must have a normative philosophical foundation, an assumption that Foucault obviously does not endorse. On the one hand, he rejects traditional Enlightenment norms; moreover he shows how the new, insidious disciplinary norms insinuate themselves into every aspect of our daily lives. On the other hand, his genealogies are clearly critical and evaluative; at the very least they implicitly appeal to a norm of antidomination or resisting oppression. Most critics emphasize Foucault's rejection of norms and charge Foucault with relativism. However, many of the same critics recognize the critical and evaluative aspects of Foucault's work, and so they claim that Foucault's work is paradoxical, because one cannot both reject norms and do social criticism at the same time. My aim is to do justice to Foucault by trying to make sense of his complicated relationship to norms. I argue that Foucault's skeptical approach apparent in his genealogies relies on commitments to antidomination and freedom, but that this does not land him back in an Enlightenment position. Foucault reworks traditional Enlightenment notions, such as freedom, so that they are understood as thoroughly social and historicized.

I argue for a more sympathetic reading of Foucault that attempts to make sense of his genealogical work as critique and links this notion of critique with his later writings on critique and freedom. I argue that his rejection of norms is well justified given his observations on how they can function. Foucault employs a skeptical method that allows him to question and criticize both social and philosophical norms. Yet, as his critics point out, Foucault's analyses are not value free. He clearly opposes domination, although he does not endorse universal norms. I argue below that his opposition to domination can be seen as part of a skeptical method that continually questions hegemonic and reified power relations. This skepticism allows him to strategically appeal to norms without necessarily endorsing them. Jana Sawicki suggests that Foucault's discourse does not preclude the possibility of appealing to norms such as rights, liberties, and justice.[7] Indeed, Foucault's implicit appeal to norms, such as freedom from domination, may be strategic because it allows him to do an immanent critique without explicitly invoking the modern categories he criticizes. I suggest that Foucault's apparent "normative confusion" functions productively in his work to criticize traditional Enlightenment norms and social norms while allowing for a reconceptualization of normative notions such as freedom and critique. I argue that these reworked normative notions can provide some grounding for a feminist politics.

FEMINIST CRITICS

Most feminist critics focus on Foucault's genealogical work to demonstrate the paucity of resources in Foucault for a robust feminist politics. Drawing mainly on *Discipline and Punish* and *The History of Sexuality Volume One*, they claim that Foucault's theory of power results in a subject determined by social forces beyond her control. Indeed much of the impact of Foucault's genealogical work comes from the chilling recognition that his analysis is correct; we are, in large part, determined by social forces beyond our control. Yet, if subjects are wholly constituted through discursive practices and social institutions, if there is "no outside to power," how is critique possible?[8]

As we have seen, there is no agreement among feminists about the usefulness of Foucault's work. Many feminists, such as Sandra Lee Bartky, Susan Bordo, Judith Butler, Jana Sawicki, and Ladelle McWhorter, find his work promising and productive for feminist theory. Yet many feminists remain skeptical about engaging with Foucault's work, and some are absolutely vociferous in their condemnation of Foucault. On the issue of norms two of the most influential feminist criticisms of Foucault are raised by Nancy Fraser and Nancy Hartsock.[9] Both Fraser and Hartsock caution that Foucault's lack of a normative framework spells trouble for feminism, which must rely on norms such as autonomy, rights, and freedom in order to derive its normative force. Hartsock warns feminists that Foucault's rejection of Enlightenment values, combined with his notion of power, results in the evisceration of a politics of social change. I show that her criticism of Foucault derives its force from a misreading of his notion of power. Fraser is more ambivalent than Hartsock about the usefulness of Foucault's work. She provides a persuasive reading of Foucault as "normatively confused," that is, she points out that his genealogies rely on normative notions that he does not justify. Yet she and other critics may be holding Foucault to too rigid a standard. As I have discussed above, Foucault does reject ahistorical, universal norms, yet as I demonstrate in this chapter he invokes new normative notions of critique and freedom.

In her influential article, "Foucault on Power: A Theory for Women?" Nancy Hartsock warns that "postmodernism represents a dangerous approach for any marginalized group to adopt."[10] Focusing on the work of Michel Foucault, she claims that his work cannot help feminists or other marginalized people in their struggles. She gives two related reasons for this. First, she claims that Foucault writes from the perspective of the dominator or the colonizer. Second, she claims that Foucault's theory of power does not take into account systematically unequal relations of power. To justify her claim that Foucault's perspective is that of the colonizer or dominator, Hartsock offers the fact that his world is profoundly alien to her. She does not recognize the world he describes, which she sees as determined by power relations, a world in which subjects have little if any choice. She also notes that Foucault calls for only the exposure of and resistance to power relations, not their overthrow. She suggests this may be because he sees power as "ever expanding and invading."[11] And she interprets his unwillingness to discuss what might replace the present system as his recognition of "the dangers of going beyond resistance to power."[12] But as I discuss below this is a misunderstanding of Foucault's notion of power. The idea that one could go beyond resistance to seize or overthrow power reinvokes the liberal notion of power as emanating from a state or as held by individuals. Hartsock also cites Foucault's suspicion of scientific claims and his rejection of Marxism as a science as evidence that he holds a dominant perspective. But Hartsock's positioning of Foucault as a dominator ignores certain specificities of the situation. In regard to this last point, she ignores the cultural and historical specificity of Foucault's criticism of Marxism. It is quite different for Foucault to criticize Marxism given its position of dominance in France at the time and his former membership in the French Communist Party, than for someone to criticize it from a liberal position. Moreover, often his criticisms were directed at what he saw as the historical failures of Marxism, for instance, the totalitarianism of Stalinist Russia. Her earlier claim, that because she does not recognize Foucault's world he is a dominator, also ignores the specificity of the situation. An underlying assumption here is that as a woman she is part of a marginalized group, and if Foucault's perspective differs so radically from her perspective this can only be a reflection of his privilege as a white European male intellectual. This, of course, ignores Foucault's homosexuality, which positions him as marginal to the dominant heterosexual culture. Hartsock's assumption that the primary division of power is between men and women reveals an oversimplified view of power and social relations that has become increasingly problematic in feminist theory. Although sex/gender is obviously an important axis of stratification for feminist analyses, privileging it obscures other important axes of domination, such as race, sexual orientation, and class. I examine this further in chapter 5, where I discuss identity politics.

Hartsock relates her second point, that systematically unequal power relations vanish in Foucault's work, to her first, saying, "domination, viewed from above, is more likely to appear as equality."[13] Hartsock interprets Foucault's conception of power as dealing primarily with individuals, rather than groups of individuals or the domination of one group by another. In some sense, this is right because Foucault does not believe that power can be held either by an individual or a group. But from this she draws the conclusion that "his account makes room for only abstract individuals, not women, men, or workers."[14] As I shall argue in chapter 3, his conception of subjectivity is far from a notion of an abstract individual. Moreover, in *The History of Sexuality Volume One* and *Discipline and Punish*, he discusses class differences, for instance, on the way that power operates on the body of the bourgeoisie in the deployment of sexuality.[15] And while it is true that he does not systematically discuss sex or gender differences, feminists have successfully extended his work to do so. Hartsock is especially critical of Foucault's image of power as a net and as capillary. She claims that his conception of power as a network "carries implications of equality and agency rather than the systematic domination of the many by the few."[16] She interprets his claim that power comes from below as implying that those at the bottom are responsible for their situations. And she believes that the image of power as capillary implies that power is everywhere. This in itself is consistent with some things that Foucault says about power, but should be seen in the context of his other claims. Instead, Hartsock draws the completely unwarranted conclusion that because power is everywhere, it is "ultimately nowhere."[17] She concludes that Foucault's complete rejection of Modernity leaves marginalized groups without the hope of creating a new and more just society. She agrees with other critics that "because Foucault refuses both the ground of foundationalism and the 'ungrounded hope' endorsed by liberals such as Rorty, he stands on no ground at all and thus fails to give any reasons for resistance."[18] Although Foucault does refuse the ground of foundationalism with its notions of objective, ahistorical, and universal truth, he is not entirely without hope for social and political change. His genealogical method encourages attention to domination, and to the situation of those relegated to the margins of society. And as I shall discuss later, he links his suspicion of political and social practices to a hopefulness about the future.

In "Postmodernism and Political Change: Issues for Feminist Theory," Hartsock once again warns of the danger for feminists in adopting a postmodern perspective. Although she admits that feminists share with postmodernists an interest in developing nontotalizing theories, she believes the postmodern approach is fundamentally flawed. She contrasts the God's-eye view of Enlightenment thinkers and the incipient relativism of postmodern thinkers; she poses a choice between "omnipotent God" or "impotent critic."[19] She places Foucault in the "impotent critic" camp with postmodern thinkers.[20] She accuses Foucault of undermining the possibility for social criticism by rejecting Enlightenment commitments to the neutrality and the universality of reason without offering any satisfactory alternative. She claims that Foucault's project is marred, on the one hand, by his rejection of Enlightenment values, and contrarily, by his implicit reliance on those same values. Hartsock enumerates the characteristic features of the "Enlightenment." First, there was an assumption that objective knowledge was possible, and this was based on the idea that reason alone could offer a view of the world that was nonperspectival, the view from everywhere. Relatedly, reason was assumed to be neutral and the scientific method was privileged and thought to yield increasingly better knowledge. Third, based on this shared capacity to reason, the Enlightenment held that human nature was universal. Fourth, this emphasis on reason and human universality presumed the transcendence of historical and cultural specificity, as well as of the body. Finally, knowledge and power were assumed to be not only separate, but antithetical. As knowledge increased, power lost its hold. Conversely, if power was everywhere, knowledge and truth were hopelessly compromised.

Hartsock finds Foucault's project epistemologically flawed because he rejects what she calls the "god-trick"—the view of everything from nowhere that typifies the Enlightenment view of knowledge—without offering an alternative.[21] She takes his rejection of the view from everywhere and his view of truth as produced through power relations to imply that "if one cannot see everything from nowhere, one cannot really see anything at all."[22] But this accusation misses the point of Foucault's genealogies; he criticizes Enlightenment assumptions not to show that knowledge is impossible, but to show that our search for a transcendental knowledge needs to replaced by local, specific, historical knowledges. In this, he is closer to a Nietzschean perspectivism than to the position that we cannot have any knowledge whatsoever. Furthermore, Hartsock claims that his rejection of objective knowledge results in a relativism that makes any politics for social change untenable. She accuses Foucault of pessimism and passivity. In her words, "Foucault's is a world in which things move, rather than people, a world in which subjects become obliterated or rather, recreated as objects, a world in which passivity or refusal represent the only possible choices."[23] She believes that Foucault's rejection of transcendence leaves him without the resources to argue for social change, and that instead all his philosophy offers is a history of subjugation. Contrary to Hartsock, I demonstrate that Foucault's notion of power does not result in determinism and can account for systematic asymmetries of power, and that he advocates social change.

To pose the choice between "omnipotent God" or "impotent critic" assumes that one must endorse Enlightenment norms in order to engage in social criticism.

However, a variety of contemporary approaches from existentialism to pragmatism to feminism engage in social criticism without necessarily endorsing Enlightenment values. Even Hartsock's own approach attempts to carve out an alternative that rejects Enlightenment reliance on universal reason, but does not lapse into relativism. Like these other approaches, Foucault's approach recognizes that critique occurs from within social institutions, practices, and power relations.

Nancy Fraser is more sympathetic to the possibility that Foucault's work may be useful for social and political critique. In "Michel Foucault: A 'Young Conservative'?" Fraser credits Foucault with a novel approach to social criticism, "Foucault has succeeded in producing a species of *Kulturkritik* that does not rely on—indeed that explicitly repudiates—the subject-object framework in all its guises."[24] However, later in the same article she retracts this praise because Foucault does not provide a nonfoundationalist justification for his criticisms.[25] For Fraser, the issue of normative justification is the central issue for assessing the usefulness of Foucault's work for social and political criticism.

In her "Foucault on Modern Power: Empirical Insights and Normative Confusions," Fraser raises crucial questions regarding the status of normative justification in Foucault's work. She credits Foucault with developing an account of power that improves on the traditional liberal notion insofar as it is able to capture the ways that power operates through practices, and infiltrates into the deepest level of the social body as well as individual bodies. In developing this empirical account of power, she says, Foucault brackets the issue of normative justification. However, the issue of justification cannot stay bracketed, and upon further examination Fraser finds Foucault "normatively confused." She attributes Foucault's normative confusion to the fact that he seems to employ his notion of power equivocally. On the one hand, he presents power as normatively neutral when he claims that it is productive and ineliminable. On the other hand, Foucault clearly calls for resistance to domination, but he fails to provide reasons for this. Once Foucault rejects Modernity and the Enlightenment notions of truth, freedom, rights, and human dignity, on what basis can he criticize domination?

In "Michel Foucault: A Young Conservative?" Fraser addresses this issue with respect to Habermas's critique of Foucault's stance regarding modernity. Habermas contends that Foucault's rejection of modernity is theoretically paradoxical as well as politically suspect. The claim that it is theoretically paradoxical relates to the issue of normative justification discussed earlier; Foucault's critique of modernism seems to rely on the very categories and assumptions it rejects. Moreover, the absence of specific alternatives for social and political change make it politically suspect. Fraser rightly points out that Habermas fails to distinguish between Foucault's rejection of humanism and his total rejection of modernity. This is an important distinction because Foucault himself distinguishes among modernity, Enlightenment, and humanism.[26] While he is quite critical of humanism, he endorses the critical impulse of the Enlightenment. I will argue that the notions of critique and freedom he salvages from the Enlightenment provide some normative basis for social criticism. Many readers of Foucault overlook this distinction among Enlightenment, humanism, and modernity. Hartsock, for instance, accuses Foucault of a wholesale rejection of the Enlightenment. Having judiciously selected humanism as the target of Foucault's critique, Fraser suggests three possible interpretations of Foucault's rejection of humanism. The first she calls conceptual or philosophical; this involves the rejection of humanism as the legacy of Cartesian dualism. This is fairly unproblematic as many Continental philosophers have pointed out problems with the dualism inherent in humanism. The second interpretation is strategic rejectionism. The strategic rejectionist interpretation holds that humanism should be rejected because it has failed to realize its ideal of increasing freedom, but has instead resulted in an increasing social control through discipline and normalization. This view of humanism, and the possible reasons for its rejection, depends on historical facts. The third interpretation is that Foucault's critique of humanism is a substantive normative rejection of humanism, that is, he thinks that humanism is undesirable in and of itself. This would mean, for instance, that autonomy and freedom perfectly realized are still simply the outcome of dominating, subjectifying practices. This third interpretation is, of course, the strongest statement of Foucault's rejection of humanism.[27] But Fraser argues that Foucault does not provide sufficient grounds for rejecting such an outcome, for if society has instantiated such humanist ideals, and individuals are self surveilling, autonomous beings, then the only obstacle to accepting this as a positive outcome is Foucault's characterization of it as the result of subjection and domination. On this point she accuses Foucault of a genetic fallacy, and offers an alternative description of this humanist society as the result of the developing of communicative competencies. She concludes that in order for Foucault to justify his rejection of humanism he will have to appeal to some alternative, posthumanist ethical paradigm. But this she claims he has not done. However, she notes that feminists have also been engaged in a critique of humanism and autonomy, and suggests that we look to feminist work for an alternative normative paradigm. The recurring issue for Fraser is that of normative justification. If Foucault is an anti-foundationalist, what form of justification can he appeal to?

The problem of normative justification in Foucault's work that Fraser raises is a difficult one. A full treatment of this issue is beyond the scope of this project, but I will briefly sketch three possible responses. First, I examine the possibility that social criticism is possible without philosophy. Second, I pursue Ladelle McWhorter's suggestion that Foucault's primary targets for change are practices, not beliefs. And third, I draw on Todd May's argument that foundational justification is impossible, so Foucault's critique is justified as an immanent critique. In their influential article, "Social Criticism Without Philosophy: An Encounter Between Feminism and Postmodernism," Nancy Fraser and Linda Nicholson explore the possibility of doing social criticism without relying on a normative philosophical framework. In general, postmodernism rejects metanarratives, that is, large-scale historical narratives that seek to explain the march of history in terms of the increasing progress toward the triumph of reason and freedom. Using Jean-François Lyotard as representative of these postmodern tendencies, they point out that after his rejection of metanarratives, he concludes that social criticism must be "local, *ad hoc*, and non-theoretical."[28] Such a focus on the merely local would not serve feminist interests because there is no place for generalizations or a critique of relations of domination and subordination. After examining new paradigms of feminist social criticism, they conclude that a hybridization of postmodernism and feminism might yield a paradigm for social criticism without philosophy. Specifically, they suggest that a postmodern feminist theory would need to retain some large historical narratives, and analyses of societal macrostructures. But these analyses would have to be culturally and historically specific. Finally, this new form of social criticism would be nonuniversalist and would give up the idea of a universal subject of history.[29] I contend that Foucault's genealogies fit the bill for this new paradigm of social criticism without philosophy. His culturally and historically specific narratives reveal general trends, as well as the shifts and asymmetries of power. They are neither metanarratives, nor entirely local. He also clearly rejects the idea of a universal subject of history, and other forms of universality.

In *Bodies and Pleasures* Ladelle McWhorter points out that Foucault directs our attention to bodies as the primary target for the operation of power.[30] If power operates at the level of bodies and practices, then so must effective resistance. So, McWhorter suggests Foucault may be justified in rejecting normative foundations for social criticism, and for refusing to put a different framework in their place. Instead, perhaps we should examine our practices as possible sites of resistance and transformation. In his later writings Foucault discusses *askêsis* and practices of the self as practices that result in self-transformation. McWhorter provides examples of the transformative effect of these practices with respect to her own life and Foucault's life. I agree with McWhorter that Foucault offers a new paradigm for social criticism that requires new responses; his shift in emphasis from beliefs and reason to bodies and practices may render the question of justification irrelevant. In chapter 6, I discuss his notion of practices of the self as practices aimed at social and political change.

In *Between Genealogy and Epistemology*, Todd May argues for the possibility of justification without foundations. He questions the whole idea of foundationalist

justification, which relies for its force on indubitable claims. The process of justification involves giving reasons for what one holds to be true, but these reasons, in
turn, rely on other claims and the inference from one to another. Thus, justification
happens within language, not by appeal to something outside of it. This view of justification allows for critique without appealing to foundations; in fact the very possibility of such an appeal is rejected. As we have seen, Foucault rejects the notion of
transcendent, ahistorical universal truth that underlies foundationalist justification.
A view of justification that is contextual, located in language and social practices allows for the possibility that Foucault can reject this notion of truth and still engage
in social criticism. As May says, "Genealogy can be called a radical political empir-
ics, wresting transcendental concepts and claims from their comfortable position at
the foundation of knowledge, inciting suspicion about whatever appears in the guise
of nature or necessity, provoking distrust of the transhistorical and the eternal—all
by a tracing of historical lineages, an analysis of emergence and descent, that
requires nothing more than a belief in historical fact."[31]

As I see it, holding Foucault to foundationalist standards of justification
may be part of the problem. Fraser herself suggests that her reading of Foucault
may emphasize what she calls his "transgressive strand," which aims to transcend
or overthrow humanism, rather than his "immanent strand," which is more like a
"critical conscience" pointing out humanism's failures and contradictions.[32] My
reading of Foucault emphasizes this immanent strand, and I find his critique valuable in spite of the fact that he does not offer an alternative normative framework.
One could argue that it would be difficult, or even self-contradictory, for Foucault
to provide such a framework given his suspicion about how norms can operate. In
this chapter, I argue that Foucault employs what I call a "skeptical method" that allows him to reject the ahistorical, universal claims that underlie humanism and
foundationalism, while still engaging in social criticism. In fact, Foucault's social
criticism derives much of its force from his insistence that we question norms.

GENEALOGY AS CRITIQUE

Even a cursory reading of *Discipline and Punish* and *The History of Sexuality
Volume One* reveals a critical stance towards the penal system and the institution of
sexuality.[33] Foucault's genealogies interweave descriptive and prescriptive aspects,
producing what one might call "critical description."[34] This critical description offers
a perspective on historical events that differs from the established account. The genealogical method is not simply history, but functions as social criticism. Discussing
his research project in "Two Lectures," Foucault describes genealogies as antisciences
because they challenge the unity of theoretical, historical, or scientific knowledge.

This challenge occurs because genealogies focus on what Foucault calls "subjugated knowledges," that is, knowledges that have been excluded or disqualified. He identifies two types of excluded or disqualified knowledge: erudite and popular. Erudite knowledge refers to formal theoretical or scientific knowledge that has been buried or ignored. Popular knowledge refers to knowledge that has been disqualified as formal historical knowledge; it is a particular, local, regional knowledge. Those who serve as sources for popular subjugated knowledges are often on the margins of society, such as psychiatric patients or delinquents. These subjugated knowledges form the basis of what Foucault calls genealogy. He says, "Let us give the term genealogy to the union of erudite knowledge and local memories [popular knowledge] which allows us to establish a historical knowledge of struggles and to make use of this knowledge tactically today."[35] Genealogies provide an unorthodox perspective on institutions and social practices. This perspective may challenge the official historical account and may undermine our deep-seated assumptions about the way things were or the way things are. Genealogies most assuredly challenge the status quo. Foucault claims, "it is through the re-appearance of this knowledge, of these local popular knowledges, these disqualified knowledges, that criticism performs its work."[36] Genealogy performs part of the critical task of philosophy by questioning domination. Foucault's commitment to antidomination is apparent. For example, Foucault is clearly critical of the intensification of the disciplinary and dominating techniques that produce docile bodies—bodies "that may be subjected, used, transformed and improved."[37] His genealogies trace the historical influences that led to present-day practices. Foucault writes what he calls "a history of the present," not to understand the past, but to understand the present.[38] A history of the present allows one to see how the present came to be the way it is; it exposes the contingency of historical forces that created the present. Recognizing the historical contingency that led up to the present implies that things could be otherwise. Foucault's detailed, if idiosyncratic, accounts of the histories of the penal system, madness, and sexuality highlight the contingency behind what are now seen as the inevitable outcomes of historical forces.[39] Foucault intends his genealogies to be tools for current political and social struggles. Far from morally neutral, Foucault's histories condemn the increase of social control over individuals through disciplinary power, and through the process of normalization as a result of advances in the social sciences. In *Discipline and Punish*, for example, Foucault looks at the way that "[a] whole set of assessing, diagnostic, prognostic, normative judgments concerning the criminal have become lodged in the framework of penal judgment."[40] Foucault's work illuminates the multiple influences—legislative, economic, medical, scientific, technological—that led up to the penal system as contemporary institution.

Foucault's *The History of Sexuality Volume One* takes issue with the repressive hypothesis regarding sexuality. The repressive hypothesis holds that at the beginning of the seventeenth century there was a certain openness about sexual activity that was notably lacking in the nineteenth century. By the nineteenth century, standards of Victorian propriety and prudishness had come to hold sway. Most people believe that these standards of sexuality are still influential today in Western society. Victorian standards of sexual morality involve repression, which operates through the silencing of talk about sex and the regulation of sexual behavior. This regulation of sexual behavior took place through legislation, social policy, and social sanctions. An underlying assumption of the repressive hypothesis is that the relationship between sex and power is characterized by repression. As we shall see, Foucault questions not only this relationship between sex and power, but also the characterization of power as primarily negative. He entertains three doubts about the repressive hypothesis that he explores in *The History of Sexuality Volume One*. He asks: Is repression a historically established fact? Do the workings of power belong to the category of repression? And, is critical discourse part of the same historical network that produced repression? He argues that, contrary to the repressive hypothesis, discourse about sex proliferated from the seventeenth through the nineteenth century, particularly through scientific, medical, psychological, and religious discourse. He discusses the new categories and types of sexuality that arose—zoophiles, zooerasts, automonosexuals, mixoscophiles, gynecomasts, presbyophiles, sexoesthetic inverts, and dyspareunist women.[41] Foucault offers historical evidence that runs counter to the claim that talk about sex was silenced through repression. He demonstrates that power functions not only to limit discourse about sexuality, but to produce new discourses about sexuality. And, he claims that the critical discourse about repression by those interested in sexual liberation, such as Herbert Marcuse, is a part of the same historical network that produced repression. In other words, theories of sexual liberation buy into some of the same assumptions as the repressive hypothesis, for example, that power is negative and limiting and that sex is the privileged locus of truth about the subject. Foucault tells a different story about the history of sexuality than the widely accepted repressive hypothesis. He shows how issues of sex and subjectivity came to be tied together, develops a new notion of power, and provides a number of specific historical examples. For instance, he discusses the hysterization of women's bodies, stating that the female body was thoroughly saturated with sexuality. Hysteria, as primarily a female malady, was thought to be linked to women's reproductive system; it was associated with a wandering womb. Foucault points out that one of the ways that sex has been defined was as wholly constituting women's bodies. With the example of the hysterization of women it is easy to see the political stakes involved in the understanding of sex, as it is with Foucault's other examples of the control of children's sexuality, the social regulation of reproductive behavior, and the psychiatrization of perverse pleasure. Women's thoroughgoing association with sex serves to mark out appropriate social and political spaces for women. For instance, in the contemporary United States one popular argument by the unenlightened against having a woman president is that her monthly menstrual cycle may make her emotions unreliable and she may threaten national security by initiating a war.

Foucault points out that sex functions as a unifying concept and an explanatory category. Because of its fundamental role in both our understanding of who we are as individuals and in social organization, the concept of sex is rarely questioned. Foucault's analysis points out how contingent historical practices shape our concept of sex. In turn, he shows how sex and sexuality play a fundamental role in the regulation of our moral and social behavior. So, Foucault's genealogy raises questions about many of the things that we take for granted, for example, that sex is a natural biological category, that particular behaviors are unnatural, and that one's sex prescribes what an individual can do.

Throughout *The History of Sexuality Volume One*, Foucault cautions us against taking the explosion of discourse around sexuality as liberatory, claiming instead that this proliferation of discourse is an exercise of power. The power exercised in the deployment of sexuality has multiple effects. It results in an increase of social control over the individual and it links together questions of sex and subjectivity. The discourse of sexuality is central both to social organization and to the constitution of subjectivity. This has led some to believe that the discourse of sexuality and its dominating, normalizing effects are inescapable. Yet Foucault indicates that just as the discourse of sexuality arose at a specific historical moment, it may not be the dominant discourse in the future. For example, at the end of *The History of Sexuality Volume One*, Foucault leaves open the possibility that some day society may be organized differently: "[M]oreover, we need to consider the *possibility that one day, perhaps in a different economy of bodies and pleasures* (emphasis added), ..."[42] Foucault's genealogy as social criticism, combined with his speculation that in the future society may be less normalizing if it operates in a "different economy of bodies and pleasures," implies that social change is both possible and desirable. This is contrary to the passivity and immobility that Hartsock claims is the outcome of Foucault's theorizing.[43]

In his genealogy of the penal system, *Discipline and Punish*, Foucault again questions the notion that our social practices and institutions have led to increasing freedom. He traces practices of punishment from the late seventeen-hundreds through the mid-eighteen hundreds. *Discipline and Punish* describes the transition in methods of punishment from execution and torture in the late eighteenth century to incarceration in the mid-nineteenth century. Foucault points out that this transition involves a corresponding shift in the target of punishment from body alone to body and soul. And he discusses how changes in practices of punishment relate to changes in our ideas about what is significant about the crime. In the eighteenth century the main issue was the guilt of the alleged suspect, but beginning in the nineteenth century the concern was with the nature of the crime. Determining what type of crime was committed helped to assess how best to punish the person, and the nature of the crime came to be seen as revealing the criminal character of the person involved. Foucault notes the way that power operates both on the body and on the soul. What he calls the microphysics of power operates on the body through the imposition of a schedule, through forced activity, and through perpetual surveillance. Power also operates on the soul by creating particular types of subjectivity: the criminal, the delinquent, the pervert. I discuss the ways that power operates on the body in more detail in chapter 4.

In spite of critics' claims to the contrary, Foucault's genealogies operate as social criticism. He questions the standard historical notion of progress by pointing out that some practices and institutions that were intended to increase freedom actually increased domination. But pointing out this unwelcome consequence of social practices and institutions by no means makes Foucault a quietist. In some genealogical works, there is explicit evidence that Foucault advocates social change. At the end of *Discipline and Punish*, Foucault leaves no doubt that through his critical description of the penal institution, disciplinary society, and the process of normalization, he intends to move us to political action to promote social change:

> That, consequently, the notions of institutions of repression, rejection, exclusion, marginalization, are not adequate to describe, at the very centre of the carceral city, the formation of the insidious leniencies, unavowable petty cruelties, small acts of cunning, calculated methods, techniques, 'sciences' that permit the fabrication of the disciplinary individual. In this central and centralized humanity, the effect and instrument of complex power relations, bodies and forces subjected by multiple mechanisms of 'incarceration,' objects for discourses that are themselves elements for this strategy, *we must hear the distant roar of battle* (emphasis added).[44]

Coming at the end of more than three hundred pages of historical analysis and critical description, this passage leaves little doubt that the aim of Foucault's genealogical analysis here is critical. Moreover, Foucault says that his interpretations of history are meant to illuminate certain aspects of the situation and to be used for current political struggles. Foucault puts it this way, "I am making an interpretation of history, and the problem is that of knowing—but I don't resolve the problem—how these analyses can possibly be utilized in the current situation."[45] I suggest that when we take into account Foucault's later work, and Foucault's own commitment to political activism, this helps us to understand Foucault's overall project as social criticism and as tools for political intervention.

Foucault's genealogies are a form of social criticism. He consistently emphasizes the contingency of historical processes, indicating that things *could* be otherwise. Furthermore, his focus on aspects of power such as domination and normalization indicate that things *should* be otherwise. But if his genealogies are forms of critique, as I have argued above, on what basis is that critique justified? Does Foucault lack a sufficient normative ethical framework, as some feminist critics have argued?[46] Or does he implicitly rely on the very normative framework of the Enlightenment that he explicitly rejects, as other feminist critics claim?[47] I argue that Foucault's relationship to norms is ambivalent; he rejects traditional norms because he is rightly suspicious of their normalizing power. Yet his skepticism about norms is a form of critical engagement with social and political issues. He reformulates a Kantian notion of critique in his later writings that appeals to the idea of freedom. However, this notion of freedom is not simply the reintroduction of a traditional Enlightenment norm, but rather it is a constrained, contextualized, historicized freedom that emerges out of particular practices and situations.

Foucault's *Discipline and Punish*, like *The History of Sexuality Volume One*, calls into question the idea that reforms in social practices and institutions are necessarily better, lead to more humane treatment, or increase freedom. In fact, both historical studies challenge this traditional interpretation. Foucault's critics have taken issue with his analyses and drawn varying conclusions. Some, such as Martha Nussbaum and Nancy Hartsock, have decided that the upshot of Foucault's genealogical analyses is that we can never be free, and they accuse him of determinism, quietism, pessimism, or nihilism. Others claim that Foucault must in fact be relying on the very notions he rejects, such as truth and freedom, in order for his argument to have critical force.[48] There is no doubt that Foucault rejects a traditional notion of freedom as free from external constraint or outside power relations. However, this does not mean he eschews all notions of freedom. In his later work he advocates the practice of freedom as a critical exercise. And as I shall discuss in the next section, he acknowledges that different degrees of freedom are possible in different social and political circumstances. What Foucault's genealogies reveal, though, is that it is a mistake to think of freedom as simply the absence of explicit force or unjust laws. Certainly these are important in influencing the forms that practices of freedom may take. Foucault affirms this in an interview: "I don't want to say that the state isn't important; what I want to say is that relations of power and hence the analysis that must be made of them, necessarily extend beyond the limits of the state."[49] Because power operates through normalizing social practices, conceptions of freedom must include resistance to those practices. As I shall discuss, freedom for Foucault involves nonnormalizing institutions and practices. Foucault's genealogies derive their critical force in part from the critique of freedom as a universal norm. For Foucault, freedom is not a universal norm or a final realizable state, and thinking that it is may blind us to the ways that new institutions and practices may result in new forms of domination. However, domination is not total because not all power is normalizing, disciplinary power.[50] Power itself is neither good nor bad; it is equally implicated in both resistance and domination. Foucault engages in social criticism with the understanding that there have been, are, and will be institutions and practices that are nondominating and nonnormalizing. But these exist alongside, and may become, practices and institutions that dominate and normalize. For Foucault, there is no utopian state where power ceases to operate and freedom is guaranteed. Nonetheless, he advocates for an increase in options and a decrease in the hold that normalizing disciplines have over an individual. Because he has impugned the very standards of justification that his critics believe he must rely on, his argument does not meet their standards for justification. But Foucault advocates social criticism not from some transcendental or foundational basis, but as an immanent critique located within particular social and historical contexts, and from one's specific situation.

I have argued, *contra* Hartsock, that Foucault's work is engaged social criticism that advocates social and political change. She sees his conception of power as equally held by all and inescapable as a primary impediment to social and political change. Without distinctions among groups of people and the recognition that power is not equally held by all, Hartsock claims that political transformation is impossible. But Foucault does make distinctions among groups of people, for instance, social scientists, medical doctors, and psychiatrists versus their patients and clients. He also makes class distinctions, distinguishing the bourgeois family with respect to how they were affected by the deployment of sexuality. Foucault associates class consciousness with the affirmation of the body, and notes that sexuality produces specific class effects.[51] He claims that the bourgeoisie created their own sexuality and body, "a 'class' body with its health, hygiene, descent and race."[52] As I show below, Foucault's notion of power can account for systematic asymmetry between groups of people.

PROBLEMS WITH POWER

As we have seen, Foucault's critics have a problem accepting his ideas as politically useful. In some cases, at least part of this problem results from a misunderstanding of Foucault's conception of power. There is good reason for this misunderstanding because Foucault himself is not clear about the functioning or limits of power. He provides an "analytics of power," rather than a theory of power.[53] This is consistent with Foucault's general approach because an "analytics of power" is contextual and historical, yet still generalizable.[54] Foucault is not making universal claims about what power is or the way that power functions. Nonetheless, power is a central concept in his work and arguably one of his most important contributions to contemporary social theory. Power as a concept of analysis is indispensable for feminist theory and practice.[55] Thus, examining Foucault's analytics of power is essential for judging whether or not his work might be useful for feminists.

Foucault rejects the traditional model of power wherein power is conceived of as only negative, repressive, and limiting. He calls this traditional model of power the juridico-discursive model. In the juridico-discursive model, power comes from above, from a sovereign or government leader. The main characteristics of the juridico-discursive model of power are: (1) a negative relation, (2) the insistence of the rule, (3) the cycle of prohibition, (4) the logic of censorship, (5) the uniformity of apparatus.[56] In other words, the juridico-discursive model of power seeks to limit behavior by imposing rules, prohibiting certain behaviors, and limiting one's access to forbidden things and ideas mainly through the imposition and enforcement of laws imposed by the state. This traditional model views power as unilateral and negative. Contrary to this, Foucault claims that power can be positive and productive. He urges us to have a more complex understanding of power. Foucault first reconceptualizes power in *The History of Sexuality Volume One*.[57] Foucault characterizes power as relational; it is the "multiplicity of force relations immanent in the sphere in which they constitute their own organization."[58] Because it is relational it is omnipresent; it is constantly produced among and between persons, institutions, things, and groups of persons. Power is mobile, local, heterogeneous, and unstable. Power comes from everywhere; it is exercised from innumerable points. Foucault emphasizes the ubiquity of power; it comes from below, not solely from above as in the juridico-discursive model of power. And relations of power are immanent in other relationships, such as economic, knowledge, and sexual relationships. As Foucault says, "Power is everywhere; not because it embraces everything, but because it comes from everywhere."[59] Power is not possessed. And power relations are both intentional and nonsubjective.[60]

This last claim, that power relations are both intentional and nonsubjective, may seem contradictory. After all, isn't it subjects who have intentions? It may help to explicate this claim. Foucault holds that power is all pervasive, that it is relational, and that it can be understood through the strategies by which it takes effect. So, in each manifestation of power in the strategies and the relations among individuals, institutions, and things, aims, goals, and objectives are revealed. For example, the "war on masturbation" against children in the nineteenth century had a specific explicit objective—to stop or reduce the activity of masturbation among children. On Foucault's reading, it also had other less explicit objectives, for instance, to increase the power of state control over the individual and the family. In the sense that local and specific power relations have aims, goals, and objectives, power is intentional. Yet Foucault also claims that power is nonsubjective. This claim is frequently cited as one of the reasons that Foucault's theory cannot be used by emancipatory social movements such as feminism. Feminists ask, "If there is no subject wielding power, then how are we to assign blame and responsibility, or to effect any sort of a change in the balance of power relations?" As I will demonstrate, this is a misunderstanding of Foucault's rather complicated notion of power.

Foucault's claim that power is nonsubjective is consistent with his claim that it is not possessed by anyone. It cannot be possessed because it is relational, shifting, mobile, and unstable. Power is nonsubjective in the sense that individuals do not *have* power, rather they participate in it. Much of that participation is beyond the control of the individual, because she is entangled in a web of relationships and institutions. And even that which is within one's control has unintended consequences and effects.[61] The local and specific aims, objectives, and goals interact with other local and specific aims, objectives, and goals, resulting in effects and consequences that are not the plan of any one person, or even any group of people. Thus, because there are specific aims, objectives, and goals, power is intentional. Yet because power is neither possessed nor controlled by individuals, it is nonsubjective. A specific example from *The History of Sexuality Volume One* may help to illuminate the way that power can be both intentional and nonsubjective. Foucault discusses how in the nineteenth century science, medicine, and the law worked together to mark some people as sexually deviant. Although these discourses (as well as various others, such as religious discourse, psychiatry, and psychology) functioned together to create categories of perverts and to criminalize those classified as such, this classification, categorization, and criminalization were not the work of any one person, or even any one group of people. And this is precisely Foucault's point—power operates in ways that are beyond our control. Still, we inevitably participate in these power relations, making conscious decisions about what to do and how to do it. Yet the impact and consequences of our actions, particularly with regard to the larger social and cultural scheme of things, is beyond us.[62] Thus, power is nonsubjective, in part because it always supersedes any person or group of persons, but more importantly, because it is relational, existing only between and among persons, institutions, discourses, practices, and objects.

Foucault's analytics of power has generated much discussion among political and social theorists. There are two main criticisms of his conception of power; the first is related to the issue of norms, and the second to the issue of agency and the possibility of resistance. As is well known, Foucault holds that power and knowledge are inseparable. He claims that all knowledge is formed within relations and networks of power; power produces knowledge, and in turn, knowledge produces power. This aspect of Foucault's conception of power has far-reaching epistemic and political-ethical consequences.[63] As we have seen, many critics have gone so far as to claim that Foucault's conception of power-knowledge commits him to relativism or nihilism, and therefore renders his work useless for emancipatory social and political movements.[64] The second main criticism of Foucault's conception of power is that it does not allow for resistance to dominant social forces. Most commonly, critics claim that because Foucault's power is omnipresent and there is no outside to power, emancipation or freedom is impossible.[65] An additional problem with Foucault's concept of power particularly pertinent to feminists is the criticism that his idea of power has a leveling effect—that is, because it runs through all relations it cannot make sense of gender dominance or any consistent asymmetry of power.

Foucault speaks directly to this last concern in his later work. Although he does reject hierarchical and unilateral models of power, he does not believe that power is distributed or exercised equally. In "The Subject and Power" and "The Ethics of Concern for Self as a Practice of Freedom," Foucault distinguishes between power and domination. Whereas power is always subject to reversal, states of domination are static, ossified relations of power. Relations of domination are particular formations of power—"the locking together of power relations with the relations of strategy."[66] Domination is a state of asymmetrical power relations that persists over time and may seem fixed. This may seem to add weight to critics' claims that Foucault's account of power precludes social and political change. However, states of domination are subject to reversal through collective action.[67] His notion of a state of domination is reminiscent of the traditional juridico-discursive model of power. Although power is still not held by individuals or groups, the notion of domination accounts for systematic asymmetries of power among individuals or groups. Nothing in Foucault's work precludes having both micro- and macro-levels of analysis. Foucault acknowledges more than once that although power is pervasive it is not equally distributed.[68] His methodological recommendation is that we reverse the usual order of an analysis of power. Rather than a "from the top down" analysis such as Marxism, we should conduct what Foucault calls "ascending analyses of power." This type of analysis moves from the local and particular to the more general in order to capture the myriad forms and techniques of power.[69]

Foucault's notion of power involves complex and overlapping relations among the concepts of domination, power, liberation, freedom, reversal, and resistance. Undoubtedly, this has contributed to some misreadings of it. I will provide a schematic overview of Foucault's use of these terms in an effort to clarify the relationship among them. Power does not exclude freedom, but implies it. Nor does domination exclude freedom, although freedom is more limited under states of domination. In response to a question about how freedom is possible if power is everywhere, Foucault answers, ". . . if there are relations of power in every social field, this is because there is freedom everywhere. Of course, states of domination do indeed exist. In a great many cases, power relations are fixed in such a way that they are perpetually asymmetrical and allow an extremely limited margin of freedom."[70] Even though options are more limited in states of domination, resistance is possible. Foucault's example of a state of domination—conventional marital structure in the eighteenth and nineteenth centuries—offers some limited options to women short of reversing the gendered power relations: "they could deceive their husbands, pilfer money from them, refuse them sex."[71] Two literary examples draw on precisely these strategies to demonstrate the potential for women's resistance in situations of male gender dominance. *Lysistrata* remains a classic example of women's power and determination to change things through their individual actions (of refusing sex) and the collective power that this engenders. Nora in Ibsen's *A Doll's House* deceives her husband and 'pilfers' money to save his life. In spite of her fragile and flighty persona, she comes off as a character of remarkable strength and courage, even if a bit manipulative. Feminists may be less than satisfied with deception, stealing, and chastity as forms of women's resistance, particularly because these activities seem to buy into damaging and inaccurate stereotypes about women. But Foucault does not rule out the possibility of other kinds of strategies that can actually change the situation of gender domination more generally. Among the specific types of resistance that he mentions are, "violent resistance, flight, deception, strategies capable of reversing the situation."[72] Feminist interests may be best served by acknowledging that resistance can occur in a variety of situations in a variety of forms both collective and individual.

Freedom for Foucault is never outside of power relations, but occurs when power relations shift through reversal or resistance. Reversal takes place when the balance of power shifts, giving one person or group of persons the upper hand (at least temporarily). Foucault uses the example of a game of chess; there are always power relations in play—among the pieces, between the players—but the balance of power shifts with each move. Resistance, too, involves shifts and changes in power relations. So both reversal of power and resistance to power can be individual or collective. And shifting power relations can end a situation of domination, and increase possibilities for freedom. The fact that resistance is possible even in situations of domination—the prolonged, static, locking together of power relations—bodes well for social change. Finally, although Foucault explicitly rejects the repressive model of power that views freedom or liberation as the freedom of the individual from power, he does use the term liberation in a specific context. He believes that in a situation of domination by one group of people over another, for instance, the colonizers over the colonized, liberation is possible.[73] Liberation here involves the end of the state of domination of the colonizer over the colonized. The end of domination does not mean the end of power, but it does result in expanded possibilities for freedom. Freedom is not a final state to be realized, but occurs only in its exercise through reversal, resistance, and other practices of freedom.

Foucault's notion of power illuminates both its negative aspect (domination) and its positive aspect (production of new objects, discourses, resistance). Power functions ambivalently for Foucault. In its negative aspect it serves to limit, to dominate, to normalize; this traditional understanding of power is akin to what feminists call "power over." In its productive, positive aspect, power creates new possibilities, produces new things, ideas, and relations; this is akin to what feminists call "empowerment." Foucault's notion of power covers both of these aspects; confusion results when his idea of power is reduced to just one aspect, "power over." "Power over" is synonymous with domination. Feminists need a concept of domination to explain men's power over women. Domination fails to explain, however, the ability to exercise power in a noncoercive way either individually or collectively. Feminists call this noncoercive exercise of power "empowerment." Empowerment involves two aspects of power, "power to" and "power with." "Power to" can be thought of as the ability of the individual to creatively transform her situation. "Power with" refers to the collective aspect of power; again, power is noncoercive. In this model, one's abilities are enhanced, not restricted, by the power of the others in the group. Moreover, the power of the collective is greater than the power of the individual to creatively transform the situation. Empowerment is productive, creative, transformative, and can be either individual or collective. Both of these conceptions of power are present in Foucault's discussion of power, and both are necessary for feminist theory and practice.

FOUCAULT'S SKEPTICISM

As we have seen, critics question the political relevance of Foucault's work given his lack of normative notions that they claim are necessary to justify appeals to rights, equality, and justice. Some even claim that Foucault's stance is downright dangerous to emancipatory social and political movements. I suggest that Foucault is rightly suspicious of norms. Foucault attacks norms at two levels—social norms and philosophical norms. As I have already discussed, he objects to philosophical norms because they purport universality. In their book, *Social Norms*, Michael Hechter and Karl-Dieter Opp define norms as "cultural phenomena that prescribe and proscribe behavior in specific circumstances."[74] Social norms regulate social behavior and are so fundamental to human existence that it is hard to imagine how exchange and interaction could take place without them. Although social norms play a significant role in sociological studies and have become increasingly important in contemporary analyses in a variety of disciplines such as political science, anthropology, economics, legal studies, and philosophy, there is no consensus about what norms are, how they are enforced, or how they emerge. What is clear, however, is the tremendously important role they play in regulating behavior. Of course, social norms alone are not responsible for regulating behavior in contemporary society; the state plays an important role in regulating behavior primarily through legal norms. However, legal norms differ from social norms in a number of ways. According to Hechter and Opp, "Social norms, by contrast [to legal norms], often are spontaneous rather than deliberately planned (hence, of uncertain origin), unwritten (hence, their content and rules for application are often imprecise), and enforced informally (although the resulting sanctions can sometimes be a matter of life and death)."[75] Because of their fundamental role in facilitating social interaction and regulating individual behavior, social norms are often viewed as primarily positive. The examples that Hechter and Opp give in their introduction to *Social Norms* are revealing; social norms "instruct people not to kill, not to injure others, to keep their promises, to abide by the Golden Rule and so forth."[76] While these examples of social norms are primarily positive, social norms can function negatively as well, excluding individuals and behaviors that do not fit with the dominant group's conceptions and values. Social norms, especially those established and perpetuated by social science, have a normalizing effect. Foucault's genealogical work makes clear the dangers of norms. The dividing practices that concern Foucault in his genealogical work evaluate, judge, and categorize—they divide the criminal from the noncriminal, the pervert from the nonpervert. Social norms are established within discourses, institutions, and practices that are embedded in normative discourses. Scientific discourse purports to be true and objective, yet the "truth" about the smaller size of the cranium of women and Blacks was used to justify our subordination to white men. Normative notions themselves can serve to disempower, exclude, and justify the status quo.[77] Thus, it is not surprising that Foucault urges us to be suspicious of them.

Normalizing practices are the central concern of Foucault's genealogical work. In *The History of Sexuality Volume One*, he demonstrates how the discourse of sexuality created new categories of deviant and pervert, while simultaneously encroaching upon the sphere of private life by exercising control over the family, and inserting itself into our psyches by changing our conception of ourselves into sexual subjects. In *Discipline and Punish*, he illustrates how practices of punishment, even while they have become more humane (we no longer draw and quarter people), operate in a deeper and more insidious way through constant surveillance. Furthermore, Foucault demonstrates that whereas punishment used to operate on the body alone, e.g., through execution, it now operates at the level of the soul through self-surveillance and self-monitoring. *Madness and Civilization* provides a third example of the dangers of normalization. In his history of madness, Foucault points out the ways in which madness has been increasingly marginalized. Here again his critical description compels us to look closely at the "progress" of the treatment of the mad. Certainly, extensive mental health networks and appropriate drugs are preferable to the confinement and restraint of the mentally ill that was so prevalent even in the United States less than a century ago. But his long-term historical perspective reveals that what looked like advances in the treatment of the mad—for instance, the medicalization of madness and the practice of performing lobotomies—are now viewed as inadequate and primitive forms of treatment. In fact, his history of madness reveals that what often looked like advances were not (most people would rather be exiled from their city than lobotomized). By extension then, his analyses and critical descriptions lead one to question current practices.

An oft-quoted phrase of Foucault's, "My point is not that everything is bad, but that everything is dangerous, which is not exactly the same as bad," is almost as often misconstrued.[78] Some critics conclude that if everything is dangerous then we ought not act to promote social change because one course of action is as good as another. But Foucault explicitly denies this. In an April 1983 discussion at Berkeley, Foucault responds to Charles Taylor's questioning about his politics.[79] Foucault states, "I disagree with Richard Rorty that everything is O.K., and that all truth games and political games are equally good. . . . for me, nothing is very good; everything is dangerous; *but everything is not equally dangerous* (emphasis added)."[80] Some courses of action, institutions, and social practices are indeed better than others, namely those that are nonnormalizing. But no way of being, institution, or practice is nonnormalizing in itself or permanently. That is why Foucault urges continual vigilance with respect to social and political institutions. Throughout the discussion at Berkeley, Foucault claims that intellectuals and philosophers need to be critical and distrustful of government and political structures. Foucault claims that this critical and distrustful attitude is not anarchistic or apathetic, but activist. This reiterates Foucault's point in "On the Genealogy of Ethics" that links the recognition of danger with activism: "If everything is dangerous, then we always have something to do. So my position leads not to apathy but to a hyper- and pessimistic activism."[81] Later in the April 1983 discussion at Berkeley, Foucault links his advocacy of distrust and suspicion with hope—"And if you are suspicious, it is because, of course, you have a certain hope. . . . And we don't have to renounce our hope because we are suspicious, or renounce our suspicion because we have hope."[82]

As I have demonstrated above, Foucault's suspicion and skepticism run throughout his genealogies. But contrary to critics' claims that this skepticism results in pessimism, fatalism, and nihilism, it seems to indicate a certain hopefulness about the future. If, as Hartsock assumes, hope is an indication of the possibility for social change, Foucault's explicit connection between suspicion and hope indicates that he believes that social change is possible. Moreover, I have argued that his genealogies employ a skeptical method that can serve as a political intervention. Thus, his skepticism is a form of social criticism.

Foucault makes his skepticism explicit in an article he wrote for the *Dictionnaire des Philosophes*.[83] In this short essay on his own work, Foucault endorses three methodological principles; the first principle advocates a systematic skepticism with respect to all anthropological universals.[84] This skepticism guides his philosophical investigations. Foucault acknowledges a more general skepticism in his response to a question posed to him in an interview shortly before his death. The interviewers asked: "Insofar as you don't affirm any universal truth but raise paradoxes in thought and make of philosophy a permanent question, are you a skeptic?" To which Foucault replied, "Absolutely."[85] It is this skepticism that is interpreted as relativism by his critics. But the rejection of universals does not necessarily result in relativism. Relativists do, of course, reject the idea of universal truth. But this position quickly devolves into the notion that there are no truths. While his work undermines the notion of universal truths about universal subjects, it simultaneously explores what truths we hold as subjects, how we came to hold these truths, and how these truths constitute us as subjects. Situated at the level of concrete practices, discourses, and institutions, Foucault's analyses reveal particular truths in their historical contingency.

It is not so much the question of truth or falsity that animates Foucault's explorations, but the conditions under which questions of truth and falsity emerge. In this sense, Foucault's project is Kantian. He investigates the conditions under which knowledge is possible, and the criteria used to establish truths. Foucault, writing under the pseudonym Maurice Florence, says, "If Foucault is indeed perfectly at home in the philosophical tradition, it is in the critical tradition of Kant. . . ."[86] The affinity between Kant's critical project and Foucault's critical project is brought out again in Foucault's essay "What Is Enlightenment?" It is here that Foucault identifies two distinct aspects of Enlightenment thinking. One aspect is the tendency to search for universal truths or a transcendental standpoint. The second aspect of Enlightenment thinking that Foucault identifies is critique, or the ability to raise questions about the present. Foucault reformulates a Kantian notion of critique, locating it in Kant's later works, such as Kant's essay "What Is Enlightenment?" For Foucault the significance of Kant's essay lies in its interrogation of the present. Foucault believes that it is no longer possible to engage in transcendental criticism or to hope to discover universal truths. Instead he says we must pursue a "historical investigation into the events that have led us to constitute ourselves and to recognize ourselves as subjects of what we are doing, thinking, saying."[87] It is this type of historical investigation that Foucault pursues in his genealogies. In "What Is Enlightenment?" Foucault explicitly advocates the type of critical attitude that is methodologically implicit in his genealogies. He urges us to adopt what he calls a historico-critical attitude; this attitude is experimental. By this, Foucault means that the possibilities for change should not be determined in advance by some abstract and universal plan or by an ideal of freedom. The historico-critical attitude is concerned both with historical inquiry and contemporary reality and aims to produce social change. Foucault says that the historico-critical attitude should serve "both to grasp the points where change is possible and desirable, and to determine the precise form this change should take."[88] Foucault advocates social and political change, but cautions that this change should be specific and local. He believes that the humanist ideals of freedom and truth are questionable, and that global solutions that are abstract and universal may serve to dominate rather than free and thus subvert the very goal that they support. The rejection of universal truth does not result in an inability to engage in social criticism. Rather the historical investigation Foucault proposes involves examination and critique of social institutions and the ways they constitute subjectivity. According to Foucault, interrogating the present, exploring the historical antecedents of our self-constitution, and examining our fundamental assumptions are the paramount tasks for philosophy. Foucault states, "In its critical aspect—and I mean critical in a broad sense—philosophy is that which calls into question domination at every level and in every form in which it exists, whether political, economic, sexual, institutional, or what have you."[89]

The notion of critique that Foucault retrieves from Kant provides another critical tool for questioning domination. Unlike Kant, Foucault does not seek to identify the limits of knowledge or its universal structures, but is concerned instead with the ways that specific discourses shape and structure our subjectivity. For Foucault, critique will always in part be concerned with subjectivity because subjectivity is not antecedent to discourses, institutions, and practices. But because subjectivity is produced through social and institutional norms and practices, critique must simultaneously question social and political institutions. If critique involves coming to understand the historical and social antecedents of one's thought, action, and speech and recognizing that these historical and social situations have shaped one, then changing oneself requires changing the social and political contexts that shape individuals. Foucault's notion of critique goes some way towards establishing a more positive goal than simply antidomination, namely freedom. Foucault says critique ". . . is seeking to give new impetus . . . to the undefined work of freedom . . . as work carried out by ourselves upon ourselves as free beings."[90] The undefined work of freedom lurks in the background of Foucault's genealogical texts. But Foucault's notion of freedom differs from the Enlightenment notion of freedom. Kant's freedom, for example, relies on a noumenal world. For Foucault, freedom has to do with the possibility of new forms of subjectivity that are historically and socially constituted, not in escaping the social and historical altogether. His skepticism opens up the possibility for critique; it allows him to question the normalizing function of norms from within a situated social and historical context. Although Foucault draws the notion of critique from the Enlightenment, he continues to reject the Enlightenment notion of freedom.[91] Critique and freedom, as Foucault discusses them in his later work, are both important for understanding his work as social criticism with the goal of antidomination. His position is often seen as deconstructive because he does not articulate a positive goal like freedom. But in addition to his new conception of freedom, Foucault expresses positive commitments to innovation, self–transformation, creativity, and social change in his work; I discuss this further in chapter 6.

For Foucault, social criticism is not a theoretical exercise divorced from one's life. He was politically active for much of his adult life. His political and social activism included participating in demonstrations, membership in Leftist political parties, speaking on behalf of prison reform, and founding the *Groupes d'Informations sur les Prisons,* as well as writing for radical journals and the popular press.[92] Foucault raises the question, "How can one define a work amid the millions of traces left by someone after his death?"[93] Although he raises this issue with regard to general questions about authorship and the unity of an author's work, the issue has particular relevance to the interpretation of Foucault's own work. Foucault's untimely death leaves many questions unanswered. In the midst of a multivolume series on the history of sexuality, Foucault's work had come increasingly to focus on ethics and subjectivity. Some scholars contend that this focus on ethics and subjectivity in Foucault's later work constitutes a dramatic break from his earlier work, which they see as lacking an adequate notion of the subject and as apolitical. I have argued that Foucault's middle work focuses on the normalizing practices that constitute subjectivity, and is thus centrally concerned with ethics, politics, and subjectivity. Sorting through the question of what defines a work, what ought to be included or excluded from consideration of an author's *oeuvre* is no easy task. I do not intend to provide a general or definitive answer to this complex question here, but I believe that including Foucault's interviews and essays, as well as his political activism, gives us a broader sense of his work and is consistent with the notion in his later writings that one's life is a work of art.

For Foucault, the critical investigation that characterizes a philosophical attitude is an ongoing task that defines a life. Foucault's historical analyses intersect with his concern for important contemporary social issues. For instance, during the time he researched and wrote *Discipline and Punish,* he engaged in activism regarding prison issues. Foucault's interviews, and his articles in the popular press, demonstrate his consistent engagement with political issues. Foucault's interviews and articles in the popular press should be included in his *oeuvre* because he himself considered them important and because they provide an important supplement to understanding his significant theoretical texts.[94] Moreover, Foucault's political activism should also count as evidence that he advocated social change. While discussing his ideas about the relationship between philosophical work and politics, Foucault says, "The key to the personal poetic attitude of a philosopher is not to be sought in his ideas, as if it could be deduced from them, but rather in his philosophy-as-life, in his philosophical life, his ethos."[95] He notes that philosophy can be used politically in ways that are counter to its theoretical commitments, citing cases of philosophers who held the universal values of Kant and the Stoics writing things in support of the Nazi regime in the 1930s. Foucault also points out that sometimes philosophers whose work advocates political action do not themselves engage in it. He criticizes the philosophers of engagement—Jean-Paul Sartre, Simone de Beauvoir, and Maurice Merleau-Ponty—for their lack of involvement in the French Resistance during World War II. This suggests that Foucault believed that a philosopher's political and social commitment ought not to be judged on the basis of her philosophical, theoretical work alone, but also on the basis of her actual political involvement.

In his later works, he proposed that one's life should be a work of art. And that this entailed ethical work on one's self. "From the idea that the self is not given to us, I think there is only one practical consequence: we have to create ourselves as a work of art."[96] Creating oneself as a work of art is an ethical project.[97] In his later work, especially *The Use of Pleasure, The Care of the Self,* and his interviews, Foucault makes the connection between self-creation and ethics. He views self-creation as inextricable from ethics; his discussions of the self as a work of art, the stylization of the self, and the aesthetics of existence involve ethical self-transformation in a social and political context. For Foucault, self-transformation takes place through work on the self, and involves what he calls techniques of the self. Foucault sometimes referred to writing philosophy as a transformative process. Recall that he defined philosophy broadly as the questioning of domination at every level. Combined with his remarks about work on the self as an ethical project, one can see some continuity between Foucault's theoretical writings and his political activism. To sum up, if one takes Foucault's claims that the critical investigation that characterizes a philosophical attitude defines a life, that the work of an author has vague and ambiguous boundaries and that one's work on oneself (but always in social and political contexts) is the paramount ethical task, then the case can be made that one should not only include all of Foucault's published work in his corpus, but also that his own "aesthetics of existence" regarding his political activism should be seen as part of his attempt to create a new nondisciplinary, nonnormalizing ethics.[98]

CONCLUSION: FOUCAULT AND FEMINIST RESISTANCE

Many feminists resist Foucault. They find his theory of resistance inadequate to facilitate social and political change; and his lack of a normative framework unable to ground what they see as necessary claims to justice, rights, and freedom that undergird emancipatory social and political movements. I have argued that Foucault offers a form of critique based on his skeptical method that does not rely on traditional Enlightenment norms. I have also explicated his notion of power in an attempt to defend his position against widespread misreading. Finally, I have shown how Foucault's later work urges us to think of our very lives as the material for ethical transformation. Foucault's later work echoes the feminist claim that "the personal is political" and that theory and practice are inseparable.

Why should feminists embrace Foucault? Because he provides a compelling account of social norms. He graphically illustrates the damage that norms can do through the process of marginalization and exclusion of those who do not conform to them. Foucault's work illustrates the ways that norms operate at the level of the body itself. Feminists should be sympathetic to the damage that norms can do. Although they masquerade as neutral, all too often norms universalize the perspective of the dominant. As both feminists and Foucault have noted, the universal norms of humanism incorporate an ideal of rationality that is constituted through the exclusion of otherness. And as feminists have argued, this ideal of rationality is coded as masculine. Moreover, it is not just the philosophical norms of humanism that support the perspective of the dominant group, social norms serve to promote and sustain the values of the dominant group. Much feminist work is devoted to illuminating the ways that gender norms in patriarchal societies serve to disempower women.

A first step in resisting norms is to recognize them and to recognize them as potentially damaging. The obvious next step is to somehow resist the norms that are damaging. Foucault's genealogies draw attention to the damage that norms can do, but feminist critics worry that Foucault fails to provide an account of resistance. Given his notion of power as omnipresent, this seems to leave us mired in networks of power, domination and norms from which there is no escape. Earlier I discussed this misconception of Foucault's notion of power. But because the misconception is so prevalent, Foucault's own direct rebuttal to this idea of power as inescapable bears repeating here. Foucault himself says, "Should it be said that one is always 'inside' power, [that] there is no 'escaping it, [that] there is no absolute outside where it is concerned, because one is always subject to the law in any case? . . . *This would be to misunderstand the strictly relational character of power relationships* (emphasis added)."[99]

I offer an interpretation of Foucault's notion of power that remains faithful to what he himself said, but also provides the space to think about freedom as redefined. Here I elaborate on Foucault's notion of power with respect to feminist resistance. Although power is everywhere, according to Foucault, freedom is still possible. In fact, freedom and power are necessarily connected. If there is no possibility for freedom, then there is no relationship of power, but rather a state of domination. One of the problems with Foucault's very rich notion of power is that he fails to adequately distinguish among different types of power, and to clarify the many different levels at which power operates. In spite of this, I believe that Foucault offers the richest account of power available in social and political theory, and that it is particularly useful to feminists. He makes a distinction between power and domination, and he allows for resistance in both cases. Like most feminist theorists, Foucault wants to allow that power exists and operates on the interpersonal, micropolitical level, as well as the structural, macropolitical level. His account of power helps to elucidate the ways that gender inflects power relationships. Foucault's ideas about resistance to domination correspond to some feminists' interest in theorizing the possibility of agency under oppression. And he allows for collective social and political transformation through the reversal of power or the end of a state of domination.

Once the widespread misconception that Foucault's account of power is solely an account of domination is laid to rest, feminists might be less wary of Foucault's ideas. Although feminists who resist Foucault may still do so, they should recognize that resistance is not only possible given Foucault's account of power, it is necessary to it. Given its importance, it may seem strange that Foucault did not say more about resistance. Even some feminists who are sympathetic to Foucault, such as Jana Sawicki and Linda Alcoff, claim that resistance is undertheorized in Foucault's work. Foucault addresses the absence of specific solutions to social and political problems in an interview: "It is always useful to understand the historical contingency of things, to see how and why things got to be as they are. But I am not the only person equipped to show these things, and I want to avoid suggesting that certain developments were necessary or unavoidable. . . . Of course, there are useful things I can contribute, but again, I want to avoid imposing my own scheme or plan."[100]

Foucault's hesitancy to set a specific agenda for social and political change is consistent with his approach of eschewing general, abstract, universal solutions.

Instead Foucault advocates political interventions that are specific to the situation. While his writings and interviews do not spell out solutions to social and political problems, his life as an activist provides many examples of specific and local resistance. Feminists have become increasingly cautious about advocating abstract and universal solutions. Radical feminist critiques showed the ways that overlooking the specificity of women's experience results in a perspective that, while ostensibly gender neutral, is in fact male, because male experience is taken as paradigmatic. Multicultural feminists criticized the radical feminist notion of "women's experience" for ignoring racial, ethnic, and cultural differences among women. Multicultural feminists argued that radical feminists fell prey to the very problems of abstraction and false universalizing that they abjured in the liberal feminist position. Significant criticisms of feminist positions that seem to assume that women's experience is homogeneous have also been made on the basis of sexual orientation and class. Feminist theory is still in the process of evolving. Yet if the criticisms by multicultural feminists, lesbian feminists, and working class feminists are to be taken into account, then it appears that feminists, like Foucault, need to reject abstract and universal solutions to political problems in favor of specific, local resistance. I suggest that feminists, rather than looking to Foucault for examples of resistance, look to the history of women's resistance and feminism. What does or would feminist resistance look like?

In her article, "Femininity, Resistance and Sabotage," Sarah Lucia Hoagland looks at sabotage as a form of resistance to oppression, (in Foucault's terms this would be resistance under a state of domination because of the persistent asymmetry of gender roles).[101] Hoagland uses the example of a former beauty queen trapped in a traditional, patriarchal marriage who is expected to perform all the domestic duties, such as cooking and cleaning, flawlessly. Yet she burns dinner whenever her husband brings the boss home unexpectedly. And she periodically packs raw eggs for her husband's lunch. Hoagland's example shows how resistance is possible even in situations of oppression or domination. It also shows that sometimes resistance relies on deception. And, even more significantly, it shows that resistance may involve the active subversion of power by using power against itself. For instance, in this example the feminine stereotype of flightiness serves to protect the woman from blame for her actions. The gender norms that prescribe this woman's social role as housewife serve to constrain her activities. Yet the gender norms that unfairly stereotype beautiful women as flighty provide a safe avenue of resistance that in fact undermines the gender norm that women are (by nature) domestic. This strategy of using power to resist power runs throughout examples of women's resistance to patriarchal power.

A second example is the Mothers of the Plaza de Mayo in Argentina. The Mothers of the Plaza de Mayo is a political group composed of women whose children disappeared under the repressive governmental regime in Argentina during the 1970s and 1980s. During this time, the military government systematically disappeared people numbering in the thousands. The disappeared were abducted, often in the middle of the night, with no warning and no trace of their whereabouts left behind. Although the military government claimed that the disappeared had been arrested as political agitators, many of the disappeared had no political ties and included students, blue collar workers, writers, scientists, journalist, lawyers, professors, labor leaders, doctors, psychiatrists, and religious leaders. Because Argentine society is still somewhat traditional in terms of gender roles, it was the women of the families who searched for their missing children because the fathers had to go to work. When the mothers of the disappeared inquired into their daughter's or son's whereabouts, they were shuffled from government agency to government agency or met with staunch denial. The mothers of the disappeared began their efforts to find their children individually, but began to share their stories in the waiting rooms of various government agencies. Soon they began to meet in their homes and churches to coordinate their efforts to find their children, and to seek support from international human rights groups, such as Amnesty International. After a while, the mothers decided to meet in front of the government offices at the Plaza de Mayo. They first met there on April 30, 1977, and since that time have held weekly meetings and demonstrations at the Plaza de Mayo. The Mothers of the Plaza de Mayo went on to draw international attention to the plight of the disappeared in Argentina and to continue to press for prosecution of those responsible for the disappearances. The mothers' political activism both grew out of and subverted gender norms: "When they began their frantic search for their children, they were primarily homemakers, content with their absorption in family and household and expressing little interest in the world beyond. They had been socialized into these roles by a traditional Argentine society that regards the male as the dominant figure, the sole participant in public life and the undisputed head of the home."[102] The mothers used the gender norms of traditional Argentine society that honored and valued motherhood even as it excluded women from the public sphere.

Invoking their status as culturally revered mothers helped to protect the women in Argentina who demonstrated on behalf of those who had disappeared. Drawing on their socially and culturally revered status as mothers was a way of using the power of the social, political, and cultural norms that sanctified motherhood and the family. These social and political norms served the dominant power by perpetuating the traditional roles and status of women and thus reinforcing the status quo. Originally a way of keeping women in their place at home and circumscribing their power, this technique of domination failed when women used the very same stereotype of virtuous motherhood to call attention to the government's abuse of power.[103] While drawing on traditional gender norms, the mothers also subverted them as they became political activists and public figures. The work of the Mothers of the Plaza de Mayo is an instance of feminist resistance insofar as it demonstrates the collective political power of women. And it is compatible with Foucault's ideas about power and resistance; according to Foucault, power operates at least in part through social norms. The example of the Mothers of the Plaza de Mayo shows how norms can constrain and foster resistance at the same time.

Foucault's relationship to norms is complex, but I have argued that this allows him both to question norms and to develop critical social analyses. In his genealogical work, the link between ethics and politics can be found in the link between self-constitution and social norms. To resist normalization is at once both ethical and political. Feminists should be sympathetic to resisting norms as a form of political action. Gender norms have perpetuated women's oppression in myriad ways. For example, feminine stereotypes such as physical weakness and emotional instability have historically restricted women's opportunities in the workplace. Foucault's call for new forms of subjectivity and individualization imply new social and political structures, since for him the process of "subjectification" has always and will always take place in a historically, socially, and culturally specific framework. As feminists have become more deeply entrenched in disciplinary and institutional structures, we might benefit from adopting Foucault's skepticism. However, as we will see in the next chapter, feminists have reservations about Foucault's notion of subjectivity as well.

Chapter 3

▶•◀

FOUCAULT AND THE SUBJECT OF FEMINISM

Feminists lodge two seemingly contradictory complaints against Foucault's notion of the subject. On the one hand, some feminists accuse Foucault of abolishing subjectivity altogether. On the other hand, some feminists claim that Foucault proposes a subject that is wholly determined by outside forces. Both complaints rest upon the connection between subjectivity and moral and political agency. Moral and political agency are necessary for feminist theory and practice insofar as they are linked to the possibility of individual transformation and social change. Historically, the possibility of moral agency has presupposed a conception of a unified rational subject. Although assumed to be necessary, this conception of a unified rational subject has recently been challenged by postmodern theories. In general, the argument between those who hold that a unified conception of subjectivity is necessary to moral agency and those who challenge this rests upon a split between those who believe that we need modernist humanist assumptions to undergird social, ethical, and political theory, and those who wish to dispense with modernist notions. Most feminist theorists fall into the first group, for as discussed earlier, feminism is a liberation philosophy that requires an emancipatory politics. Foucault, of course, falls into the second group.[1] In this chapter, I argue that one finds an alternative to the modern conception of the subject in Foucault's work that is useful to feminists. I discuss Foucault's rejection of some of the prevalent conceptions of the subject in philosophy; it is clear, for instance, that he rejects the Cartesian *cogito*, and the more recent turn to the philosophy of the subject articulated in existentialism and phenomenology. Moreover, he is clearly suspicious of notions of subjectivity in psychological discourse. In spite of his rejection of these very specific ideas of subjectivity, Foucault does not reject the idea of subjectivity altogether. In fact, I argue that he provides a way of thinking about subjectivity that is both compatible with and useful to feminist theory and practice. Feminists need a conception of the subject that can account both for processes of normalization

53

and for resistance to norms. As even his critics would agree, Foucault's genealogical writings offer a powerful account of the process of how norms constitute subjectivity. But feminist critics worry that a subject thoroughly constituted through social norms lacks a basis for resistance to those norms. Foucault's later work offers a view of the self that is socially constituted and capable of autonomy and engaging in practices of freedom. However, when Foucault's later work has not been ignored by feminists, it has been criticized as presenting a view of the self that, while now capable of autonomy and freedom, is hopelessly subjectivist, individualist, and aesthetic.[2] I try to demonstrate that his genealogy of the subject, including his later works, offers an account of subjectivity that is both socially constituted and capable of resistance.

In this chapter, I address feminist criticisms of Foucault's notion of the subject. First, I examine the criticism that Foucault does away with the notion of subjectivity altogether. I argue that his rejection of the rational subject of Modernity parallels feminist criticisms of the Modern subject, for instance, in liberal political theory, as excessively rational and impossibly atomistic. Feminists have developed new understandings of subjectivity that do not isolate rationality as the *sine qua non* of the subject, and that account for the real situation of sociality, interdependence, and human development. I explore similarities and differences between the influential feminist account of the self in care ethics and Foucault's notion of the self. The relational self in care ethics provides an account of the self that emphasizes the importance of social roles and relationships. However, its undifferentiated focus on women's experience has led to charges by feminists of ahistoricism and false universalizing. Foucault's conception of subjectivity avoids charges of ahistoricism and universalism that have been directed at this relational self. I suggest that Foucault's genealogical approach can provide a model for feminist inquiries of the subject. His approach, like contemporary feminist approaches, emphasizes historical and cultural specificity and embodiment.

FEMINIST CRITICS

Feminist suspicions that Foucault is destroying the subject are widespread. Rosi Braidotti puts it this way: "The combination of conceptual elements is quite paradoxical: deconstructing, dismissing, or displacing the notion of the rational subject at the very historical moment when women are beginning to have access to the use of discourse, power and pleasure.... The truth of the matter is: one cannot deconstruct a subjectivity one has never been fully granted."[3] For feminists such as Braidotti, the deconstruction of the rational subject has bad consequences for women, (at the very least the timing is wrong). The rational subject has been the basis upon which claims to equality, rights, and freedom have typically been made. But as feminists such as Braidotti argue, women have yet to be granted the full status of rational subject and the realization of equal rights that follows from this status. Nancy Hartsock shares Braidotti's suspicion about postmodern attempts to decenter the subject. She asks, "Why is it that just at the moment when so many of us who have been silenced begin to demand the right to name ourselves, to act as subjects rather than objects of history, that just then the concept of subjecthood becomes problematic?"[4] If the subject 'disappears' who speaks or acts?[5] On what basis can political claims be made? Who is doing the choosing in moral and ethical situations? Feminists raise important questions about the disappearance, decentering, deconstruction, and fragmentation of the subject at this historical moment. So long as political discourse relies on an idea of the subject that is unified and rational, feminists will have a stake in defending this notion of subjectivity. Thus, the concept of subjectivity has important implications for politics.

Correlatively, concepts of subjectivity have important implications for ethics and moral theory as well.[6] Unified and rational subjectivity is seen as requisite for moral agency. In traditional philosophical accounts, moral agency relies upon the notion of freedom. In fact, the problem of agency has generally been construed as the determinism/free will debate. Freedom, in turn, often relies upon metaphysical assumptions (for instance, in Descartes the notion of freedom depends on the will, and in Kant, freedom depends on the noumenal world). The free will/determinism debate casts the issue as a dilemma in which agency is antithetical to considerations of the natural, material world. Thus, moral agency relies on a notion of subjectivity that is not determined by outside forces nor fragmented. Foucault rejects the terms of this debate. As Gilles Deleuze notes, "Three centuries ago certain fools were astonished because Spinoza wished to see the liberation of man, even though he did not believe in his liberty or even in his particular existence. Today new fools, or even the same ones reincarnated, are astonished because the Foucault who had spoken of the death of man took part in political struggle. In opposition to Foucault, they invoke a universal and eternal consciousness of the rights of man which must not be subjected to analysis."[7] Foucault clearly reconceives of freedom as occurring within, not outside of, power relations. Yet the dualistic thinking that associates power relations with determinism and opposes these to freedom continues to inform the debate about political and moral agency, and thus conceptions of subjectivity. Foucault not only criticizes this dualistic thinking, much of his work offers an alternative to this problematic assumption. I pursue this line further in chapter 4 when I demonstrate how Foucault attempts to avoid dualism in his conception of the body-as-subject.

While some feminists criticize Foucault for obliterating subjectivity because of his claims about the death and disappearance of Man, other feminists criticize

Foucault for conceiving subjectivity as an always subjected docile body enmeshed in relations of power. This latter group of feminists claim that the result of Foucault's genealogical investigation of subjectivity as produced through discourses and practices results in determinism. They view Foucault's subject as totally determined because it is enmeshed in relationships of power and is produced as effect through disciplines and practices. Lois McNay claims, "The emphasis that Foucault places on the effects of power upon the body results in a reduction of social agents to passive bodies and cannot explain how individuals may act in an autonomous fashion. This lack of a rounded theory of subjectivity or agency conflicts with a fundamental aim of the feminist project to rediscover and re-evaluate the experiences of women."[8] McNay contrasts the "social agent" to the "passive body." This contrast recapitulates a view of subjectivity that Foucault tries to avoid. For him, bodies are both active and passive; it is bodies that resist and increase their forces through discipline, as well as being shaped by disciplinary practices. Moreover, Foucault's subject will never be capable of autonomy in the Kantian sense. For Kant, autonomy and freedom consist in exercising one's rationality through giving oneself the rational law. As feminists have shown, notions of autonomy that purport to be free of all empirical influence ignore basic facts about human development and sociality.[9] Foucault does have a notion of self-governance in his later works—the self's work on itself or care for the self—that could be understood as a reconception of autonomy. Significantly, unlike for Kant, for Foucault self-governance takes place within social relationships and with reference to cultural and historical traditions. In what follows, I argue that feminists should not be so quick to dismiss Foucault's subject as a passive body incapable of autonomy. I propose that his rejection of an *a priori* subject is in line with much of feminist theory and further that his reconception of the subject as embodied and constituted through social norms may also be consistent with feminist goals.

FOUCAULT'S CHALLENGE TO SUBJECTIVITY

On some readings, feminist suspicion of Foucault seems to be well founded. After all, his proclamations about the "death of Man" and the death of the author clearly attack the idea of subjectivity. Conversely, his claim that the subject is an effect of power lends credence to his critics' charge that Foucault holds a deterministic view of the subject. Below I show how feminist critics may have come to interpret Foucault's notion of the subject in such diametrically opposing ways. These contradictory criticisms of Foucault correspond to critics' focus on specific works; critics who focus on his earlier archaeological work claim that he advocates the abolition of the subject; critics who focus on his middle genealogical work claim that his account of subjectivity is deterministic. But to say that these contradictory interpretations of Foucault result from the difference in his own position over the years is too simple. Likewise, to say that Foucault simply contradicts himself is too facile a dismissal. I try to provide a broader view of Foucault's notions of subjectivity and the self by examining feminist criticisms of Foucault, and exploring possible continuities in Foucault's work by taking the subject as the theme of his research.[10]

Foucault's call for the "death of Man" can be found near the end of *The Order of Things*. Having discussed the limits of representation, Foucault turns his attention to philosophy's attempts to represent human subjectivity. From Descartes through phenomenology, he finds representations of subjectivity woefully inadequate, caught as they are in the analytic of finitude—the empirico-transcendental double. Foucault states, "In our day . . . it is not so much the absence or the death of god that is affirmed as the end of man."[11] Coupled with his predictions that "man will disappear," that "man is in the process of perishing," "that man would be erased, like a face drawn in the sand at the edge of the sea," and that man is a recent invention, it is little wonder that feminist critics accuse Foucault of deconstructing subjectivity.[12] Moreover, *The Order of Things* is not the only place that Foucault attacks the notion of the subject. In *The Archaeology of Knowledge*, Foucault refers to the "different positions that the discoursing subject may occupy."[13] Rather than seeing the subject as having a unifying or synthetic function, Foucault's analysis looks at the way that "the various enunciative modalities manifest his [the subject's] dispersion."[14] And, perhaps less directly, Foucault's essay "What Is an Author?" challenges the idea of subjectivity. In it, he questions the unity of an author's work, and the relationship between an author and her work. Foucault challenges prevailing conceptions of subjectivity as unified, transcendental, and synthesizing, referring respectively to Descartes, Kant, and Hegel. He also rejects the idea that subjectivity is synonymous with consciousness, a philosophical problem that begins with Descartes and continues through the phenomenologists. Foucault argues against these notions and in favor of the dispersion, disappearance, and death of the subject. As we have seen, feminists object to this.

But feminists object no less to the determined subject found in Foucault's genealogical works. In *Discipline and Punish*, Foucault develops an analysis of the microphysics of power; he examines the way that the power-knowledge complex "invest[s] human bodies and subjugate[s] them by turning them into objects of knowledge."[15] Foucault explores the "body as the object and target of power."[16] He develops an analysis of the methods and techniques used to subject the body; he calls these methods and techniques disciplines. Disciplines operate on the body, affecting behavior, movement, gestures, and attitudes. Disciplines produce docile bodies; bodies "that may be subjected, used, transformed and improved."[17] Foucault claims that the classical age discovered the body as an object of control, but that the eighteenth century heralded new forms of power and control over individual bodies. These new forms of power and control operated on a different scale, insidiously permeating individual bodies. The result is a new level of control concerned with details such as gestures and movements and not simply the body as a whole. Foucault's discussion of the disciplines, combined with his discussion of new forms of surveillance, makes a convincing case for the near total domination of individuals by these new forms of power and control. It is no wonder that feminists look (again and again) to these sections of Foucault's work to criticize his notion of subjectivity. However, as I have argued in chapter 2, Foucault is critical of the new forms of domination that have emerged since the 1800s. His concept of power helps to illuminate the myriad ways that power functions not only through the state, but also through social norms. Just as there are strategies to fight state power, there are strategies to resist normalizing disciplinary power.

In *The History of Sexuality Volume One*, Foucault analyzes the relationship between subjectivity and power. He claims that the subject is produced through power rather than being outside of or antecendent to power relations. One of the ways that power produces subjects is through the process of confession; "[t]he truthful confession was inscribed at the heart of the procedures of individualization by power."[18] One confesses the truth about oneself, and in so doing becomes ensnared in the production of truth, the production of self, and relations of power. For Foucault, confession is an example of the reversal of the traditional relationship between truth and power. Instead of being freed, the one who confesses contributes to her own subjection by articulating the truth about herself. Through the ritual of confession, one is constituted as a subject in both senses of the word [*assujettir*], to be a subject and to be subjugated or subjected. Individuals participate in their own self-constitution through confession, but simultaneously they produce themselves with reference to the demands of power to speak the truth about themselves. In speaking about oneself, one is both subject to and subject of; "[t]he confession is a ritual of discourse where the subject who speaks coincides with the subject of the statement. . . ."[19] Interpreters have made much of this double sense of subjection. In fact, critics focus on the claim that one becomes a subject through subjection. This has often been read as further evidence that Foucault's subject is passive, docile, and totally dominated by outside forces. But this collapses the tension between these two aspects of becoming subject [*l'assujettissement*]. Just as his notion of power has two aspects, domination, which constrains, and the productive aspect, which engenders, his idea of the subject who is constituted by power also has two aspects; subjects play an active role in their own production.

Similarly, the disciplines both enable and constrain. And the subjects produced through them are not only damaged and limited by them but also gain

strength, skills, and resources. Two brief examples may help to illustrate this. Honi
Fern Haber discusses the female bodybuilder as an example of Foucauldian resistance.[20] The female bodybuilder's muscular body challenges the accepted, conventional norms of the stereotypical female body. Haber argues that this unconventional
body can serve as a point of Foucauldian resistance. What I would like to draw attention to is the way that a "discipline" both enables and constrains. The discipline
of weight lifting requires regulation of bodily habits and daily routines. It also requires regulation and control at the level of gestures and movements; one must lift
weights properly or risk sustaining an injury that will preclude further weight-lifting
activity, at least temporarily. But through discipline, one acquires new skills, new
strength and (perhaps) a different relationship to one's body. Moreover, the challenge
that female bodybuilders present to traditional gender norms may have broader social and political ramifications. Appropriate social and political roles for women have
historically been prescribed by gender norms. Women's assumed lack of physical
strength has limited their access to some fields that require physical strength. Gender norms are both produced through and challenged by disciplinary practices.

In "Foucault, Femininity, and the Modernization of Patriarchal Power,"
Sandra Lee Bartky discusses the ways that women take up and are subject to particular disciplinary practices associated with femininity.[21] She, too, shows the ambivalent character of the disciplines. Women engage in a variety of disciplinary
practices including weight control, cosmetic surgery, and applying make-up. As
Bartky notes, some of these disciplinary practices, such as the ritual of using cosmetics, not only subject women to dominating external forces, but also produce
particular skills, talents, and capabilities. For instance, while engaging in the discipline of applying make-up, women may hone their sense of color, gain a greater
sense of design, and foster their creative abilities. Nonetheless, these abilities arise
in the context of the patriarchal imperative to "beautify oneself."

The relationships among power, disciplines, discourse, and subjectivity are
complex. Disciplines produce subjects, discourses produce subjects, subjects are
the effect of power.[22] In turn, disciplines, discourses, and power are each themselves complex; power is relational, discourses are polyvalent, and disciplines are
multifarious. Subjects thus produced are likewise complex, both she who is
speaking and she who is spoken of, both dominated and resisters, both constrained and enabled by various disciplines, practices, and institutions. Feminist
critics such as Lois McNay and Nancy Hartsock who claim that Foucault offers
only a notion of a passive subject determined by power relations miss the complexity of Foucault's account of subjectivity. Although Foucault's genealogical
works may appear to yield a determined subject, they sketch out a new way to
think about subjectivity that breaks from the traditional philosophical dilemma
of viewing self and sociality as mutually exclusive. Feminists especially should

be sympathetic to this approach because it parallels some recent developments in feminist moral theory.

To sum up, feminist critics find evidence in Foucault's genealogical work for their claim that Foucault's subject is thoroughly enmeshed in power relations, produced by disciplines and through discourse. Thus, they conclude Foucault presents us with a determined subject, a passive body incapable of autonomy. Other feminist critics look to Foucault's archaeological work to provide support for their claim that Foucault calls for the disappearance and dissolution of man, and they conclude that he wants to do away with subjectivity altogether. Several factors mitigate against these contrary readings of Foucault. First, as I have shown, even in his genealogical works Foucault's subject is not portrayed simply as the passive recipient of social forces. Rather subjectivity, like power, discourse, and discipline, needs to be understood as multivalent and complexly constructed. Second, focusing only on Foucault's middle (genealogical) works does not do justice to his ideas about subjectivity, especially since it is widely acknowledged that it is his later works that focus on subjectivity. It is these later works—*The History of Sexuality Volumes Two* and *Three*, his work on the technologies of the self, and on governmentality—that deal with the process of subjectification, the active process of the subject constituting herself. Thus, no account of Foucault's subject can be complete without taking into consideration these later works. Third, Foucault had much to say about subjectivity in his essays and interviews, and including a consideration of what he said there helps to flesh out his ideas about subjectivity. As I demonstrate below, attention to these materials can help to make sense of the seeming contradiction between his view, on the one hand, that man is disappearing, and on the other hand, that the subject is determined by social forces.

FOUCAULT'S REFUSAL

Foucault does explicitly reject the subject of the Enlightenment. "Because what troubles me with these analyses which prioritise ideology is that there is always presupposed a human subject on the lines of the model provided by classical philosophy, endowed with a consciousness which power is thought to seize on."[23] The Enlightenment model of subjectivity equates consciousness with the self. This is epitomized by Descartes' famous formulation, "I think, therefore I am." Descartes' influential view of subjectivity not only assumes the priority of consciousness to subjectivity but questions the relationship between mind (consciousness) and body. The Cartesian view of subjectivity with its emphasis on consciousness and its problematic assumptions about the relationship between mind and body has been supplanted by subsequent philosophical understandings of subjectivity and the mind-body relationship. Phenomenology and existential-ism represent important philosophical approaches to these issues. I cannot go into the variety of positions represented by the wide range of thinkers considered phenomenologists and existentialists, but in general phenomenology and existential philosophy focus on lived experience. This focus on lived experience includes attention to the dimension of embodiment, the social production of meaning, historical specificity, and material cultural practices. Phenomenological and existential approaches provide a viable alternative to much of what is problematic about Enlightenment conceptions of subjectivity typified by Descartes' view. But Foucault rejects as well the subject of phenomenology and existentialism. "One has to dispense with the constituent subject, to get rid of the subject itself, that's to say, to arrive at an analysis which can account for the constitution of the subject within a historical framework. And this is what I would call genealogy, that is a form of history which can account for the constitution of knowledges, discourses, domains of objects etc., without having to make reference to a subject which is either transcendental in relation to the field of events or runs its empty sameness throughout the course of history."[24] This rejection of the subject worries feminists who argue that we must retain a notion of the subject in order to have political and moral agency.

But what is Foucault refusing when he refuses the subject? Foucault's opposition to the Cartesian *cogito* is well documented.[25] But surely his wariness of accepting a Cartesian notion of subjectivity is not what feminists object to, because many feminists also reject a Cartesian notion of subjectivity. In an interview shortly before his death Foucault responds to the question, "But you have always 'refused' that we speak to you about the subject in general?" by saying, "What I refused was precisely that you first of all set up a theory of the subject . . . What I wanted to know was how the subject constituted himself, in such and such a determined form. . . . I had to reject a certain *a priori* theory of the subject in order to make this analysis of the relationships which can exist between the constitution of the subject or different forms of the subject and games of truth, practices of power and so forth."[26] His denial of the subject here is not a denial of the subject *tout court*, but a hesitation to begin from a particular theory of the subject. Foucault refuses the subject as the condition for the possibility of experience, claiming instead that it is experience that results in a subject or subjects.[27] When asked whether his books prior to *The History of Sexuality* "ruin the sovereignty of the subject," Foucault replies that he wanted to return to the problem of the subject and follow its developments through history to analyze "the combination of processes by which the subject exists with its different problems and obstacles and through forms which are far from being completed."[28] Foucault does not reject the subject altogether, but refuses a particular formulation of it. Foucault refuses conceptions of subjectivity that assume an *a priori* notion of the subject either as the condition for the possibility of experience (which he ascribes to phenomenology and existentialism) or as transcendental consciousness (which he attributes to Descartes and Kant). But these conceptions of subjectivity hardly exhaust the possibilities for conceiving of the self. As he says, "subjectivity . . . is of course only one of the given possibilities of organization of a self-consciousness."[29] For Foucault, subjectivity is a historically and culturally specific way of conceptualizing the self. He associates the emergence of the desiring subject with Christianity because of its concern with deciphering, controlling, and confessing sexual desire. He points out that Greek thought did not have a theory of subjectivity or a conception of the subject. Foucault does not deny that the Greeks were interested in issues of the self such as self-mastery and self-knowledge. The Greeks, like later philosophers, were interested in defining the conditions for experience, or as Foucault puts it, problematizing experience. Different historical epochs problematize experience differently and for the Greeks the result of the problematization of experience was not the subject, but the individual. Foucault claims that there is no theory of the subject in Greek philosophy and hence no subject.[30] As he says, "What was missing in classical antiquity was the problematization of the constitution of the self as subject."[31] For Foucault, the notion of subjectivity is fraught with problems. He is especially critical of the tie among subjectivity, sexuality, and truth, which he traces in *The History of Sexuality Volume One*. This particular form of subjectivity was constituted through the practices of Christianity, notably confession, but continues to influence current Western conceptions of morality. Foucault believes that a subject-centered morality has run its course. His objections to anthropological universals discussed in chapter 2 carry over to conceptions of subjectivity and morality. However, his rejection of universals should not be seen as a disinterest in moral and ethical questions. His studies of Antiquity are an exploration of an ethics that does not rely on a universal moral code, and an elaboration of a process of subjectivization that does not result in a (Modern, or in his terms, Classical) subject.[32] Foucault's attack on the subject can be seen as specific to the subjectivity of what he calls the Classical Age. His genealogies reveal the normalizing character of the disciplines that constitute subjectivity; this should prompt us to investigate nonnormalizing ways of existence. In Foucault's view, refusing what we are would enable us to liberate ourselves from the type of individuality (subjectivity) that has imposed itself on us through disciplines and practices for the last several centuries. The refusal to be what we are, to be a subject and hence subjected, opens up new possibilities for being.

Foucault's call to get rid of the subject is directed towards contemporary conceptions of subjectivity, which he finds problematic.[33] Rather than abandoning the notion of the subject, Foucault wishes to trace its development; ". . . we should try to discover how it is that subjects are gradually, progressively, really and materially constituted through a multiplicity of organisms, forces, energies, materials, desires, thoughts, etc."[34] His remarks make clear that his refusal of the subject is the refusal to take what is a particular historical form of consciousness as universal and ahistorical. It is not meant as a complete dismissal of the theoretical problematization of the self. In the introduction to *The Use of Pleasure*, Foucault describes his genealogical project in *The History of Sexuality* series as a shift from self to subject, as well as a genealogy of sexuality.[35] Many scholars argue that Foucault's later work—volumes two and three of *The History of Sexuality* and various interviews and articles—belatedly introduces an active and autonomous notion of the self.[36] This active self is especially apparent in *The Care of the Self,* where Foucault analyzes the self's relation to self. Critics raise two problems for this active subject of the late Foucault; they view it as inconsistent with his earlier work (particularly *Discipline and Punish*). And while some see it as a corrective to the overly passive view of the subject in Foucault's middle works, they criticize his new focus on the self as primarily aesthetic and individualistic.[37] On the issue of continuity, I heed Foucault's claims that his last work developed out of his earlier work and that the subject is the general theme of his research.[38] I provide a reading of his genealogical works that accounts for resistance, and I connect this to the practices of the self that he discusses in his later works. I argue that the self that Foucault discusses in *The History of Sexuality Volumes Two* and *Three* is relational and ethical. My reading of Foucault's later work emphasizes his portrayal of this self as social and relational, as depending upon relations to others.[39] Foucault's focus on the "ethical subject of sexual conduct" in volumes two and three of *The History of Sexuality* invites comparison with other views of the ethical subject. I draw some parallels between Foucault's discussion of the care of the self and the feminist idea of a relational self in care ethics. And I point out commonalities between Foucault's criticism of a transparent, rational subjectivity, and feminist criticisms of the atomistic, rational subject. I demonstrate that Foucault and feminists agree about the pervasiveness of power and the correlative expansion of the political. Moreover, power and subjectivity are inextricably linked in Foucault. If we consider carefully what Foucault says about the subject and power, and take seriously his distinction between power and domination, Foucault's subject seems constituted by social relations, yet capable of resistance. This social subject capable of resistance that emerges out of my reading of Foucault is compatible both with feminist aims of capturing the specificity of women's experience and the political and social transformations necessary to end the oppression of women.

FOUCAULT'S GENEALOGY OF THE SUBJECT

By his own description, most of Foucault's work is devoted to an exploration of what constitutes human subjectivity. The processes through which human beings are made into subjects Foucault calls "modes of objectification." His work has dealt with three modes of objectification that follow a rough chronology of Foucault's work. The first mode of objectification deals with modes of inquiry that assume the status of sciences, such as economics, linguistics, or biology. His archaeological work explores these modes of objectification and the subjects produced by them, for example, the productive subject and the speaking subject. The second mode of objectification Foucault calls "dividing practices," where the subject is either divided from others, e.g., the criminal from the noncriminal, or divided within herself. Foucault's genealogical work is concerned with these dividing practices that examine the ways that institutions objectify the subject. Much of the debate about the usefulness of Foucault to feminism is concerned with Foucault's institutional analyses, especially *Discipline and Punish*. The third mode of objectification is really subjectification, that is, an analysis of how individuals turn themselves into subjects, e.g., the sexual subject. Foucault focuses on this mode of objectification in volumes two and three of *The History of Sexuality* and in his work on the practices of the self. Although it is this third mode of objectification that is concerned with the active constitution of the subject, there has been little attention to it by feminists.[40] This oversight is unfortunate, since the later works of Foucault, assorted articles and interviews, and volumes two and three of *The History of Sexuality* contain a view of the self that has affinities to recent feminist moral theory.

Understanding power is central to understanding Foucault's analysis of subjectivity. As discussed in chapter 2, Foucault explicitly rejects the paradigm of power as repression, arguing that power is not only negative but also productive. He rejects the juridical model of power wherein power is characterized as repressive, rule-based, uniform, and prohibitive. According to this model the subject is constituted as one who obeys this negative unilateral power. Foucault characterizes power as positive and productive. Indeed, he states that the subject herself is an effect of power. Power is everywhere, a multiplicity of force relations; it is always local and unstable. Power is action that runs through and between things; power is first and foremost relational.[41] Not only is power always a relationship, but power relationships exist everywhere. Foucault's relational view of power improves on the juridico-discursive model of power. His view illuminates how power pervades the social body: "Between each point of a social body, between a man and a woman, in a family, between a teacher and a pupil, between the one who knows and the one who doesn't, there pass relations of power which are not the pure and simple projection of the great sovereign power over individuals; rather they are the mobile and concrete ground upon which power comes to be anchored, they are the conditions of the possibility for its functioning."[42] Foucault's analysis of power as omnipresent and dispersed coincides with feminist claims that power is present in many arenas of life that on a traditional liberal view were considered private or apolitical, such as the family and the classroom. Likewise, both feminists and Foucault expand the realm of the political to include issues previously considered private, such as personal relationships, sex, and the body.

Although the political is pervasive, it is not all-powerful. Recognizing that relations of power are everywhere does introduce politics into all social interactions. But far from reinforcing the status quo, this recognition is a prerequisite to analyzing and changing social relations. As I discuss in chapter 6, in consciousness-raising groups women questioned the disciplines and practices of femininity and developed individual and collective resistance to them. One of the key insights of the early Women's Liberation movement was that the political is present in everyday life. Feminists pointed out the gender politics in domestic relationships, in doctor-patient relationships, and even within Leftist political groups. For feminists, the notion that the "personal is political" opened up a vast array of relationships and power structures to constructive criticism. Foucault, too, recognizes the pervasiveness of politics in everyday life: "To say that 'everything is political' is to recognize this omnipresence of relations of force and their immanence to a political field."[43] The pervasiveness of power and its effect on all aspects of our daily life is a significant move away from the traditional liberal understanding of a centralized political power emanating from the state. Foucault's understanding of power as pervasive supports feminist challenges to the public/private split and encourages extending the analysis of power dynamics to interpersonal relationships.

As discussed in chapter 2, feminists object that the omnipresence of power seems to inhibit the possibility for agency and resistance on the part of the subject. But Foucault is quite clear that power is always subject to reversal and that freedom is a condition of the possibility for power's existence. In "The Subject and Power," Foucault puts it this way: "Power is exercised only over free subjects, and only insofar as they are free. By this we mean individual or collective subjects who are faced with a field of possibilities in which several ways of behaving, several reactions and diverse comportments may be realized. Where the determining factors saturate the whole there is no relationship of power."[44] The possibility of reversal distinguishes power from domination; relationships of domination are static relationships of power. Whereas relations of power exist everywhere, relations or states of domination are a consolidation of power by a social group. When domination occurs at the societal level, reversal is possible only through revolution or collective resistance.[45] While subjectivity is constituted through discourses of truth that are imbued with relationships of power, this nonetheless does not automatically preclude the possibility of moral and political agency or resistance. Indeed, without the possibility of resistance there can be no power in Foucault's sense, only domination.

It is through power and its constitution of the subject that resistance is possible. There is a certain reciprocity between the subject and power; "The individual is an effect of power, and at the same time, or precisely to the extent to which it is that effect, it is the element of its articulation."[46] In other words, the subject is both an effect of power and a vehicle of power. Foucault explicitly rejects the idea that individuals are merely the "inert or consenting" target of power; as he says, "individuals are the vehicles of power, not its points of application."[47] Rejecting the paradigm of power as only repressive, it is easier to see that the claim "power is everywhere" need not result in the totalization of dominating forces. Power has not only a negative but also a positive aspect; it produces subjects, disciplines, and discourses. As I discussed in chapter 2, Foucault's genealogical work discusses both these aspects of power, although critics generally focus on only one aspect.[48] This lopsided view of power results in a similarly distorted view of the subject. If power is simply a negative, totalizing, dominating force, then the subject is correspondingly limited, restricted, and dominated.

While in his genealogies Foucault examined the role of institutions in constituting the subject, his later work deals with the active constitution of the subject, the role the subject plays in self-constitution. Considerable debate attends how to read Foucault's work; some scholars such as Peter Dews[49] argue that the later work reveals an abrupt theoretical shift, while Foucault views it as developing out of earlier work.[50] Even within Foucault's earlier work, many have noted inconsistencies regarding his simultaneous dismissal of the subject and preoccupation with subjectivity, and his implicit appeal to normative concepts such as freedom, truth, and justice.[51] Admittedly, there is a certain tension in Foucault's work. The many different contradictory interpretations by Foucault's critics and his champions serve to exacerbate this tension. My aim is not to eliminate this tension but to use it productively.[52] I read Foucault's later work as continuing to focus on subjectivity as socially constituted and historically variable.

Earlier I discussed the central role that confession plays in producing modern subjectivity. In *The History of Sexuality Volume One*, Foucault argues that while confession apparently gives the individual greater freedom through the articulation of the truth about herself, it in fact contributes to the process of subjectification because it takes place within relations of power and ties one to one's identity. Confession individualizes through the process of producing the truth about oneself. However, this process of individualization is not a solo enterprise. This production of the truth about oneself takes place within a social context. One of the ways that sexual confession was codified in scientific terms was through the method of interpretation. Foucault puts it this way, "The truth did not reside solely in the subject who, by confessing, would reveal it wholly formed. It was constituted in two stages: present but incomplete, blind to itself, in the one who spoke, it could only reach completion in the one who assimilated and recorded it."[53] The process of individualization depends on social relations with others. Admittedly, in *The History of Sexuality Volume One*, Foucault focuses on the ways that subjectivity has been produced through normalizing social relations, practices, and institutions. However, his focus on normalizing practices and institutions is historically specific; in volumes two and three of *The History of Sexuality*, Foucault explores the ways that cultural practices and traditions shape individual behavior without becoming normalizing. The practice of telling the truth about oneself through confession is central not only to the production of the discourse of sexuality and the corresponding scientific and medical institutions that sprung up around it, but also to the shift in the constitution of the subject. As mentioned earlier, the constitution of the subject takes different forms in different historical epochs and cultures. One of the decisive factors in the shift from the constitution of the self during Antiquity to the constitution of subjectivity, which according to Foucault takes place around the fourth century A. D., was Christianity. Through specific religious practices such as the examination of one's conscience and confession, Christianity exhorted one to examine every thought and confess every desire. Engaging in this process of self-reflection involved deciphering the self, or what Foucault calls a hermeneutic of the self. Foucault's project of doing a genealogy of the desiring subject led him to an examination of the roots of morality in Antiquity.

The History of Sexuality Volumes Two and Three trace the continuities and the changes of the discourses of sexuality from the ancient Greek to the early Roman period. *The Use of Pleasure* analyzes specific "practices of the self" and the series of problematizations out of which arose the discourse of sexuality and the desiring subject. Practices of the self refers to the specific practices one engages in to live an ethical life. The task of becoming an ethical subject was achieved not through universalizing principles, but through individualized action. Becoming an ethical subject involved overcoming the conflict between passion and reason by moderating one's desires. Having a proper relationship to the pleasures was achieved through regimen. Regimen, both diet and regulation of sexual pleasure, is a way of forming oneself as a subject with proper concern for the body. This use of pleasure through regimen holds an important place in the story of the constitution of the subject because it is in part through these bodily practices that one becomes an ethical subject.[54] Foucault locates the formation of the subject in the history of ethics: "a history of 'ethics' understood as the elaboration of a form of relation to self that enables an individual to fashion himself into a subject of ethical conduct."[55] This relation to the self involved moderation of one's desires. This exercise of moderation in turn produced self-mastery. Self-mastery involved not simply restraint, but also discipline through exercising and training in the gymnasium. It is notable that Foucault talks of discipline here without talking of it as normalizing. François Ewald points out that modernity is characterized by normativity, and that it is in the context of modernity that disciplines became normative.[56] In chapter 2, I made a distinction between philosophical and social norms; philosophical norms are universal and ahistorical, social norms are cultural phenomena that prescribe behavior. I argued that Foucault was rightly suspicious of norms insofar as they normalize behavior. But I do not think that Foucault holds that all social norms or even all disciplinary practices normalize in the same way. His objection to norms that impose universal principles does not indict social norms embedded in specific historical and cultural practices that are constitutive of social interaction. However, I do think that a certain ambiguity on this issue plagues Foucault's work and makes him vulnerable to criticisms regarding the seemingly inescapable domination of the subject through normalizing disciplines and practices. As I have pointed out, subjectivity itself is a historically specific conception of the self that emerged out of normalizing disciplinary practices. The self of Antiquity that Foucault describes in *The Use of Pleasure* and *The Care of the Self* does not engage in normalizing disciplinary practices. Indeed, the ancient self could not engage in normalizing disciplinary practices because they are linked to specific historical circumstances such as the influence of Christianity, the rise of science, and the emergence of the social sciences. It is in Foucault's later work on Antiquity that one finds a notion of the self that engages in (nonnormalizing) disciplinary practices that seem to increase rather than decrease freedom.

AESTHETICS OF EXISTENCE: LIFE AS A WORK OF ART

Commentators on Foucault willingly admit that his later work takes an ethical turn, but some find that this turn leads to a dead end. They claim that Foucault's ethical subject is individualistic and aesthetic. Foucault proposes that we think of our lives as a work of art. He invokes the notion of an aesthetics of existence wherein one's ethical choices are guided by aesthetic considerations. Critics claim that Foucault's later work focuses on the self without concern for others or attention to moral and political issues; this leaves Foucault's work on ethics open to charges that are raised against his earlier work—that is, that it is nihilistic, relativistic, and apolitical. More specifically, feminists who look to Foucault's later work to provide a counterpoint to what they see as the failure of his earlier work to adequately deal with issues of autonomy, agency, and collective action raise new challenges. Although Foucault's ideas about the care of the self and practices of freedom provide some resources for thinking about autonomy and agency, feminists claim that Foucault's view of the self in his later works is masculinist, atomistic, or solipsistic, and divorced from ethical and political considerations because of his focus on the aesthetics of existence. Jean Grimshaw notes three problems with Foucault's notion of the self in his later works.[57] First, because Foucault draws on ancient Greece as the source of his ideas about care of the self and practices of the self, he perpetuates the bias in ancient Greek society and thought that only elite men can be ethical subjects. Second, she claims that Foucault's aesthetic approach to morality is solipsistic, and fails to acknowledge collective goals and aspirations. Finally, she claims that Foucault's concern with self-mastery and care of the self leads to a subject-centered approach to morality that does not take into account the effects of one's action on others. Similar criticisms are raised by feminists Jane Flax and Lois McNay. Flax says of Foucault's notion of an aesthetics of existence, "Such a constant remaking of the self presupposes a socially isolated and individualistic view of the self."[58] She points out that such a notion of the self is hard to reconcile with feminist interests in enduring relationships, or participation in a political community. Lois McNay says that the central problem with Foucault's aesthetics of existence is that it "privileges an undialectical and disengaged theory of the self."[59] She claims that Foucault's call for our lives to become works of art implies an "active agent freely choosing modalities through which he or she constructs a relation with the self."[60] This active, atomistic self that feminists find in the later Foucault is no more suited to feminist aims than the passive, determined subject critics found in his earlier work. Indeed, from the point of view of his critics, it seems that Foucault has come full circle. While critics view his notion of the subject in his genealogical works as passive, completely enmeshed in social relationships, and thoroughly politicized, they view his idea of the self in his later works as active, isolated, atomistic, and divorced from political and ethical concerns. But each of these readings overemphasizes one aspect of Foucault's genealogy of subjectivity. I have argued that the notion of subjectivity found in Foucault's genealogical works can be seen as a resisting and active subject, as well as a disciplined and normalized subject. And I shall argue that his notion of the self in his later works retains a grounding in social relationships, practices, and institutions. In chapter 6, I show that Foucault's idea of an aesthetics of existence relates to both ethics and politics.

Foucault uses the terms "art of existence," "aesthetics of existence," "stylistics of life," and "life as a work of art" in his later books, essays, and interviews. He notes that in ancient Greece the concern was with leading a beautiful life, but that in the contemporary world we tend to relate ethical issues to scientific knowledge.

Although we cannot return to the world of ancient Greece, the historical study of it can be instructive. Antiquity offers a different paradigm for ethics, that of aesthetics, rather than science. Not surprisingly given his suspicion of the human sciences throughout his work, Foucault advocates the aesthetic paradigm. One of the attractive features of the aesthetic paradigm is that it is not universal and is therefore not normalizing. Thus, an aesthetics of existence is consistent with the positive recommendations for change that Foucault makes throughout his work; for him invention, innovation, creativity, and transformation should characterize our relationship to ourselves. As Jean Grimshaw and other feminist critics point out, in Antiquity the possibility for leading a beautiful life was limited to a small group of elite males. Admittedly, *The History of Sexuality Volumes Two* and *Three* do focus on the construction of male ethical subjectivity, from the concern with virility to the proper relationship for men both with their wives and with boys. But Foucault emphatically denies that he looks to the Greeks for an alternative or answer to our contemporary problems.[61] His study of Antiquity teaches us the same lesson that his earlier genealogies do, that what may seem like necessary connections, for example, between ethics and science, are historically contingent, and not the result of human nature or anthropological universals. So, what Foucault takes from his study of Antiquity is not a specific solution, but a new way of thinking about the connection between ethics and aesthetics. Departing from the exclusivity of the Greeks, where the beautiful life was the prerogative of elite males, he asks, "But couldn't everyone's life become a work of art?"[62] Foucault explicitly distinguishes his proposal that one's life could be a work of art from the contemporary obsession with perfecting one's lifestyle, which is characterized by attention to superficial details. For Foucault, life as a work of art is characterized by creativity, and attained through work on the self. Work on the self involves the intensification of relations to oneself; this intensification of relations to self is characterized by self-mastery and self-knowledge. Work on oneself and the correlative intensification of relations to self contribute to the formation of ethical subjectivity. This work on oneself occurs through specific practices of the self. Foucault's notion of one's life as a work of art involves ethical work; one elaborates one's life in terms of aesthetic values. Creating oneself as a work of art is not a fleeting task that changes daily; it is an ongoing project that involves constant work. This project is not complete until the end of one's life.[63] An aesthetics of existence is thus an ongoing project that requires ethical work. This contrasts with our current understanding of ethics, which Foucault sees as tied to the scientific paradigm, and relies on the notion of a true self. He rejects the notion that there is a true self, or deep self, to be discovered. He says, "[f]rom the idea that the self is not given to us, I think that there is only one practical consequence; we have to create ourselves as a work of art."[64] He notes that his view of what it means to create oneself as a work of art is closer to Nietzsche's view than to Sartre's. Nietzsche states that giving style to one's life involves long practice and daily work.[65] This fits with my characterization above. Given the stability and long-term commitment that making one's life a work of art involves, the criticism by Flax and McNay that an aesthetics of the self presupposes a voluntaristic notion of the self, where the self is continually remade, seems off-base. In fact, Flax associates Foucault's view with Sartre's, despite the fact that Foucault explicitly dissociates his view from Sartre's view of aesthetic creation and radical choice.[66] I find it helpful to think about Foucault's proposal to make one's life a work of art in terms of the actual process of artistic creation, for instance, a large drawing or painting. One makes certain choices along the way, but these choices are with reference to a particular vision of the end product. The vision of the end product may change along the way, and one exercises one's creativity in each and every choice of color, line, and form. The project requires daily work in a sustained direction. An artist does not go to the same large canvas every morning with a radically new vision in mind; if she did, it would be impossible to create art. She must persist in her task in order to create a work of art. Foucault's call for us to create our lives as a work of art likewise requires persistence and daily work. A beautiful life requires ethical work, work on ourselves through practices of the self. It is this connection between ethics and aesthetics that Foucault explores in his later work. Thus, Foucault's turn to aesthetics is not a retreat from ethics, as critics claim, but an attempt to return to ethics without the baggage of the Modern notion of the true self.

Contrary to critics' claims that Foucault advocates an aesthetic notion of the self that is removed from social and political engagement, I have demonstrated that his aesthetics of existence requires ethical work on one's self. Moreover, practices of the self have a social dimension. Whether done individually or collectively, practices of the self draw upon the conventions, rules, and customs of the culture. One of the main practices of the self that Foucault analyzes in his later works is care of the self. Care of the self implies a relationship with others in at least two ways. It enables one to occupy one's proper social role; "the care of the self enables one to occupy his rightful position in the city, the community, or interpersonal relationships."[67] And it requires the help of a guide or a close friend; "one needs a guide, a counsellor, a friend, someone who will be truthful with you."[68] Care of the self, then, implies social relationships. These social relationships include interpersonal relationships such as friendship and one's relation to others in the *polis*. Assuming one's proper place in the *polis* requires ethical work and the exercise of self-mastery. Care of the self concerns relations with others. Foucault says that care of the self is a history of subjectivity concerned with "the government of the self by oneself in its articulation with relations with others."[69]

Foucault situates his studies on the care of the self at the intersection between his earlier projects of the histories of subjectivity and the analysis of forms of governmentality.[70] Foucault claims that the principle "gnothi seauton" (know yourself) replaced the principle "epimeleia heautou" (care for yourself) in Greek thought. He examines the practices or techniques that fostered this care for one-self. *The Use of Pleasure* problematizes sexual ethics. Foucault examines the areas of dietetics, economics, and erotics. Foucault traces the practices and attitudes related to sexual pleasure. The use of pleasure is not regulated by prohibitions the way that contemporary sexual morality is, but is moderated by the subject's proper at-titude and relationship to his own desires. Foucault finds that the practices of diet, household management, and erotic relationships stylize, rather than codify, sexual conduct. In *The Care of the Self,* he focuses on four practices, the interpretation of dreams, the medical regimen, the marital relation, and erotic relations with boys. Care of the self involves an intensification of relations with oneself and the exer-cise of self-mastery. Self-mastery takes the form of exercising control over one's appetites, such as diet and sex, and also attention to one's bodily practices, such as exercise. These bodily practices, for Foucault, constitute a significant aspect of ethics. Ethics is concerned with behavior and modes of conduct. Foucault con-trasts ethics to a second aspect of morality which is concerned with universal norms. His focus throughout *The History of Sexuality Volumes Two* and *Three* is on the aspect of morality concerned with behavior, "the manner in which one ought to form oneself as an ethical subject acting in reference to the prescriptive ele-ments that make up the code."[71]

Foucault distinguishes four aspects of ethical conduct: (1) ethical substance, (2) mode of subjection, (3) ethical work, and (4) telos.[72] Ethical substance deals with the material of moral conduct, e.g., feelings, intentions, behavior, and acts. Ethical substance is the answer to the question, "What part of myself is concerned with moral conduct?" The mode of subjection has to do with the way that people recognize their obligation. In other words, which rules are followed and why? Does one behave ethically because of divine law, natural law, rational rule, beauti-fication of the self? Ethical work involves the specific practices one must engage in to achieve one's ethical aims. Foucault refers to these practices as practices of the self or ascetics [*askêsis*], these practices aim at self-transformation; they include self-examination, moderation, and complete renunciation. Finally, teleology deals with the aims and goals of our ethical conduct. What kind of person do we aspire to be when we act in a moral way—immortal, pure, free, masters of ourselves? Moral conduct, then, is not simply a matter of following rules or laws. It involves these four aspects, wherein the ethical subject works on himself; "this requires him to act upon himself, to monitor, test, improve and transform himself. There is no specific moral action that does not refer to a unified moral conduct; no moral con-duct that does not call for the forming of oneself as an ethical subject; and no forming of the ethical subject without 'modes of subjectivation' and an 'ascetics' or 'practices of the self' that support them."[73]

The History of Sexuality Volumes Two and *Three* are detailed explorations into the practices of the self of Antiquity; they comprise a history of ethics through an examination of these practices. One becomes an ethical subject through action. Care of the self includes knowing oneself, attending to oneself, transforming oneself. Foucault connects care of the self in the Greco-Roman world with individual liberty, and he claims that these practices permeated ethical thought from Plato until the later Stoics. He notes a shift in the relationship to the self that happened during the Christian era when care of the self was associated with egoism, selfishness, and individual interest. But in antiquity ethics as a practice of liberty centered on the imperative, "Care for Yourself." As noted, this care for the self is not simply individualistic, it "implies complex relations with others . . . relationship with others is present throughout the development of care for self."[74] The techniques of the self that Foucault explores in his later writings concern cultivation of the self in a social context.

This cultivation of the self contributes to establishing social practices, discourses, and institutions. As Foucault says, "It [the cultivation of the self] also took the form of an attitude, a mode of behavior; it became instilled in ways of living; it evolved into procedures, practices and formulas that people reflected on, developed, perfected and taught. It thus came to constitute a social practice, giving rise to relationships between individuals, to exchanges and communications, and at times even to institutions."[75] Cultivation of the self is inseparable from the social context in which it takes place; it both depends upon and gives rise to relationships. The techniques of the self involved in cultivating the self were part of a tradition that was communicated and taught to others. Foucault states, "I would say that if now I am interested in fact in the way the subject constitutes himself in an active fashion, by the practices of self, these practices are nevertheless not something the individual invents."[76] Throughout his analyses of the interpretation of dreams, medicine, the marital relation, and erotic relations with boys, Foucault explores the relationship of the self to the self. As mentioned earlier, the proper ethical relationship was self-mastery. Mastery of the self required an intensification of relation to self by which one constituted oneself as a subject of one's acts. However, this intensification of self relations does not necessarily result in individualism.

Foucault distinguishes three senses of individualism: the intensity of the relations to the self which involves work on oneself, the valuing of private life such as the family and domestic sphere, and what he calls the "individualistic attitude." The individualistic attitude is the view that individuals are separate from social groups and institutions. He suggests that the intensification of the relations to self may be independent of the individualistic attitude of the singular subject.[77] Care of the self and the attendant intensification of the relation of self to self relied on communication with others: "Around the care of the self, there developed an entire activity of speaking and writing in which the work of oneself on oneself and communication with others were linked together. Here we touch on one of the most important aspects of this activity devoted to oneself: it constituted, not an exercise in solitude but a true social practice."[78] Foucault argues that this new mode of the subject is not simply a response to social and economic changes. "Hence the cultivation of the self would not be the necessary consequence of these social modifications; it would not be their expression in the sphere of ideology; rather, it would constitute an original response to them, in the form of a new stylistics of existence."[79] This new stylistics of existence formed out of the practices of the self is a result of the subject active in her own self constitution, not simply the passive recipient of economic and social determinants.

Foucault's subject as sketched out in his later works is constituted through disciplines and social practices but not determined by them. Foucault's discussion of the subject of Modernity (the Classical Age) is instructive. He demonstrates the ways in which the constitution of subjectivity is invested by power through normalizing disciplines and practices. However, his account of the pre-Modern subject in his studies of Antiquity demonstrate alternative forms of self-constitution. I explore these practices of the self more fully in chapter 6. For now, I wish to call attention to a feature common to the problematization of the self in Foucault's studies of Antiquity and the Classical (Modern) age. In both cases, selves or subjects are formed through practices, are enmeshed in social relationships, and exist within institutional matrices. Moreover, as will become clear in the following chapter, for Foucault notions of the self and subjectivity are inseparable from embodiment and bodily practices.

THE RELATIONAL FEMINIST SUBJECT

It would be impossible to capture the range and variety of feminist notions of the subject. However, like Foucault, most feminist theorists reject the notion of the Enlightenment subject as disembodied consciousness. Recent feminist analysis focuses on the embodied subject embedded in a social context. Challenges to the Enlightenment subject by feminists come from a variety of perspectives. Here I focus on feminist criticisms of the atomistic individualism underlying liberal political theory and the reconception of the moral subject found in care ethics. I trace some similarities between the relational self central to care ethics and the actively self-constituting subject in Foucault's later works.[80] Both avoid the false dilemma that pits the sociality of the self against moral and political agency.

As feminists have pointed out, the conception of the subject in liberal political theory is problematic on several different counts.[81] Although there are significant differences among the specific philosophical views that are referred to alternately as liberalism, humanism, Enlightenment thinking, or Modernity, here I rehearse what are generally taken to be the common features of these views. The assumption of a universal rational subject has often meant the exclusion of women, because historically women have been associated with emotions and the body. Women have been viewed as less rational than men. Moreover, the assumed universality of the subject erases differences that may be constitutive of subjectivity, such as gender or race. By ignoring such particularity, the presumed neutrality of universality implicitly favors the white, male citizen. The focus on rationality and universality abstracts from all other features about the self, particularly its material, embodied basis. Not only is the body ignored in this view, but social relations are assumed to be voluntary and entered into by fully developed adults. As many feminists have pointed out, this ignores undeniable features of the human situation. Notably, it ignores the fact that people do not spring like mushrooms from the earth, but are born into families and are completely dependent on them for the nurturance and support that will allow them to grow into adulthood.[82] This assumption of radical separateness, or atomism, obscures the work of caretaking generally done by women. And it assumes that the individual is prior to social relations. Yet as feminists argue, to be born is to enter into social relations. Social relations are constitutive of a subject in fundamental ways, from an infant's dependence on adult caretakers (usually the mother) for satisfaction of material needs, to learning to use language, to developing a capacity for rationality. Furthermore, beyond an infant's dependence on her family to nurture and provide for her, even as adults all human beings exist in a complex web of relationships. These relationships include both personal relationships and impersonal relationships, such as economic interdependence. The liberal view of the subject misrepresents the extent to which subjects are separate from one another, and outside of institutional arrangements.

The criticisms of this view of the subject implicit in liberal theory as rationalistic, isolated, and disembodied come from a variety of feminist perspectives, including liberal feminism. Liberal feminists, such as Susan Moller Okin, have pointed out the masculine bias of liberal political theory because its assumption of voluntary, contractual relationships ignores the fact that the family, not the individual, is the basic social unit.[83] Some radical feminists, on the other hand, question conventional notions of the family and the traditional role of mothering. Radical feminists are more likely to find fault with the liberal view of the self because its focus on rationality and abstraction from the body overlooks the facts of embodiment and sexual difference. Marxist and socialist feminists think that the liberal view of the self does not account for the historical situatedness of the self and the effects of social practices, especially the impact of the sexual division of labor. Feminist critical social theorists, such as Seyla Benhabib, believe that a view of the self should include some account of the development of rationality and communicative capacity. Multicultural feminists stress the importance of racial and ethnic identity to a notion of the self; global feminists believe that culture, religion, and colonialism play a role in the conception of the self. Postmodern feminists agree with multicultural and global feminists that differences among women should be acknowledged and taken into account when theorizing about subjectivity. But postmodern feminists balk both at fixed categories of identity that reify difference and at the universality of the liberal view that obscures difference.

To sum up, feminists criticize the liberal view of the subject on several counts, because of its presumed universality that obscures difference, including sexual difference; because of its rationality that has historically excluded women; and because of its abstraction from the concrete, material world, both in terms of the erasure of the body and the neglect of the social relationships and institutions on which every subject depends. Note that many of these criticisms are shared by Foucault; he vigorously and consistently objects to a notion of the subject that is universal and rational. He views the subject as constituted through social relations and institutions. And, he objects to the emphasis placed on consciousness in most theories of subjectivity; for him subjectivity is embodied. Some feminists have turned to object-relations psychology for a view of subjectivity that captures the social and relational aspect of subjectivity. I discuss this below and point out the similarities and differences between this view and my reading of Foucault's view of the subject.

Deontological moral theory has its historical roots in Kant, but remains one of the most prominent contemporary moral theories. It emphasizes notions of duty, obligation, and justice. Deontology holds that the moral point of view is impartial, that moral autonomy depends on resisting socialization, and that moral agents ought to follow universalizable moral rules. Feminist moral theory challenges this paradigm of moral agents as independent, autonomous, justice-oriented bearers of rights. Carol Gilligan criticizes Lawrence Kohlberg's theory of moral development for privileging the use of universal principles by autonomous moral agents. In contrast to the traditional view of the moral agent as autonomous, Gilligan argues that the ethic of care comes out of a sense of self that is relational.[84] Drawing on Nancy Chodorow's object relations theory, which holds that a person's identity develops out of her early relational experiences, Gilligan argues that girls develop a sense of self that is relational because they do not need to differentiate themselves from their primary caretaker as dramatically as boys.[85] Both Chodorow and Gilligan criticize as masculinist the view that moral autonomy is characterized by separation. Their criticisms indicate an implicit normative view that the ideal for both genders is a sense of self as connected to others. Gilligan characterizes moral maturity as the convergence of the ethic of care and the ethic of justice. She notes that moral theory needs to acknowledge the importance of relationships in order to deal with the complexity of human experience. Chodorow draws the general conclusion that: "becoming a person is the same thing as becoming a person in relationship and in social context."[86]

Gilligan's ethic of care emphasizes attachment to others, responsibility to relationships, and non-violence. She contrasts these features to the assumption of separateness, the notion of equality between individuals, and the idea of justice that characterize the ethic of justice. One of Gilligan's main objections to the application of the ethic of justice to all moral situations is its reliance on universal principles. In applying universal principles, the moral agent abstracts not only from the particular circumstances of the situation, but also from her own identity and life history. Gilligan found that relationships and social roles were fundamental to the justification that women provided for their solutions to moral problems. Moreover, her research demonstrated that the significance that her female subjects placed on care and relationships was not taken into account by traditional models of moral reasoning. Indeed, the deontological model of moral reasoning explicitly encourages the repudiation of relationships with its emphasis on impartiality. Gilligan's care ethics presents a view of the subject as constituted through and sustained by relationships with others. Furthermore, in care ethics these relationships are assumed to be reciprocal, mutual, and caring. Moral decisions are made from within a network of relationships with an eye toward enhancing the relationship and not harming others. On this view, the moral imperative is an injunction to care. The care perspective includes a responsibility to others and to relationships, a contextual, nonhierarchical view of moral reasoning, and a conception of the self that is interdependent and relational.

The relation self of care ethics, like Foucault's as sketched out above, arises through social relations. Because the self emerges through social relations, moral agency and autonomy are not viewed as contrary to socialization, but as arising from it. One of Gilligan's research subjects describes a moral dilemma as "a network of connection, a web of relationships that is sustained by a process of communication."[87] This emphasis on communication echoes Foucault's claim cited above that care of the self relied on communication with others. Gilligan's ethic of care redefines the moral subject as relational. Correlatively, for Gilligan, endorsing a relational moral subject involves a move away from universal principles. In care ethics, moral action arises from within a network of social relations, and depends upon the particular situation and the individual involved. This move away from universal principles and toward individual action within a network of social relations parallels the distinction Foucault makes between morality as a universal code and ethics as the behavior and conduct of the individual.

Feminist philosophers have expanded on Gilligan's care ethics approach, proposing a self both social and capable of resistance. Diana Meyers reformulates autonomy as a competency acquired through socialization. This reformulation overcomes the dichotomy between viewing autonomy as the resistance to social-ization and viewing the self as social.[88] Seyla Benhabib, too, offers a view of a so-cial self capable of autonomy while recognizing that we are embedded in social networks: "[T]he web of human affairs in which we are immersed are not simply like clothes which we out grow or like shoes we leave behind. They are ties that bind; ties that shape our moral identities, our needs, our visions of the good life. The autonomous self is not the disembodied self."[89] This feminist reconceiving of the subject gives weight to the network of relationships and social roles that con-stitute subjects while still allowing for moral agency. This social self—a self who is relational and situated within specific historical and political circumstances—pre-dominates in recent feminist moral theory.[90]

While I have emphasized what I see as the similarities between the feminist view of the self in care ethics and Foucault's view of the self, there are significant differences as well. In contrast to the view of social relations as mutual and recip-rocal in care ethics, Foucault often seems to view social relations as strategic and agonistic. For instance, Foucault suggests that we should analyze power relations in terms of struggle, conflict, or war.[91] And for Foucault, all relations between in-dividuals are strategic because they are relations of power.[92] Often these strategic relations are confrontational or agonistic where individuals are pitted against one another. But strategic relations can also refer to relations between individuals that are benign, even beneficial, such as good pedagogical relations between a teacher and a student. Foucault's notion of relationships as strategic and often agonistic differs from Gilligan's portrayal of relationships as mutual and nurturing. There are important differences in their views of the social as well. Gilligan focuses on interpersonal relationships, first with respect to the relationships within the fam-ily that shape the gendered identities of women and men, and then with respect to the relationships between friends, lovers, and family that inform moral decision making. Gilligan's psychological approach focuses on identity as socially con-structed and she emphasizes the importance of identity for moral reasoning. As we shall see in chapter 5, Foucault questions the usefulness of notions of identity. His view of the social is significantly different from Gilligan's emphasis on the in-terpersonal. Foucault focuses on larger-scale social practices and institutions. He looks at the ways that changes in the law, in medicine, in religious practices, in the economy, in architecture, in technology, and in various fields of disciplinary knowledge such as psychiatry, linguistics, etc., affect and transform particular prac-tices like punishment or the practices involved in sexuality. Foucault's view of the social is historically and materially rooted. Much recent feminist work in ethics and moral theory expands on the ideas in care ethics, while feminist ethicists and political theorists have paid relatively little attention to Foucault. Given the differences between the ideas of the self and the social in care ethics and Foucault, can Foucault's ideas provide any resources for feminists?

CONCLUSION

Foucault and feminist care ethicists do agree that the subject is socially constituted through a network of discourses, institutions, and practices, but their views of the self and the social are fundamentally different. I have argued that feminist concerns about Foucault's subject are misplaced. He rejects only particular forms of subjectivity, i.e., the humanistic subject and its successors in existentialism. Furthermore, I have shown that he is right to reject this notion of the subject because it is abstract, atomistic, rationalist, and disembodied. Feminists likewise reject disembodied, atomistic, rationalist conceptions of the subject. Yet why should feminists adopt Foucault's subject when a notion of a relational and social subject is already available within feminist theory?

In spite of its contribution to undermining the masculinist bias in ethics, care ethics has been criticized by feminists on several counts. First, it has been criticized for romanticizing relationships as always nurturing and caring. Second, feminists argue that the care ethic is formed under conditions of patriarchal oppression and that it continues to serve the interests of the patriarchy. Ignoring this inequality of power, they say, contributes to women's continued subordination. Third, care ethics reinforces stereotypical gender roles by valorizing care and nuturance, traits typically associated with women. Fourth, critics claim that care ethics engages in false universalization because it neglects important race and class differences among women. Fifth, the object relations theory that care ethics is based upon has been criticized as ahistorical and acultural because it assumes that the process of identity formation remains constant in different cultures and historical periods.[93] These feminist criticisms of care ethics can be instructive for selecting the salient features for a feminist theory of subjectivity. Perhaps first and foremost, a feminist theory of subjectivity must include an analysis and critique of power. This analysis of power should include both the recognition that asymmetries of power exist between individuals, and among groups of individuals, and the recognition that relations of power shape subjectivity. A feminist theory of subjectivity needs to take into account the diversity among women; to this end it should be culturally and historically specific and it should reflect the variation of race, class, ethnicity, sexual orientation, physical ability, age, and religion even among women from the same historical and cultural period. A feminist theory of

subjectivity needs to account for gendered subjectivities without somehow reinforcing stereotypical or essentialist notions of gender; it needs to examine the
complex relationships among gender, sex, and sexual orientation. Finally, a feminist theory of subjectivity must begin with the body. All of this implies that a feminist theory of subjectivity must be firmly grounded in real, historical, material
practices and institutions.

Foucault's genealogy of the subject is explicitly historicized and thus not
vulnerable to criticisms such as ahistoricism that plague object relations theories.
Additionally, he locates the formation of subjectivity in specific social and cultural
practices that can accommodate feminists' concerns about the complicated relationships among sex, gender, and sexuality. Foucault provides an analysis of power
and an implicit critique of domination that is useful for exploring asymmetries of
power between individuals and groups as well as examining the ways that power
shapes subjectivity. And his conception of subjectivity begins with the body. However, feminists have criticized Foucault's account of the subject as androcentric.
This androcentrism reveals itself in Foucault's earlier work by an inattention to
gender and in his later work through his explicit focus on the male ethical subject.[94] Because Foucault's genealogy of the subject in *The Use of Pleasure* and *The
Care of the Self* is explicitly a male subject it cannot be adopted by feminists who
want to resist a male bias inherent to the construction of subjectivity. His exclusive
focus on the male subject in the elitist and male-dominated societies of classical
Greece and Rome ignores inequalities of gender and class. Only free men become
ethical subjects through the care of the self. However, Foucault's genealogy of the
male subject helps to expose the construction of masculinity and de-naturalize the
subject as male. A genealogy of the male subject does not preclude feminist genealogies of the female subject. Investigations of the constitution of the female
subject may raise important questions about the conditions under which women
become constituted as subjects.

In the following chapters, I examine what such a genealogy of a feminist
subject might look like in the contemporary United States. In chapter 4, I discuss
embodiment and the disciplines specific to the feminine female body. In chapter
5, I look at the way that binary categories of sex, gender, and sexuality structure
our ways of thinking about sexuality, subjectivity, bodies, and desire. In chapter 6,
I look at consciousness-raising as a possible feminist technique of the self and I
explore the way it helped to construct both community and individual identity for
contemporary feminists. I conclude by showing how Foucault's notions of subjectivity, body, identity, and politics can help feminists negotiate current issues in
sexual politics.

Chapter 4

▶●◀

FOUCAULT AND THE BODY: A FEMINIST REAPPRAISAL

The body plays a central role in contemporary feminist theory. Recently feminists have focused increasingly on the body—as a source of knowledge, as a site of resistance, and as the locus of subjectivity.[1] Feminists have taken mainstream, traditional philosophy to task for embracing mind/body dualism and for associating women with the body and men with the mind. Early feminist work, such as the work of anthropologists Mary Douglas, Sherry Ortner, and Michelle Rosaldo, makes a compelling case that women have been associated with the body, nature, and emotion; that these terms have been opposed to mind, culture, and reason, which are associated with men; and that the former have been systematically devalued. Feminist philosophers have also traced the association of women with body and nature (and their devaluation) in the history of philosophy.[2] Feminist critics of the Enlightenment decry the overemphasis of reason and the disembodied conception of subjectivity characteristic of this philosophical tradition.

As some feminist philosophers have noted, the body plays a central role in the work of Michel Foucault.[3] Foucault's notion of the body has at least three features that are significant for feminist theory. First, both Foucault and feminism reject dualism and the binary thinking that accompanies it. As I have discussed in chapter 3, he criticizes mainstream philosophy from Descartes to Sartre for identifying subjectivity with consciousness. Second, Foucault politicizes the body, and his notions of disciplinary practices and micropower are useful tools for feminist analyses of the body, especially to illuminate the patriarchal power of feminine cultural norms. Foucault's genealogical work explores the body as a site of the operation and exercise of power. One of Foucault's main concerns, for instance, in *Discipline and Punish* and *The History of Sexuality Volume One*, is the way that social norms operate on the body. Feminists share this concern about the way that social norms, especially patriarchal norms, affect bodies. Third, Foucault prioritizes the body; the body and its investment by power are significant issues for Foucault. One of the effects of power on the body is subjectivity; thus questions of subjectivity are inseparable from questions of the body. So, for Foucault as for feminists, subjectivity is always embodied. Thus, there are significant parallels between Foucault and feminism on the issue of the body: both reject mind/body dualism, both view the body as a site of political struggle, and both view the body as central to subjectivity and agency. Not only are there parallels between Foucault and feminism on the issue of the body, feminists have drawn directly upon Foucault's work. Feminists have taken up Foucault's notion of the body in interesting and important ways, using his ideas of disciplinary practices and micropower to explore the construction of femininity. In spite of these parallels, even feminists who are sympathetic to Foucault's work take issue with his notion of the body.

As I pointed out in chapter 3, discussion of moral and political agency generally takes place within the dualistic framework of the determinism/free will debate. The dualistic assumptions that underlie most philosophical discussions about agency inform our thinking about bodies as well. The typical dualist view holds that the body is inert, passive, and unthinking (in contrast to the active, thinking mind). According to this view, the body is conceived of as part of nature, a material object consisting of organs, appetites, and biological functions. This naturalistic view of the body stands in sharp contrast to the social inscription view. In the social inscription view, the body is seen as conditioned by its historical situation. Bodies, both in their materiality and in our conceptions of them, are shaped by historical and cultural forces. In its strongest version, the social inscription position holds that the body is constituted by these forces, and thus seen as determined by them. Surprisingly, Foucault's account of the body is interpreted as supporting both of these contradictory positions.[4] As we shall see, feminist critics find each of these positions untenable because the social inscription view undermines agency, while the naturalistic view is not consistent with Foucault's view of the body as an effect of power. Moreover, feminist critics accuse Foucault of androcentrism because he makes no mention of sex or gender difference in his discussion of the body.

In this chapter, I address three significant feminist criticisms of Foucault's notion of the body. First, some feminists accuse Foucault of androcentrism because his descriptions of bodily disciplines and practices are not sex/gender specific; furthermore, when he does specify sex-specific practices or disciplines, he speaks explicitly of male practices. I demonstrate that, although Foucault himself does not analyze sex/gender differences, his work has been extremely useful for feminist analyses. Second, some feminist critics argue that Foucault implicitly relies on a natural or prediscursive body. Critics point out that Foucault holds that the body is an effect of power; this combined with his claim that "the body is an inscribed surface of events" seems to result in a deterministic conception of the embodied subject.[5] Yet Foucault also claims that the body is a source of resistance.

This seems to result in a paradox: if the body is a template for cultural inscription, then it must exist prior to this cultural inscription. As Judith Butler puts it: "By maintaining a body prior to its cultural inscription, Foucault appears to assume a materiality prior to signification and form."[6] For Foucault, as for Nietzsche, the body is the site for the cultural inscription of values. And as Butler points out, the body as the site of cultural inscription implies a prior materiality; something to be inscribed. After all, without a notion of body that somehow exceeds its social significance, how is resistance possible? This is precisely the problem for the third group of feminist critics—Foucault's notion of the body seems to be completely determined by social and cultural forces. This has the unwelcome effect of undermining women's agency. Lois McNay claims; "Foucault's understanding of individuals as passive bodies has the effect, albeit unintentional, of pushing women back into this position of passivity and silence."[7] This criticism of Foucault's notion of the body as determined parallels feminist criticisms that his notion of the subject is determined. This is not surprising since Foucault claims that both the subject and the body are "effects of power." And, as discussed earlier, his notion of power is widely misunderstood. Power produces not only docile bodies, but resistant bodies. I shall argue that Foucault's feminist critics overprivilege the social inscription model of the body. I demonstrate that Foucault's complex and elusive model of the body may be best thought of as oscillating among a social inscription model, a model of internalization, and a model of interpretation. Acknowledging this complexity in Foucault's notion of the body helps to illuminate how the body is both shaped through normalizing disciplinary practices and resists those practices. Because Foucault's account of the body emphasizes the role that social norms play in shaping the body and constituting subjectivity, it is useful to feminists who need a theory of the body that can account for gender norms. And as Butler's Foucauldian feminist arguments reveal, Foucault's ideas are also useful for destabilizing and undermining gender norms. Thus, Foucault's notion of the body is particularly well suited to feminist concerns because it illuminates both the power of social norms and the possibilities for resistance to those norms.

FOUCAULT'S BODY

Foucault's objections to mind/body dualism and its attendant overemphasis on consciousness can be found in his major texts as well as in his interviews and essays. As discussed in chapter 3, Foucault disagrees with the model of subjectivity found in traditional philosophy, where mind or consciousness is primary and is thought to exist somehow outside of power relations. The body for Foucault is more than the locus of subjectivity; it is the very condition of subjectivity. For

Foucault, consciousness and subjectivity are not separable from the body. In fact, in *Discipline and Punish*, Foucault claims that power operates on the body to produce the soul, and the concepts of psyche, subjectivity, personality, and consciousness. Yet he states that these concepts are no less real for having been produced by power. His view that the soul is "the present correlative of a certain technology of power over the body" is consistent with his critique of humanism and his project of a genealogy of subjectivity.[8] Soul, consciousness, psyche, subjectivity, and personality are each specific ways of conceptualizing human interiority. Each way of thinking about human interiority arose at a particular time, within a particular context. Foucault differentiates the humanist soul that emerged out of particular practices of punishment, supervision, and restraint from the soul of Christian theology.[9] In some ways, the humanist soul provided a justification for the changes in the exercise of power in the practice of punishment. If a criminal is seen as capable of rehabilitation, then practices of punishment must focus on reform, on changing the attitude and behavior of the criminal, rather than on retribution. As is clear from his analysis in *Discipline and Punish*, Foucault does not believe that reforms in punishment, for instance, the move from execution to incarceration, necessarily mean that power is no longer exercised on the body. Power is simply exercised in different ways. One of the results of the changes in the exercise of power that occurred during the eighteenth century were new conceptions of interiority, namely, humanist conceptions of subjectivity and of the soul. Having rejected metaphysical dualism, Foucault cannot posit a mind, soul, psyche, or subjectivity that is somehow prior to or apart from the body. In fact, he inverts the usual relationship between body and soul, saying, "The soul is the effect and instrument of a political anatomy; the soul is the prison of the body."[10] Power through its effect on the body produces an interiority (the soul), and in turn, it is in part through this interiority that power is exercised on the body. Gilles Deleuze, in his well-known commentary on Foucault's work, refers to Foucault's notion of subjectivity as a "folding" or doubling. The inside is an operation of the outside; the exterior produces the interior by a doubling, a folding, a reflection back on itself.[11] This idea of Foucault's conception of subjectivity as a folding supports my view that for Foucault subjectivity and the body are inseparable; he offers an account of embodied subjectivity.

Foucault's focus on the body is consistent with his rejection of the universal subject. Notions of subjectivity that begin with the body must take cultural difference and historical specificity into account; subjects cannot be divorced from the contexts in which they develop and operate. Questions about subjectivity are therefore temporally and ontologically secondary to questions about the body. Thus, it is not surprising that for him the question of the body should take priority: "Indeed I wonder whether before one poses the question of ideology, it wouldn't be more materialist to study first the question of the body and the effects of power on it."[12] Foucault focuses on the body in his genealogical texts, *Discipline and Punish* and *The History of Sexuality Volume One*. Additionally, he discusses the body in some of his interviews and essays, as well as *The Birth of the Clinic*, *The Use of Pleasure*, and *The Care of the Self*. Although Foucault's discussion of the body can be found in several of his major texts, critics often focus on Foucault's essay "Nietzsche, Genealogy, History" to substantiate their claims that Foucault holds a social inscription account of the body that results in determinism.

Foucault's discussion of the body in "Nietzsche, Genealogy, History" takes place within his discussion of genealogy. The essay explicates Nietzsche's notion of genealogy and contrasts it to traditional history. Genealogy is characterized by two moments, *Herkunft* (descent) and *Entstehung* (emergence). The body figures importantly in both aspects of genealogy. Foucault describes descent as group affiliations, sustained by bloodlines, tradition, or social class. Descent is manifested bodily, ". . . descent attaches itself to the body. It inscribes itself in the nervous system, in temperament, in the digestive apparatus; it appears in faulty respiration, in improper diets, in the debilitated and prostrate bodies of those whose ancestors committed errors." The aspect of genealogy concerned with descent focuses primarily on the body and its history. As Foucault says, "The body—and everything that touches it: diet, climate, and soil—is the domain of *Herkunft*. The body manifests the stigmata of past experience and also gives rise to desires, failings and errors." Descent, then, is history as articulated through the body, and through particular bodies. According to Foucault, following Nietzsche, "The body is the inscribed surface of events (traced by language and dissolved by ideas), the locus of a dissociated self (adopting the illusion of a substantial unity), and a volume in perpetual disintegration. Genealogy, as an analysis of descent, is thus situated within the articulation of the body and history."[13]

The second aspect of genealogy, *Entstehung* (arising or emergence), views history as the play of dominations, and objects emerge as the result of conflicting forces and systems of subjection.[14] The play of dominations produces things and ideas; "it establishes marks of its power and engraves memories on things and even within bodies."[15] Emergence, then, is also concerned with the body, but this time as the site of contestation or struggle. Genealogy, which Foucault also calls effective history, is centrally concerned with the body. Contrasting effective history to traditional history, Foucault says, "Effective history, on the other hand, shortens its vision to those things nearest to it—the body, the nervous system, nutrition, digestion, and energies."[16] Effective history (genealogy) recognizes the influence of history on the body: "The body is molded by a great many distinct regimes; it is broken down by the rhythms of work, rest, and holidays; it is poisoned by food or values, through eating habits or moral laws; *it constructs resistances* (emphasis added)."[17] Even in this early essay, published before Foucault had developed his account of power in *The History of Sexuality Volume One* and his ideas about the disciplined body in *Discipline and Punish*, resistance figures importantly in his discussion of the body. As I discuss later, resistance may simply consist in offering new configurations of power and knowledge, an alternative discourse that shifts power relations. Bodily resistance may result from the struggle or contestation of the various regimes that constitute it. In this chapter, I suggest that Foucault's discussion of the body is multivalent, rather than paradoxical, as some critics charge. His conception of the body allows us to think of the body as both normalized and resistant. In Foucault's explication of Nietzsche's notion of genealogy, the body is inscribed by events, is molded by regimes, and is a locus of resistance. It should come as no surprise, then, that Foucault's genealogies are essentially histories of the body. Foucault's *Discipline and Punish* and *The History of Sexuality Volume One* answer Nietzsche's call for specific histories.[18]

Both *Discipline and Punish* and *The History of Sexuality Volume One* examine changes in the ways that power is exercised. Historically, power had been exercised by the king over his subjects, and with the development of nation-states, by the state over its citizens. Foucault's genealogical studies trace a change in sovereign power from the "right of death to power over life." Prior to the seventeenth century, sovereigns had the power to decide whether or not someone should be put to death if she transgressed the laws. In the seventeenth century, this power shifted from "right of death" to "power over life." Power over life was exercised in two main ways; it was exercised over individual bodies through disciplines, and it was exercised over the social body through biopolitics. In *Discipline and Punish*, Foucault examines the history of punishment as the "political technology of the body." He illustrates the ways that power operates on the body, tracing the various forms that power has taken, ranging from execution (right of death) to imprisonment (power over life). His opening example, the execution of Damiens, the regicide in 1757, graphically illustrates the way that power operates on the body. But the way in which power operates on the body changed, Foucault argues, with the advent of the social sciences, and the disciplinary advances in science, medicine, and psychiatry. As his genealogies show, these advances in knowledge have concrete consequences for practices and institutions.

Discipline and Punish details the ways that power operates on the body, through punishment and in more subtle ways through the myriad forms of regulation of time, space, and activity that each person is subject to every day. For Foucault, the body is inscribed with relations of power, and the historical changes of this power can be seen in the different ways it affects the body. Power operates on the body in various ways, and in the case of punishment, the forms have varied historically, from torture and execution in the mid-eighteenth century to incarceration in the present. By examining the concrete example of the history of punishment, he is able to trace the tangible effects of power on the body. Foucault is clear about his project's assumptions and aims:

> To analyse the political investment of the body and the microphysics of power presupposes, therefore, that one abandons—where power is concerned—the violence-ideology opposition, the metaphor of property, the model of the contract or of conquest; that—where knowledge is concerned—one abandons the opposition between what is 'interested' and what is 'disinterested', the model of knowledge and the primacy of the subject. . . . One would be concerned with the 'body politic', as a set of material elements and techniques that serve as weapons, relays, communication routes and supports for the power and knowledge relations that invest human bodies and subjugate them by turning them into objects of knowledge.[19]

For Foucault, the question of the body is inseparable from questions of knowledge and power. He describes a microphysics of power that operates on bodies through various institutions and practices. This microphysics of power affects the body at the level of gestures, as well as behavior. Foucault analyzes the ways that this microphysics of power works to produce individuals.

Perhaps the most compelling part of *Discipline and Punish* is the section on discipline, where Foucault describes the insidious and subtle techniques of power that create docile bodies. Docile bodies "may be subjected, used, transformed and improved."[20] According to Foucault, the advent of docile bodies corresponds with an increase in control and a change of the forms of control over bodies. These changes involved a change in scale (from whole body to individual parts), a change in object (from behavior to efficiency and internal organization of movements), and a change in modality (from assessment of result of activity to continual supervision of the process).[21] Foucault offers several examples to illustrate these stricter new forms of control. The shift from whole body to individual parts is exemplified by this excerpt from La Salle's book on conduct for Christian schools: "When the prayer has been said, the teacher will strike the signal once to indicate that the pupils should get up, a second time as a sign that they should salute Christ, and a third that they should sit down."[22] The shift from behavior to efficiency and the internal organization of movements can be seen in the military's change in its standards for marching troops. In the early seventeenth century, troops were simply expected to march in lines to the beat of a drum, with the entire unit raising the same foot at the same time. By the mid-eighteenth century, troops were expected to learn and use four different types of steps: the short step, the ordinary step, the double step, and the marching step. Moreover, each of these steps had to conform to specific measurements and duration. In the space of 150 years, soldiers' bodies were required to submit to increasingly complex choreographies. The shift from assessing the result of an activity to supervising the process is probably most obvious in industrial settings, where supervisors and managers sat or stood on raised platforms overseeing large rooms full of workers. Foucault goes into great detail about the way that discipline operates. He mentions four general categories: the art of distribution, which is concerned with space; the control of activity, which is concerned with time; the organization of genesis, which is concerned with efficiency; and the composition of forces, which is concerned with organizing individuals as part of a larger whole. Each of these general categories is further divided.

Distribution of space takes place through enclosure, partitioning, attention to function, separation into units. Foucault cites examples of hospitals, schools, military barracks, and factories to illustrate how discipline operates through the distribution of space. A specific example of a modern hospital may help to clarify the different aspects of the distribution of space. Recently I went to a large hospital (enclosure) for a mammogram. I was instructed to first go to the room for outpatient registration (attention to function), from there I was told to go to the finances area, a large room with sixteen individuals seated at sixteen desks separated by partitions (partitioning). After it was ascertained that my bill would be paid, I was sent to the area of the hospital called the Women's Center, where I again waited patiently. After a while, a woman in a pink uniform called my name and showed me where to get undressed, how to put on the hospital gown, where to lock up my things, and where to wait for the mammogram technician (attention to function). After another wait, the mammogram technician took me to a small room with an x-ray machine to do my mammogram (attention to function). It turned out that I needed an ultrasound as well. I was told that they did not normally do ultrasounds on Wednesdays, but they would try to squeeze me in (separation into units). After another wait, the ultrasound technician took me into the room with ultrasound equipment to do the ultrasound (attention to function). Afterwards I waited again (the longest wait) for the doctor to discuss the results with me (separation into units). So, enclosure refers to the hospital itself, or any building or space designated for a specific purpose. Partitioning is the further subdivision of that space into discreet rooms or work areas. Attention to function involves specific equipment or tools: mammograms can only be done in rooms that have x-ray equipment; ultrasounds only in rooms that have computer imaging equipment; registration and financial services require only a personal computer. The final aspect of distribution of space, separation into units, has to do with the distribution of the individual in relation to other individuals. Foucault also calls this the "rank." In the military, this is exemplified by those with higher status standing or marching at the front of the formation. The rank signifies the status of the individual relative to others, "the place one occupies in a classification."[23] In my hospital example, separation into units can be applied to the hospital's policy to only do ultrasound screening on certain days and thereby separate out the healthy patients from those who are not as healthy (ultrasounds are given when a mammogram shows an irregularity). The doctor's role in the entire process also illustrates this last aspect of rank. Her place at the top of the hierarchy of the large cast of assistants and technicians is reinforced by her place at the end of the process and her role as the expert in interpreting the results (not to mention the way the long wait reinforces her rank relative to me, the patient). As Foucault says, ". . . the disciplines create complex spaces that are at once architectural, functional and hierarchical."[24]

Control of activity is achieved by establishing timetables, applying temporal imperatives to action, correlating this action to the body as gestures, and to the manipulation of objects, and finally through adherence to the rule of non-idleness, the maximization of both speed and efficiency. Factory work provides a good example of the various aspects of control of activity. When I worked in a factory that produced parts for gas meters, the typical working day was eight and a half hours long; the work day was divided by a half-hour break in the middle for lunch, and further divided by two fifteen-minute breaks, one in the morning and one in the afternoon (timetable). Tasks in the factory required specific machines, some of which have automated parts; thus one's task is regulated by the speed of the machine (applying temporal imperatives to action). Working on a machine like a flaring machine, which flares the ends of metal tubing, or a metal lathe, which puts grooves in the sides of metal tubing, you must adjust your body so that your arms and hands can most easily perform the task (correlating action to the body as a gesture). Additionally, you learn to pick up the metal tubing so that it can be placed in the machine with a minimum of adjustments (correlating the action to the manipulation of objects). Each of these elements contributes to performing one's task smoothly, and because every movement is geared towards performing one's task well and quickly, there are no wasted movements (rule of non-idleness). Organization of genesis refers to organization of time dealing with an individual through a developmental process, for instance, military training or schooling. The composition of forces concerns the relationship among individuals in forming a larger whole through their spatial relationship to others, through their relationship in time, and through their place in the chain of command, for instance, the relationship among individuals in a military unit. Each of these aspects of discipline contributes to the formation of the modern individual. Foucault summarizes it this way: "[D]iscipline creates . . . an individuality that is endowed with four characteristics: it is cellular (by the play of spatial distribution), it is organic (by the coding of activities), it is genetic (by the accumulation of time), it is combinatory (by the composition of forces)."[25] The discipline Foucault refers to permeates individual bodies, it sets limits, it simultaneously shapes bodies and individuality. Discipline exerts itself through systems and institutions. Though *Discipline and Punish* is centrally concerned with the history of penal institutions, Foucault also draws examples from military, medical, educational, and industrial institutions, and the family. Power operates through disciplines to normalize behavior. As Foucault points out, this process of normalization is not restricted to institutions whose explicit aim is to "correct" behavior, such as prisons, but is a widespread feature of all institutions in modern society.

While *Discipline and Punish* focuses on the ways that power operates through disciplines, *The History of Sexuality Volume One* focuses on the way power operates through discourse.[26] Discourse [*dispositif*] refers to a multitude of institutions and practices, as well as disciplinary knowledge (as in the disciplines of science, medicine, psychology, anthropology, biology, etc.). Some interpretations of Foucault seem to view discourse as primarily having to do with words, or text. But it includes attention to social and political context and differentials of institutional power. For Foucault, the *dispositif* is as much about the said as the unsaid; it includes "discourses, institutions, architectural forms, regulatory decisions, laws, administrative measures, scientific statements, philosophical, moral and philanthropic propositions" and their relations.[27] In *The History of Sexuality Volume One*, Foucault sets out to "define the regime of power-knowledge-pleasure that sustains the discourse [*dispositif*] on human sexuality."[28] These discourses are part of the operation of power. According to Foucault, we are incited to speak about ourselves, to confess our sexual secrets, to see the truth about ourselves in relation to sex. Thus, the constitution of ourselves as sexual subjects comes about through the proliferation of discourses. Discourse is the conjunction of power and knowledge.[29] Yet discourse is not simply an instrument of power: "Discourses are not once and for all subservient to power or raised up against it, any more than silences are. . . . discourse can be both an instrument and an effect of power, but also a hindrance, a stumbling-block, a point of resistance and a starting point for an opposing strategy. Discourse transmits and produces power; it reinforces it, but also undermines and exposes it, renders it fragile and makes it possible to thwart it."[30]

The deployment of sexuality focuses on the body. Sexuality is deployed through a multitude of discourses—through medical and psychiatric discourse that named perversions, through legal discourse that criminalized particular sexual acts, through social discourse that located sex in the family and gave parents license to watch over their children, through religious discourse that identified some practices and desires as sinful and that exhorted one to examine one's thoughts. Foucault associates the deployment of sexuality with the rise of scientific discourse. Speaking of the nineteenth century, he says, "It was a time when the most singular pleasures were called upon to pronounce a discourse of truth concerning themselves, a discourse which had to model itself after that which spoke, not of sin and salvation, but of bodies and life processes—the discourse of science."³¹ The discourse of science and the related discourses of medicine and psychiatry began to take sex as their central question. As discussed in chapters 2 and 3, Foucault conceives of power as both prohibitive and productive. With regard to sex, the productivity of power operates by producing new categories of persons and by increasing social regulation. Foucault identifies four operations of power as productive with respect to sex. First, power functions by increasing its reach into the family. Second, power functions by creating new categories of persons according to sexual perversion. Third, this incorporation of sexual perversions into the body gave the medical-scientific establishment license to observe, poke, and prod. And fourth, the increased reach of power, combined with the normalization of particular types of sexuality, (e.g., the monogamous heterosexual couple), resulted in sexual saturation. These functions of power were novel; they operated neither through law or taboo; they served to both increase knowledge and to extend the reach of power.

Foucault claims that this proliferation of discourses about sexuality is linked to the constitution of subjectivity; sex becomes central to who we are. As sexual subjects, our embodiment is central. It is on and through the body that the discourse of sexuality is deployed. The discourse of sexuality operates both at the level of the individual body and the body politic. At the level of the body politic, the form of power that Foucault calls biopower operates through population control, public health, and genetics. At the level of the individual body, power operates through the inscription of social-cultural norms on the body, resulting in a politicization of the body. The body politic and the politics of the body mirror one another, rendering both populations and individuals docile and useful. As we shall see, feminist analyses demonstrate how cultural norms of femininity are inscribed on individual women's bodies. These norms are inscribed on the body politic as well, validating some bodies as useful for heavy lifting and manual labor and some bodies as useful in the service industry and as support staff. Many occupations are still gender segregated in the United States. Foucault's new conception of power—the "micro-physics of power"— demonstrates the way that power operates on individual bodies. Feminists have found his concepts of power and disciplinary practices useful for discussing gender norms.

FEMINIST EXTENDERS: DISCIPLINARY PRACTICES AND THE FEMININE BODY

Feminists view the body as an important site of political struggle. Reproductive issues, issues of violence against women, rape, sexuality, gender norms, and beauty ideals highlight the importance of the body to practical, political feminist struggles. In North American feminist theory, the body has functioned as the unproblematic ground of sexual difference. Since at least the 1970s, feminists have been making the distinction between sex and gender.[32] Sex refers to the anatomical, physical body and gender refers to the behavior and cultural meaning associated with biological sex. Gender was viewed as culturally and historically variable while sex was viewed as biologically given. The sex/gender distinction allowed feminists to argue against the position that "biology is destiny" and other conservative political positions that held that women's nature dictated her social roles. Feminists adopted different political strategies; liberal feminists emphasized gender equality and minimized sexual difference, whereas radical feminists emphasized sexual difference. Despite these different strategies, sex and gender were seen as distinct categories. Recently, some feminists have called into question this distinction between sex and gender.[33] Whereas before gender was viewed as the "cultural" meanings associated with the "natural" sexed body, now both gender and sex are viewed as constructed. To say that sex is constructed is not to deny the materiality of the body. It is to recognize that the body is not simply natural, but already bears the mark of cultural inscription. Sex categories are not simply given but are human constructs. The human body comes in a tremendous range and variety of shapes, features, and characteristics, including sex characteristics, yet our classification system allows for only two sexes. As we will see in chapter 5, sexual dimorphism does not adequately capture the variety and complexity of human bodies. Not only are sex categories culturally variable, they are historically variable as well; the criteria for being of a certain sex have changed over time. Embodied existence is saturated with political and cultural significance.

Foucault's view that the body is not simply given but is culturally constructed, as the "field of inscription of sociosymbolic codes" lends itself particularly well to showing how gender norms are incorporated.[34] Feminists Sandra Lee Bartky and Susan Bordo develop the idea that the body is the site of cultural inscription in interesting ways. Their analyses stress that the cultural construction of the body is always gendered. Given the centrality of the body to Foucault's analyses and his focus on sexuality, it is strange that he did not discuss gender-specific disciplinary practices. This inattention to gender has led feminists to accuse Foucault of androcentrism. Because he does not discuss sex or gender-specific disciplinary practices, his implicit assumption is that the body is sexually neutral. This presumed sex/gender neutrality, some argue, is androcentric because the neutral, universal body is always the male body (by default).[35] One feminist response to Foucault's neglect of sex and gender issues has been to extend his ideas to discuss these issues. Sandra Lee Bartky comments on Foucault's curious oversight of gender difference: "Women, like men, are subject to many of the same disciplinary practices Foucault describes. But he is blind to those disciplines that produce a modality of embodiment that is peculiarly feminine."[36] To help remedy Foucault's neglect of gender, Bartky extends Foucault's discussion of disciplinary practices to investigate female identity and subjectivity. These disciplines and practices include cosmetics, fashion, and the incorporation of bodily norms. Her analysis illuminates the ways in which the cultural norms of a patriarchal society transform women into properly feminine bodies. Susan Bordo in "Anorexia Nervosa: Psychopathology as the Crystallization of Culture" illustrates the significance of gender in the cultural malleability of the body when she points out that a disproportionate number of women suffer from anorexia nervosa.[37] The analyses by Bartky and Bordo focus on the feminine body and the disciplines particular to it. The Foucauldian framework of disciplines and practices that both use to explore female subjectivity does not simply describe the creation of passive feminine bodies, but reveals the contingency of the cultural construction of gender.

Sandra Lee Bartky's classic article "Foucault, Feminism and the Modernization of Patriarchal Power" extends Foucault's analysis of the disciplined body to women. She explores the disciplinary practices specific to women. Bartky rightfully accuses Foucault of neglecting the gender specificity of disciplines and practices. She examines the disciplinary practices specific to women, dividing them into three groups: (1) practices that aim to produce a body of a certain shape and size, (2) practices that elicit a certain repertoire of gestures, and (3) practices that encourage bodily adornment. Bartky skillfully demonstrates the ways that these practices form and shape the feminine body. She points out that these disciplinary practices collude with oppressive patriarchal structures. Standards for acceptable bodies vary culturally and historically; current fashion in the hegemonic culture prescribes slender bodies. Women engage in various disciplinary practices to produce slender and shapely bodies. These practices include exercise and dieting in various forms, e.g., aerobics, spot reducing, abdominal workouts. There is a seemingly endless array of weight loss and diet regimes as well: the high-protein, no-carbohydrate diet; the balance-between-carbohydrates-and-protein diet; the grapefruit diet; the one-type-of-fruit-a-day diet. Add cosmetic surgery to these practices and you have a full range of disciplinary practices supported by medical institutions and reinforced through cultural media such as advertising, magazines, television, and films.[38] These media reflect cultural norms that are more prescriptive than descriptive. As Foucault illustrates throughout his genealogical writings, cultural norms operate in insidious ways, through various disciplines and practices. Bartky's discussion of the feminine body illustrates how cultural norms support disciplinary practices and *vice versa*.

Her second category of feminine disciplinary practices—the practices that elicit certain gestures—further illustrates the connection between cultural norms and disciplinary practices. As documented through empirical studies and photographic portfolios, women's postures and gestures are more restricted than men's.[39] One well-known example is the difference between the ways men and women sit. Women tend to sit with their legs together or with one thigh crossed over the other, whereas men typically sit with their legs open or with an ankle crossed over a knee. In these typical postures, men invariably take up more space than women. In movement, too, women tend to take up less space. Iris Marion Young's article "Throwing Like a Girl" is a phenomenological account of the difference in motility between men and women.[40] In motion, women tend to use less of the space around them, restricting their movements. Women keep their limbs closer to their bodies in actions such as throwing a ball, and tend to take shorter strides when running. As Bartky notes, disciplinary practices involve not only the whole body, but also discrete parts of the body. Sociologist Arlie Hochschild's work on women's emotional labor is well known.[41] Her study documents the ways women working in service industries are required to smile regardless of the situation or their own emotional state. This inscription of cultural norms is in keeping with Foucault's observation that control of the body through disciplinary practices no longer simply works the body wholesale, but focuses in on specific parts.

Bartky's third category of bodily adornment deals with the body as an ornamented surface. Beginning with the skin, the cultural norms of fashion dictate that women should have smooth, soft, supple, unblemished, and wrinkle-free skin. In the contemporary United States, a woman must also be hairless, save for her head. Bartky mentions the craze to shave, wax, use depilatories, and seek out electrolysis to rid oneself of unwanted hair. In spite of the old adage, "Beauty is more than skin deep," there is an overwhelming array of products that can be applied to the skin. These include not only skin care products such as moisturizers and specialized cleansers, but also cosmetics. A visit to any drugstore in the United States will satisfy the curious about the startlingly large array of cosmetic products—seemingly every part of the face can be darkened, shadowed, highlighted, dyed, or colored. Bartky points out that little latitude is permitted; there are standards of appropriateness for how to apply makeup and how much makeup to apply in different contexts. Indeed, social sanctions are applied to women who use too much or none at all.[42] Bartky successfully demonstrates the ways that Foucault's disciplinary practices construct the feminine body. Her examples portray the way that oppressive patriarchal social norms are not simply imposed from the outside, but are internalized. Indeed, when they are not successfully internalized, social sanctions may ensue. These social sanctions range from relatively minor shunning or ostracization, to economic deprivation as the result of job loss, to threats of physical violence, for example, in cases of perceived gender transgression. In fact, sex and gender are among the most inviolate social norms.[43]

Susan Bordo offers another fruitful feminist application of Foucault's work on the body.[44] Her insightful analyses extend Foucault's notion that the body is the site of cultural inscription. But she, like Bartky, goes beyond Foucault to apply his ideas to the specific construction of the female body. Bordo provides the most sustained feminist discussion of Foucault's work on the body. Her feminist perspective stretches Foucault's ideas about the body as a site of cultural inscription and social control to account for women's experiences. A brief overview of Bordo's engagement with Foucault's body reveals the fruitfulness of applying Foucault's ideas to the specificity of women's experiences. In both "Docile Bodies" and "Anorexia Nervosa," Bordo discusses the ways in which culture constructs and pathologizes femininity. In "Docile Bodies," she examines three pathological forms that have emerged at different historical periods and that disproportionately affect women: hysteria, agoraphobia, and anorexia. These pathologies, she claims, are an extreme form of the inscription of femininity on women's bodies. Bordo notes that some feminist literature reads these pathologies as protest. Susie Orbach, for example, claims that anorexia is a form of unconscious feminist protest. The refusal of food and the subsequent reduction of body size is a silent protest, an indictment of "a culture that disdains and suppresses female hunger, that makes women ashamed of their appetites and needs, and that demands that women be constantly working on transformation of their bodies."[45] Ironically, this particular act of protest ultimately undermines the power and agency of the subject engaged in it. All too often unchecked anorexia results in death by starvation. Bordo explores the issue of anorexia in more depth in "Anorexia Nervosa"; there she chronicles the increasing obsession of North American (primarily middle-class white) women with food and the correlative rise in eating disorders. The incidence of anorexia has gone up dramatically in the last two decades. Bordo characterizes anorexia and bulimia as pathologies, but she reads them not as a deviation from hegemonic culture, but as its epitome.[46]

Bordo examines the way that the cultural imperatives of femininity get expressed through women's fixation on dieting and slenderness. She identifies two levels at which cultural practices exert power over bodies: (1) the body as the text of culture and (2) the body as the practical locus of social control. The body as the text of culture refers to the ways that our lived bodily experience is affected by the changes in social practices and cultural categories, subsequently changing our bodies themselves. Cultural practices can also exert control directly over physical bodies, for example, in the case of the anorexic's confinement to a hospital; this is the body as the practical locus of social control. Although these two levels of bodily control are distinguishable, they are not separate. They are interimbricated; the practical body is always already culturally mediated. Bordo makes a related distinction between Foucault's useful body and the intelligible body. The intelligible body is the body as an object of knowledge that is read through scientific, medical, and legal discourses. The useful (or docile) body is the result of the body being shaped by these discourses through engaging in specific disciplinary practices. As Bordo points out, the useful and intelligible body may be mutually supportive, as in the case of Victorian standards of femininity—hourglass figure, corsets, bustles, and restricted eating for women. Or they may be in tension with one another, as in the image of the contemporary slim superwoman, and the reality of the prevalence of eating disorders among those who strive to attain this ideal. Bordo's analysis of eating disorders is heavily indebted to Foucault. She adopts three important aspects of Foucault's notion of power. One, the idea that power operates through networks, discourses, and institutions; this is what Foucault calls the capillary model of power. Two, she agrees with Foucault that power is not simply repressive, but also productive and constitutive. And three, Bordo thinks an analysis of cultural discourse needs to be able to account for the "subversion of potential rebellion," the subject's collusion in her own oppression.

For doing cultural analysis, Foucault's analytics of power is clearly superior to traditional models of power. The idea that power operates through cultural and social norms, through discourses, and from below as well as from above allows for the recognition of the normalizing power of the media and visual images, as well as the discourses of science and medicine. His notion of power helps to explain the ways that cultural phenomena are developed and sustained through the interaction of cultural and social practices and individual actions. Furthermore, his idea of power takes into account the co-optation of resistance, the subject's collusion in her own oppression. Bordo's analysis of anorexia exemplifies these aspects of Foucault's notion of power. She shows how women's psychopathologies of anorexia, agoraphobia, and hysteria can be taken up as practices of resistance by individuals and/or read as practices of resistance by feminist scholars. And then she points out that these resistances are recuperated by the same oppressive patriarchal forces that spawned them, through the isolation of women in their homes, the confining of women to their beds, and the reducing of women's physical bodies. This restriction, confinement, and minimizing hardly seem like effective resistance, as Bordo points out. Bordo suggests, however, that one lesson feminists can learn from the ways that these strategies of resistance are recuperated by power is to be suspicious of the workings of power itself.

As I have argued in chapter 2, this is one of the central points in Foucault's genealogical work—suspicion about the workings of power, discourses, and institutions. If we are under continual surveillance due to the workings of power, our own power lies in the continual surveillance of power itself. We can apply Foucault's skepticism about dividing practices that mark some individuals as normal and some as abnormal, that condone some behaviors and pathologize others, to the categories of disease attributed to women. This serves to underscore Bordo's point that each of the disorders she discusses is a hyper-expression of the cultural dictates of femininity at the time; hysteria as the epitome of the fragile, emotional nineteenth-century woman, agoraphobia as the rigid adherence to the domestic role of women in the 1950s, anorexia as the slim superwoman of the 1980s and 1990s. Thus, women are pathologized for assuming the culturally dictated role, albeit in an exaggerated way. This is not to discount the ways that women are, in fact, hurt and disempowered by these disorders. But regarding the pathologization itself as part of the workings of power lends support to reading the manifestation of the pathologies in individuals as acts of resistance, while not losing sight of the damage that results. Furthermore, as Bordo's work shows, a Foucauldian analysis of power can be applied both at the larger social and cultural level to yield a political analysis. As most feminists argue, gender norms are not simply innocuous social rules or guidelines that tell one how to act and dress (although they are surely that as well); gender norms play a significant role in social organization. Moreover, the gender norms for women are not just constraining on some trivial level but encourage self-starvation (anorexia), bodily mutilation (cosmetic surgery, breast implants), and unwarranted surgical practices (Caesareans, hysterectomies, genital reconstruction). As I discuss later in this chapter, feminists can provide and have provided counterdiscourses to the hegemonic patriarchal discourse about sex and gender.

Both Bartky and Bordo admirably illustrate the ways that disciplinary practices exert power on and control over women's bodies. Each applies Foucault's concepts of discipline and power to show the specificity of the construction of the feminine body. This extension of Foucault's ideas for feminist purposes helps to remedy the gender gap in Foucault's work. Feminist critics who accuse Foucault of androcentrism and gender-blindness should consider the contribution that some of his central ideas can make to feminist analyses of gender norms. These feminist analyses show how patriarchal power works through disciplinary practices to oppress women. Foucault's conception of power as not simply juridical and prohibitive, but also as productive and as exercised on bodies through social norms can account for the ways that oppression can construct identities. Women are not simply passive objects adhering to patriarchal demands, nor are they duped by culture. There is an entire system of social rewards (and punishments) that reinforces appropriate gender behavior. Examining the ways that disciplinary practices, such as excessive dieting and the use of cosmetics, are not simply imposed upon, but are taken up by women reveals the ways in which women collude in their own oppression. Foucault himself was not unaware of the ways that bodily ideals and norms functioned to exhort one to physical perfection. Speaking of the way power operates, he says, "we find a new mode of investment [by power] which presents

itself no longer in the form of control by repression but that of control by stimulation. 'Get undressed—but be slim, good-looking, tanned!' For each move by one
adversary there is an answering one by another."[47] Bodily ideals are part of the
normative apparatus that shape our lives. Foucault clearly provides some tools for
cultural and social criticism, as the feminist analyses by Bartky and Bordo illustrate. But their analyses focus on the subject's compliance with power through
adopting disciplinary norms, rather than on resistance to it. To be fair, Bartky
briefly mentions female bodybuilders and radical lesbian communities as possible
sites of resistance to prevailing norms of feminine embodiment. Bordo also mentions female bodybuilders as a possible site of resistance. Yet in their analyses, an
account of resistance remains undeveloped, perhaps because Foucault himself
does not provide a fully developed account of resistance. As Bartky says, "Foucault
seems sometimes on the verge of depriving us of a vocabulary in which to con-
ceptualize the nature and meaning of those periodic refusals of control, which just
as much as the imposition of control, mark the course of human history."[48]

But, as before, a closer examination of what Foucault says about the body
and power reveals some resources for resistance in the complex operation of
power. Simply put, self-mastery over one's appetites, one's desires, one's body can
be a good thing if it is not taken to excess, as in the case of Bordo's anorexics. Foucault notes the complexity of the workings of power:

> Mastery and awareness of one's own body can be acquired only through
> the effect of an investment of power in the body: gymnastics, exercises,
> muscle-building, nudism, glorification of the body beautiful. All of this
> belongs to the pathway leading to the desire of one's own body, by way of
> the insistent, persistent, meticulous work of power on the bodies of chil-
> dren or soldiers, the healthy bodies. But once power produces this effect,
> *there inevitably emerge the responding claims and affirmations, those of one's
> own body against power* (emphasis added), of health against the economic
> system, of pleasure against the moral norms of sexuality, marriage and
> decency. Suddenly, what had made power strong becomes used to attack
> it. *Power, after investing itself in the body, finds itself exposed to a counter-
> attack in that same body* (emphasis added).[49]

Power operates in and through the body both as discipline and as resistance. Despite the recuperative tendency of power, Foucault calls for a "new stylistics of existence" in his later work. Not all power is disciplinary power, and in his later work
Foucault develops his idea of practices of the self that involve nonnormalizing relationships. Foucault expands on the ideas of self-mastery, self-awareness, and self-
transformation in *The Use Of Pleasure* and *The Care of the Self*, where he discusses
the proper relationship of one's self to one's body. As discussed in chapter 3, Fou-

cault's later work addresses the active constitution of the subject, the self's work on the self. This work on the self included a concern for one's body: "Theoretically, the cultivation of the self is soul-oriented, but all the concerns of the body take on a considerable importance."[50] The cultivation of the self involved a concern for the self, an attention to daily practices, such as diet and exercise. For example, ancient texts were full of advice about one's relation to one's body—what to eat, what to drink, how much to exercise, how much to sleep, how often to have sex. Taken together these constituted a regimen that one should follow to maintain good health. This concern with health and the body are integral to the formation of subjectivity; "it was a whole manner of forming oneself as a subject who had the proper, necessary, and sufficient concern for his body."[51] Concern for the body and the relationship of self-mastery were crucial to the formation of oneself as an ethical subject. Foucault's later work offers a way to think about bodily practices not as normalizing disciplines, but as practices of the self that are necessary for ethical subjectivity. Practices of the self can lead to self-transformation and to new nonnormalizing ways of being and relating. So, practices of the self provide another avenue for resistance, along with the competing claims of power and discourses.

Understandably feminist analyses have focused on the disciplinary aspect of power because it illuminates the way that gender norms operate to constrain women's behavior. Nonetheless, an articulation of feminine disciplinary practices also reveals a certain tension—if being feminine is not "natural" for women, but rather the result of social and cultural practices, then insofar as women do not conform to stereotypical gender roles they resist feminine disciplinary practices. Perhaps this tension between recognizing the effect of disciplinary practices and wanting to destabilize the categories produced through them is one of the reasons Foucault himself did not articulate gender-specific disciplinary practices in his work.

A FOUCAULDIAN FEMINIST CRITICISM OF FOUCAULT'S BODY

While Bartky and Bordo extend Foucault's ideas to account for the effect of social and cultural gender norms on the body, Judith Butler takes a Foucauldian approach to the issues of gender, sex, and sexual desire. In *Gender Trouble*, Butler deconstructs the naturalness of the categories of sex, gender, and desire by doing a genealogy. Her genealogy exposes that these categories are not natural, but are the effect of particular power formations. Following Foucault in assuming the cultural inscription of the body, Butler shows how sex and gender come to be written on the body, in part through the gestures and expressions of the body. Butler's performative theory of gender illustrates the productive aspect of power—sex categories are produced and maintained through social practices. Moreover, one of the ruses of power is to make these categories seem as though they are natural. Butler argues against the reification of these categories, she describes gender as "a doing."[52] That is, gender is produced through actions. One performs one's gender. Gender is no longer seen as the cultural expression of one's natural sex. In fact, Butler challenges the idea that sex is natural. She takes up Foucault's claim that the discourse of sexuality produces sex. She demonstrates that the categories of sex, gender, and desire are mutually reinforcing. Each of these categories is constructed as binary and this contributes to the normalization of individuals as fitting one category or the other. Moreover, membership in one category is presumed to imply membership in a set of categories—if female sex, then feminine gender, and then the desire for the opposite sex, i.e., masculine male. Butler challenges the assumption that there is a necessary relation among these categories. As she points out, this assumed harmony among sex, gender, and desire is itself held in place by the institution of compulsory heterosexuality. Often arguments against homosexuality appeal to biology and nature, most often the role of the sexes in reproduction, to shore up their belief that homosexuality is unnatural. Butler challenges not only the notion that homosexuality is unnatural, but also the distinction between natural and cultural that grounds the argument. The sex/gender distinction relies on the nature/culture distinction. In a Foucauldian move, she inverts the usual relationship between sex and gender. She argues that it is through gender performance that sex is ascribed to bodies. Thus, sex and the body are no longer seen as natural. The implication of this for feminism is that the body as the ground for sexual difference and gender identity as the rallying point for feminist politics are both challenged. I take up issues of identity in chapter 5. For most feminists, the materiality of women's bodies plays a fundamental role in feminist politics. After all, it is sexual difference that underlies women's larger role in reproduction, women's greater vulnerability to rape, and the sexual division of labor, to name just a few issues. Challenging the materiality of bodies and the naturalness of sex seems to undermine, rather than promote, feminist interests. Indeed, this is one of the objections radical feminists, as well as socialist feminists and feminist critical social theorists, have to postmodernism, both in its feminist version and in the work of Michel Foucault. But what are the ramifications of viewing the body as material, natural, and sexed?

In *Bodies That Matter*, Butler elaborates on her "performative theory of gender," this time focusing on the way that the materiality of bodies is produced. Once again using a Foucauldian framework, Butler addresses the question of the materiality of the body and the articulation of sex. Butler elaborates on a question she raises in *Gender Trouble*:

> Within those terms [the terms of the debate about free will and determinism], 'the body' appears as a passive medium on which cultural mean-

ings are inscribed or as the instrument through which an appropriative and interpretive will determines a cultural meaning for itself. In either case, the body is figured as a mere *instrument* or *medium* for which a set of cultural meanings are only externally related. But 'the body' is itself a construction, as are the myriad 'bodies' that constitute the domain of gendered subjects. Bodies cannot be said to have a signifiable existence prior to the mark of their gender; the question then emerges: To what extent does the body *come into being* in and through the mark(s) of gender? How do we reconceive the body no longer as a passive medium or instrument awaiting the enlivening capacity of a distinctly immaterial will?[53]

In *Bodies that Matter*, Butler begins by responding to criticisms of the social constructionist view of the body implied by her argument that sex and gender are constructed in *Gender Trouble*. She notes that critics attack the constructionist view of the body from two contradictory positions, some claiming that constructionism results in determinism, while others claim that it results in voluntarism. Those that claim that it results in determinism claim that if sex and gender are constructed through discourse, then there is no room for agency because there is no agent apart from discourse (this parallels feminist critics of Foucault who claim that if subjectivity is produced through power, then resistance to that power is impossible). Critics who claim that the social constructionist position results in voluntarism argue that if gender is a performance, then someone must be doing the performing. Butler objects that the critics who believe that the social constructionist position results in determinism exaggerate the power of discourse and language, assuming that they generate and determine not only meaning, but also being. This interpretation construes the social constructionist position as linguistic monism and linguistic idealism. To deflect this interpretation of social constructionism, she proposes to return to a notion of matter, not as a stable substrate, but as "a process of materialization that stabilizes over time to produce the effect of boundary, fixity, and surface we call matter."[54] In response to those critics who "seek assurances . . . that there are, minimally, sexually differentiated parts, activities, capacities, hormonal and chromosomal differences [Butler wants] to offer an absolute reassurance to [her] interlocutor, [but] some anxiety prevails."[55] Her argument in the rest of *Bodies That Matter* indicates some reasons for that anxiety. She worries that designating some things as natural, even bodily sex attributes, puts them beyond the realm of criticism and genealogical inquiry. To put it simply, if we assume that there are male and female bodies, then that may foreclose questions about what criteria we use for sex classification. Butler follows Foucault in thinking that everything has a history, including bodies and matter, and in thinking that these histories involve political stakes and political struggles.

Due to constraints of time and space, I cannot do justice to Butler's rather complicated analysis of the ways that bodies are materialized. One of her central concerns is with the regulation and normalization of bodies; she addresses the question of why some bodies matter, for instance, gender-conforming, heterosexual bodies, and some bodies do not, for instance, gender-transgressive queer bodies. Butler draws from a variety of sources, including French feminism, psychoanalytic theory, traditional philosophical texts, critical social theory, literature, film, and poststructuralism to make her argument that bodies and sex are discursively produced. She portrays through readings of texts and films the ways that gender and sexuality regulate the body.[56] She argues that her theory of gender as performativity can steer clear of the twin perils of determinism and voluntarism. It avoids voluntarism because performances of gender are compelled by social norms. It avoids determinism because gender performance may resignify or reiterate those social norms to produce new meanings. Butler uses drag as an example of gender transgression in both *Gender Trouble* and *Bodies That Matter*. In *Gender Trouble*, Butler claims that drag as a parodic performance of gender subverts gender norms. But some feminist critics objected that drag was just as likely to reinscribe gender norms as subvert them, and others thought that cross-dressing was an anemic form of resistance and hardly qualified as political. Butler admits in *Bodies That Matter* that drag functions ambivalently; it may serve to reinscribe gender norms just as well as subvert them. However, she argues that to see all gender as drag is to undermine heterosexuality as normative. This is what I see as the heart of her argument in both *Gender Trouble* and *Bodies That Matter*—the political project for feminists is to destabilize and denaturalize the whole sex/gender/sexuality system. Although drag as a political act may seem far-fetched to some feminists, the social and political stakes of the policing of normative gender categories are quite clear. As Butler mentions, it is not only in texts and films that one sees the regulation of gender norms and the price of gender transgression. Hate crimes against lesbians, gays, and transgendered people continue to increase in the United States. The regulation of sex, gender, and sexuality becomes more apparent when an individual defies the normative assumptions that circumscribe appropriate appearance and behavior.

Because Butler adopts a Foucauldian approach to feminist questions I would classify her as a Foucauldian feminist, and many feminists have engaged with her work to indirectly criticize Foucault.[57] Butler does seem to endorse Foucault's genealogical method and she uses some of his central notions, such as his reconception of power, but she is by no means uncritical of Foucault. In fact, she takes issue with Foucault's notion of the body. As discussed earlier, Foucault's account of the body has been subject to contradictory interpretations, the naturalistic view and the social inscription view. Some critics argue that Foucault's discussion of the body oscillates between these two incompatible views.[58] They wonder: How can the body be subject to power, the object of disciplinary practices, inscribed by history, as Foucault says it is, and also be a source of resistance? I have discussed some of the disciplinary practices that Foucault associated with the increased control of the body in the eighteenth century. His view of the way that power operates on the body leads some to the conclusion that disciplines and discourses completely shape the body and circumscribe one's actions. This view of the body as determined by social forces is obviously unpalatable, as feminist critics Lois McNay and Sandra Bartky have expressed. Butler's criticism of Foucault's account of the body differs slightly from the position that he simply presents a deterministic account of the body. She claims that Foucault seems to present the body on the one hand as determined by culture and on the other hand as naturalistic. She charges that Foucault implicitly relies on a prediscursive body, unmediated by culture, a natural body.[59] Elizabeth Grosz makes a similar claim in *Volatile Bodies*; she says, "'Bodies and pleasures' are the objects and targets of power, in a sense, Foucault seems to imply that they pre-exist power, that they are or may be the raw material on which power works and the sites for possible resistance to the particular forms power takes."[60] Both Butler and Grosz claim that if Foucault's account of the body relies on a model of social inscription, then there must be something that escapes this inscription in order to resist.

In "Foucault and the Paradox of Bodily Inscription," Judith Butler argues that Foucault's account of the body is paradoxical. She attributes to Foucault a cultural inscription model of the body, wherein the body is inscribed by culture and imprinted by history. Butler points out that the cultural inscription model relies on something that is inscribed; thus if Foucault claims that the body is "the inscribed surface of events . . . totally imprinted by history," he must implicitly rely on a notion of a natural or precultural body.[61] Butler takes up this issue again in *Gender Trouble*, where she draws on Foucault's essay, "Nietzsche, Genealogy, History." She discusses Nietzsche's influence on Foucault, pointing out parallels in their understanding of the way that history produces cultural values. "In a sense, for Foucault, as for Nietzsche, cultural values emerge as the result of an inscription on the body, understood as a medium, indeed, a blank page." She goes on to say that history on this view is figured as a "relentless writing instrument."[62] Butler argues that Foucault's view of history implies that the body is somehow prior to history, and before the law (of language), that is, prediscursive. Indeed, if Foucault does hold that the body is constructed through discourse, as he seems to in *The History of Sexuality Volume One*, and if he also holds that the body somehow preexists its social inscription, then his view is paradoxical. However, I shall argue that the social inscription model does not adequately portray Foucault's account of the body. Butler herself backs off from her earlier criticisms of Foucault in *Bodies That Matter*, saying, "At times it appears that for Foucault the body has a materiality that is ontologically distinct from the power relations that take the body as the site of investments. And yet, in *Discipline and Punish*, we have a different configuration of the relation of materiality and investment. There the soul is taken as an instrument of power through which the body is cultivated and formed. In a sense it acts as a power-laden schema that produces and actualizes the body itself."[63] In spite of this more nuanced view of what Foucault says about the body, Butler still finds some limitations to Foucault's view of the body. While discussing Slavoj Zizek's recent work on politics and identity, Butler agrees with him that contrary to Foucault "the subject is not a unilateral effect of prior discourses" and she notes that Zizek introduces a concept of the real which stands counter to a ". . . Foucaultian linguisticism, construed as a kind of discursive monism whereby language effectively brings into being that which it names. . . ."[64] It is not quite clear if Butler is agreeing with or criticizing Zizek's view of Foucault as a linguistic monist, but her earlier critique of Foucault, which claims that cultural values are written or inscribed on the body and that the body is a blank page, suggests that she agrees with this view. Furthermore, she is at pains to dissociate her own view from linguistic monism, which she argues is a misunderstanding of the radical social constructionist position. She rejects the position attributed to her by critics that "the meaning of construction becomes that of linguistic monism, whereby everything is only and always language."[65] In a more recent work, *The Psychic Life of Power*, she seems to be defending Foucault from this interpretation as well: "The claim that a discourse 'forms' the body is no simple one, and from the start we must distinguish how such 'forming' is not the same as a 'causing' or 'determining,' still less is it a notion that bodies are somehow made of discourse pure and simple."[66] Yet she still holds to her earlier claim that Foucault implicitly relies on a notion of the body that is pre-discursive and ontologically distinct from power relations. "Although Foucault wants on occasion to refute the possibility of a body which is not produced through power relations, sometimes his explanations require a body to maintain a materiality ontologically distinct from the power relations that take it as the site of investment."[67] I believe that Butler's criticism of Foucault as holding seemingly paradoxical views on the body rests in part on her view that Foucault holds only a social inscription model of the body. Moreover, I believe her interpretation of Foucault's notion of the body has contributed to feminist dismissals of it. As I have discussed above, the social inscription model of the body holds that values are written or inscribed on the body. This emphasis on language may seem consistent with Foucault's claim that bodies are produced through discourse as well as disciplinary practices. And, to some extent it is, because language, names, and identity categories all play important roles in the process of individualization or subjection.[68] But as I pointed out earlier Foucault's notion of *dispositif,* which is usually translated as discourse, refers to a variety of material practices and social institutions. Although quite certainly Butler knows that for Foucault discourse does not simply mean language, sometimes her writing belies this fact. Often in the course of an argument she will use "the symbolic" or ("re)signification" as a substitute for "discourse." Using these terms may contribute to readers interpreting discourse to mean simply language. Additionally, Butler's own argument for her performative theory of gender focuses on the constitutive power of language. She draws on J. L Austin's notion of the performativity of speech acts where the utterance performs an action, as in the case of baptisms, the dedication of ships, and marriage ceremonies. Butler also relies on Luis Althusser's notion of interpellation to argue for the discursive construction of sex, gender, and the body. Althusser's notion of interpellation posits that subjects are produced through being addressed, hailed, or named because this naming places the individual in a social structure relative to the name. One need only think of the university setting and the practice of calling one's colleague *Professor So-and-so* when speaking of this colleague to students.[69] Butler's use of Austin and Althusser helps to explain the constitutive role of language for producing subjectivity. And her appropriations of them illuminate the ways that hate speech and normalizing social categories can be injurious. The power of language to constitute identity is a Foucauldian insight that is important to feminists. But as feminist critics have argued, so is retaining the materiality of the body. As Susan Bordo says, "And so long as we regard the body in drag as an abstract, unsituated linguistic structure, as pure text, we may be convinced by Butler's claim that the gender system is continually being playfully destabilized and subverted from within. But subversion of cultural assumptions (despite the claims of some deconstructionists) is not something that happens in a text or to a text."[70] But does Bordo's criticism apply to Foucault as well? I argue below that it does not because his account of the body is not solely the social inscription model that Butler attributes to him.

The social inscription model does seem to imply that there is something there prior to the social inscription. In this model, cultural and social norms are viewed as "written on the body"; the body is seen as inscribed, engraved, marked. Elizabeth Grosz uses the example of tattooing and scarification to discuss how inscription operates. Butler likens inscription to writing and uses the metaphor of "the body as the blank page." While Foucault's model of cultural inscription can account for such cases of physical inscription, it also refers to the physical and social conditions that affect the body, such as environment, climate, diet, regimes. Foucault's main discussion of the inscription model is in "Nietzsche, Genealogy, History," although his most extended discussions of the body can be found in his genealogical works, *The History of Sexuality Volume One* and *Discipline and Punish,* as well as one of his early works, *The Birth of the Clinic.* The social inscription model that Butler and Grosz attribute to Foucault is only part of the story.

I suggest that Foucault's elusive and complex notion of the body oscillates between models of inscription, internalization, and interpretation. Foucault uses many verbs to describe the effect of power on the body—it is marked, engraved, molded; it is shaped and trained; it responds and increases its forces.[71] While marked and engraved seem to fit with the social inscription model, molded fits less well. And shaping, training, and responding evoke the idea of some interplay between the body and power. Moreover, a body that increases its forces implies an active body, rather than simply the passive recipient of social and cultural inscription. A closer consideration of his genealogical works reveals that the inscription model does not adequately capture the different ways that Foucault talks about the body. Foucault's work suggests several different ways to think about the body, and there is no compelling reason to privilege the social inscription account over the others. A fuller account of Foucault's ideas about the body is important for assessing what contribution his work on the body can make to a feminist articulation of the body.

Although Foucault does not use the term internalization, and would probably avoid it because of its psychological overtones, I believe it captures one of the ways that Foucault talks about the body. Foucault's vivid portrayals of disciplinary practices in *Discipline and Punish* are best thought of in terms of a model of internalization. Speaking of the useful body as the product of disciplinary power, Foucault says it is "manipulated, shaped, trained, [it] obeys, responds, becomes skilful and increases its forces."[72] Note the range of meanings conveyed by this one phrase. While being manipulated and obedient conjures up images of a passive body, training and responding rely on some sort of active body, one that is capable of internalization. This idea of the body as active is even more apparent when the body is described as becoming skillful and increasing its forces. Training and discipline both fit with a model of internalization, rather than inscription. Discipline and disciplinary practices, as discussed by Foucault, are exercises of power on the body in particular ways. In general, his descriptions of discipline and training rely on the body's internalization. Internalization occurs through repeated actions that result in habituation. While discipline meted out to prisoners and in the military may constrain the body and limit its possibilities, discipline can also function in ways that increase the power of the body, i.e., its forces and skills. Earlier, I discussed the practice of female bodybuilding as a form of resistance. If we look at the practice of weight lifting in general, we can see how discipline functions ambivalently. On the one hand, bodybuilders may simply be trying to achieve a muscular build to conform to a cultural ideal. On the other hand, engaging in the practice of weight training also increases the body's forces, in terms of strength and endurance, and develops a new set of skills specific to the practice of weight lifting. Discipline, then, functions ambivalently, like power, in one sense increasing the capacities of individuals and in another sense imposing limits.

Foucault specifically discusses exercise as a form of discipline: "Exercise is that technique by which one imposes on the body tasks that are both repetitive and different, but always graduated. . . . Exercise, having become an element in the political technology of the body and of duration, does not culminate in a beyond, but tends towards a subjection that has never reached its limit."[73] Discipline progresses toward a goal, the goal of producing the modern individual. In order for discipline to achieve its goal of producing useful and docile bodies, the body must internalize its demands. Foucault, for instance, discusses military posture as one example of the exercise of disciplinary power. The soldier adopts a certain posture as the result of specific demands, guidelines, exercises. At first these guidelines may be reinforced through physical force and adjustments. But as Foucault makes clear throughout his discussion of disciplinary practices, their distinctive feature is the way they operate insidiously on bodies, permeating them, and deriving the most power from the subsequent self-regulation of bodies.

Nowhere is this clearer than in Foucault's discussion of surveillance in *Discipline and Punish*. Surveillance, or the disciplinary gaze, was found especially in hospitals, asylums, prisons, schools, orphanages, factories, and working-class housing developments. The disciplinary gaze was made possible through some innovations in architecture, "an architecture that would operate to transform individuals: to act on those it shelters, to provide hold on their conduct, to carry the effects of power right to them, to make it possible to know them, to alter them."[74] Buildings were arranged with windows and partitions (rather than walls) to facilitate surveillance. In factories and schools, work stations and desks were arranged in long rows in large rooms with the manager or teacher keeping a watchful eye from the front of the room. But surveillance did not end with one individual supervisor, it was part of a network of power: "It was also organized as a multiple, automatic and anonymous power: for although surveillance rests on individuals, its functioning is that of a network of relations from top to bottom, but also to a certain extent from bottom to top and laterally; this network 'holds' the whole together and traverses it in its entirety with effects of power that derive from one another: supervisors, perpetually supervised. . . ."[75] The pervasiveness of the disciplinary gaze results in self-monitoring. One never knows if one is being watched, so one acts as if she is under surveillance and adjusts her behavior accordingly. Foucault's infamous example of such a system is Bentham's Panopticon.[76] The plans for this prison called for a central guard tower with prisoners in cells all around it. The walls of the cells facing the guard tower would be transparent so that the prisoners would be visible to the guards at all times. The structure was to be set up in such a way that although prisoners were always visible, the guards were not, so that the prisoners never knew whether or not they were actually being watched. Thus, those in the cells monitor their own behavior (presumably to conform to the expectations of the guards, if they were watching). Surveillance is a significant form of disciplinary power, even the mere threat of it causes individuals to alter their behavior and "transform themselves." Surveillance impacts actions, behavior, bodies. Although it begins from the "outside" through the disciplinary gaze of the guard, teacher, or manager, part of its effectiveness relies on its moving "inside" through the self-monitoring of the individual being watched.[77] The model of internalization captures this process much better than the model of inscription.

What I am calling the model of interpretation corresponds to what Foucault calls the intelligible body. The intelligible body is the body as an object of knowledge interpreted through disciplinary discourses, such as biology, physiology, psychiatry, and medicine. As he describes it, knowledge of the body is inseparable from power's investment in it: "[i]f it has been possible to constitute a knowledge of the body, this has been by way of an ensemble of military and educational disciplines. It was on the basis of power over the body that a physiological, organic, knowledge of it became possible."[78] According to Foucault, the useful body and the intelligible body are distinct but overlapping ways of understanding the body.[79] The concept of the useful body deals with the body in terms of submission and use; the concept of the intelligible body deals with the body in terms of functioning and explanation.[80] Although Foucault makes a distinction between intelligible and useful bodies, there is clearly a relationship between these ways of understanding the body. Bodies are always already invested with cultural meanings and cultural meanings inscribed on the body have real physical and political effects.

While *Discipline and Punish* deals primarily with the useful body, *The Birth of the Clinic* and *The History of Sexuality Volume One*, as well as parts of *The History of Sexuality Volumes Two* and *Three* deal mainly with the intelligible body. *The Birth of the Clinic* traces the development of medical science and the corresponding changes in the understanding of the body. Foucault describes his project as both historical and critical.[81] He discusses the changes in medicine and the medical model in the context of political, legal, religious, and technological changes. He traces the shift in the understanding of disease from the nosological model, which understood disease in terms of categories and essences, to the model of pathological anatomy, which understood disease in terms of immediate symptoms and their visible effect.

Medicine also created new understandings of the body; as the locus of disease, as the object of the medical gaze, as mystery, as tissues, as organic system, as tactile object, as visible object, and as a case history.[82] With the advent of the case history, a discourse of the individual became possible. The practice of asking a series of questions to establish the nature of the problem is an integral part of the shift in medical understanding from categories (nosological) to description (pathological). Foucault's interest in the individual as a case continues in his genealogical works. In *Discipline and Punish,* he discusses the examination as a disciplinary practice. The emphasis on writing and documentation that accompanied the examination resulted in a new type of knowledge of the individual: "the constitution of the individual as a describable, analysable object . . . a case which at one and the same time constitutes an object for a branch of knowledge and a hold for a branch of power . . . . it is the individual as he may be described, judged, measured, compared with others, in his very individuality; and it is also the individual who has to be trained or corrected, classified, normalized, excluded, etc."[83] And in *The History of Sexuality Volume One,* he notes the emergence of "a whole machinery for specifying, analyzing and investigating, [sexuality]."[84] This documentation of the individual as a case history was largely medical, scientific, and psychological, at least with respect to issues of the body, such as sex and sickness. Foucault's concept of the intelligible body, then, includes the body as understood and represented through various disciplinary discourses and practices. He calls attention to the way that power functions in these representations and understandings of the body. This concern is certainly shared by feminists, who like Foucault, are critical of the traditional medical model and the professionalization of medicine. Feminists have been wary of the power that accompanies representations of the body. Biological, medical representations of the body are deeply influenced by prevailing cultural assumptions. There are many feminist analyses of the ways in which representations of the body reflect our cultural assumptions, from the classic *Our Bodies, Ourselves* to Emily Martin's *The Woman in the Body: A Cultural Analysis of Reproduction* and Anne Fausto-Sterling's *Myths of Gender,* and more recently her *Sexing the Body.*[85]

Many readers of Foucault, both critics and champions, attribute special significance to the resistance of the body.[86] Indeed, Foucault's rallying cry for new forms of "bodies and pleasures" has spawned diverse projects, from defenses of sadomasochist practices and gay bodybuilding as projects of political transformation, to gardening and line dancing as *askêsis* of self-transformation.[87] Some critics, however, have taken issue with the privileging of bodies and pleasures as a point of resistance. Feminists Judith Butler and Elizabeth Grosz both seem to assume that if the body is to be a point of resistance, it must somehow escape cultural inscription.

Does Foucault's call for bodies and pleasures as a significant point of resistance rely on some utopian moment outside of discourse, institutions, and practices? There seems to be no reason to interpret Foucault's promotion of bodies and pleasures as utopian, relying on some notion of a natural body. Resistance is coincident with power: "They [resistances] are the odd term in relations of power; they

are inscribed in the latter as an irreducible opposite. Hence they, too, are distributed in an irregular fashion: the points, knots, or focuses of resistance are spread
over time and space at varying densities, at times mobilizing groups or individuals
in definitive ways, *inflaming certain points of the body* (emphasis added), certain
moments in life, certain types of behavior."[88] He goes on to say that resistance is
intrasubjective, it marks off "irreducible regions" in individuals, "in their bodies
and in their minds."[89] Resistance, when it happens, happens within and through
the body. It happens both through the individual body and the collective, social
body. Near the end of *The History of Sexuality Volume One*, Foucault suggests that
we think about the possibility of a "different economy of bodies and pleasures."
Presumably this different economy of bodies and pleasures emerges out of our
current situation and promotes new discourses, knowledges, and practices. In fact,
Foucault urges us to reverse sex and sexuality and try to counter the deployment of
sexuality. This reversal can only take place by countering the "grips of power with
the claims of bodies, pleasures and knowledges, in their multiplicity and their possibility of resistance."[90] This multiplicity of knowledges, bodies, and pleasures
works together as a possible site for resistance. Bodies and pleasures do not stand
outside the discourses that produce them. Nonetheless, there is no single over-
arching discourse that determines the limits and possibilities of bodies or pleasures. Although Foucault does not provide a road map of what these new bodies
and pleasures might be like, he does provide some tools to survey and criticize the
available culturally dominant discourses. He urges us to go beyond "sex-desire" to
bodies and pleasures. His discussion of how power and normalization operate
through the discourse of sexuality points to possibilities for resistance.

FEMINIST RESISTANCE TO THE DEPLOYMENT OF SEXUALITY

How important is it for feminists to resist the "deployment of sexuality" and
how might this be accomplished? Two brief examples may serve to illustrate possible feminist interventions in the deployment of sexuality and the corresponding
grip of power on women's bodies. Radical feminists Anne Koedt and Marilyn
Frye challenge normative patriarchal views of sex and women's sexuality. Anne
Koedt's classic article "The Myth of the Vaginal Orgasm" directly challenges
Freud's contention that vaginal orgasm is the proper form of sexual satisfaction for
a mature woman. She questions the standard formulation that "vaginal orgasm
equals mature sexual response." Instead Koedt looks at the way that this presump-
tive goal structures our very understanding of sexual activity itself. She examines
the implicit assumptions behind vaginal orgasm as the goal of sex; she reveals that
this goal presupposes a sexist and heterosexist definition of sex. Sex is defined as

heterosexual intercourse, and a woman is supposed to achieve sexual satisfaction in the course of bringing her (male) partner sexual satisfaction. Koedt criticizes this narrow conception of sex and points out that it is damaging to women. The damage to women was both physical and psychological. Surgery to move the clitoris closer to the vagina was one of the cures recommended for women who failed to have vaginal orgasms. Failing to live up to the sexual standards set out for them by Freud, women blamed themselves and "flocked to psychiatrists looking desperately for the hidden and terrible repression that kept them from their vaginal destiny."[91] This example illustrates Foucault's concerns about the medicalization of sex, the power of normalizing discourse, the connection between knowledge and practices such as surgery, and the pathologizing of women who fail to live up to the normative standards. Koedt deconstructs the notion of sex, and shows how normality for women is tied to sexist and heterosexist assumptions. She encourages us to question the traditional discourse of sexuality. Koedt offers an alternative discourse of sexuality. In effect, she examines the way power works to define institutions, practices, and knowledges. And she provides a competing feminist discourse on what counts as normal mature female sexuality and sexual satisfaction. Ultimately, however, the alternative discourse that Koedt offers does not challenge the notion of sexuality itself, and so does not resist the grips of power or go beyond the deployment of sexuality. Nonetheless, her alternative notion of women's sexuality offers an important moment of resistance within the discourse of sexuality.

A second example of feminist resistance to the deployment of sexuality is Marilyn Frye's article "Lesbian Sex." In her article she explores the meanings of lesbian sex and the ways these meanings connect with sexuality. The starting point for her discussion is the fact that lesbian couples have sex less than other couples. This conclusion was reached as the result of an empirical study that included lesbian couples, gay couples, heterosexual unmarried couples, and heterosexual married couples. Frye begins by noting that the fact that lesbians "had less sex" than other couples came as no surprise to her or to her friends. But then she goes on to examine what is meant by sex. Noting that on average heterosexual sex takes eight minutes, whereas lesbian sex may take thirty minutes, an hour, or an entire afternoon, Frye says: "The suspicion arises that what 85% of heterosexual married couples are doing more than once a month and what 47% of lesbians are doing less than once a month is not the same thing."[92] Frye points out that standard measures are not adequate to capture the experience of lesbian sex. Questions such as "How many times?" and "How frequently?" permit neither exactitude nor certainty. She points out that what counts as a time could be interpreted in a variety of ways: when one partner has an orgasm, only when both partners have orgasms, each time one partner touches the other's genitals. And

then there is the problem of individuation—is it a new time each time one partner gets up to go to the bathroom or to get a glass of water? Frye, like Koedt,
points out that the definition of sex is phallocentric. That is, sex is constructed
from a male point of view. Thus, with no male in the picture, (phallocentric) sex
doesn't happen. But of course, it does happen; it just escapes definition. Lesbian
sex, Frye claims, is "inarticulate, pre-linguistic, non-cognitive." There is "no linguistic community, no language, and therefore in one important sense, no knowledge."[93] Out of this lack of knowledge and the elusiveness of lesbian sex new
possibilities emerge. Lesbian sex takes place outside the dominant, discursive
framework. And Frye implies because of this, it may be a form of resistance. Although Frye would undoubtedly resist a connection between her feminist theorizing and Foucault's work, there are some parallels. Both Frye and Foucault
think it is important to examine the way that power works in discourses, institutions, and practices. Both believe that discourse (as words and knowledge) influences and shapes our perception of and participation in practices. Both valorize
"subjugated knowledges," those knowledges which have been marginalized and
act as "counter-discourses." And both think that these counter-discourses constitute resistance, at least resistance to the defining power of dominant discourse.

Frye's article also makes clear the normalizing power of dominant discourse.
If sex is defined as male orgasm, then lesbian sex doesn't count as sex. So, when social scientists measure and compare sexual activity, lesbians fall below average. As
Foucault notes, the power of normalizing discourse lies in its ability to define experience in a particular way while at the same time masking this particularity. The
dominant discourse normalizes heterosexual sex as the only kind of sex, while it
refuses to recognize lesbian sex as sex. Frye observes, "[W]e are dissatisfied with
ourselves and with our relationships because we don't have sex enough. We are so
dissatisfied that we keep a small army of therapists in business trying to help us
have sex more."[94] Frye's article exposes the workings of power that pathologize
lesbians' relative dearth of sex by pointing out the phallocentric assumptions involved in the definition of sex. If sex is defined around male orgasm, then it is no
wonder that lesbians are having relatively little of it! In her article, Frye employs
the time-honored feminist strategy of looking at an issue that views women or
lesbians as the problem, as not normal, as lacking, and by questioning the assumptions, she reveals the sexist and heterosexist bias of the discourse, and consequently revalues lesbians' experience.[95] Finally, there is a resonance with Foucault's
bodies and pleasures in Frye's call to "start with a wide field of our passions and
bodily pleasures."[96] Frye suggests that we begin with our bodies and their pleasures
to create alternative meanings to dominant discourse: "Meanings should arise
from our bodily self-knowledge, bodily play, tactile communication, the ebb and
flow of intense excitement, arousal, tension, release, comfort, discomfort, pain and

pleasure (and I make no distinctions here among bodily, emotional, intellectual and aesthetic)."[97] Bodies and pleasures, then, serve as a point of resistance to dominant, normalizing discourse for both Frye and Foucault.

Of course, there are many differences between their approaches as well. Frye emphasizes meaning while Foucault shies away from meaning and intentionality. Frye uses words like "better," "inadequate," and "positive"—evaluative, normative terms that Foucault avoids. And Frye's work is part of a larger project of feminist theory that has the specific goal of ending women's oppression; to this end she offers positive recommendations. As discussed in chapter 2, Foucault's work has been criticized for not offering solutions and for not advocating a general program for social and political change. So it is not my intention to say that Frye and Foucault are engaged in the same project, or doing the same thing, or that their work has the same effect or goal. I do want to suggest, however, that Frye's article can be seen as feminist resistance to the deployment of sexuality. She reveals the process of normalization that occurs as a result of the study by questioning the definition of what is being studied. She points out that the assumptions of the dominant heterosexist, phallocentric discourse render lesbian sex invisible through its inability to codify it. She questions the results of the study that lesbians have less sex through examining the way the definition of sex is based on standard heterosexual practice. She humorously points out that heterosexual sex may occur with more frequency, but typically does not last nearly as long. In effect, she reverses the implicit evaluation of the study that views lesbians as "less than." In the end, she recommends that lesbians look to bodily pleasures to expand the concept of "doing it." This expanded concept of sex would include a wide range of acts, activities, and attitudes. Although Frye may not go as far as Foucault's polymorphous incitement to discourse, she embraces a multiplicitous, pluralistic vision of what counts as sex. Frye does not seem to share Foucault's suspicion that these new knowledges may serve to repress the very groups that helped to articulate them. Resistance to the deployment of sexuality takes place within a field of power relations and may itself be co-opted. One can imagine that the new knowledges and languages developed out of lesbian knowledges, practices, and communities may be used in the next survey. Nonetheless, Frye's "bodily pleasures" constitute a point of resistance to the deployment of sexuality.

The articles by both Koedt and Frye, then, can be seen as feminist resistances to the deployment of sexuality. Each analyzes the dominant phallocentric, heterosexist discourse and points out the assumptions that undergird it. Both offer new knowledges (subjugated knowledges) that begin from women's experience and lesbian experience. These new knowledges that begin from bodies and pleasures can serve as counterdiscourses. These counterdiscourses help to interrupt the process of normalization that is part and parcel of the deployment of sexuality.

The deployment of sexuality—through discourses, institutions, and practices—constitutes our experience of ourselves as normal or pathological. Women's sexuality has been pathologized from the male point of view.[98] Feminist resistance, then, is a reversal of power, taking women's experience as primary and exposing the workings of phallocentric power in the dominant discourse.

CONCLUSION

For both feminists and Foucault, the body is central for thinking about subjectivity, for understanding the effects of social and cultural norms, and for developing resistance to normative practices. In this chapter, I have tried to respond to feminist criticisms of Foucault's notion of the body. I agree with feminist critics who charge that the discussion of gender and gender-specific disciplinary practices are absent from Foucault's work. However, the analyses of the disciplinary practices of femininity by Bartky and Bordo show that Foucault provides valuable conceptual tools for feminists. Moreover, I wonder if the absence of discussion of gender-specific practices in Foucault's work was strategic, helping to pave the way for the deconstruction of gender. Butler's Foucauldian argument about the production of gender and sex is very different from Bartky's and Bordo's, yet all use Foucault's insights to make their cases. There is a certain tension in Foucault's work between the body as an effect of power and the body as a source of resistance, which some have claimed is paradoxical. I have argued that Foucault offers a variety of ways to think about the body—as material, with a history, interpreted through discourses, whose interiority is produced through discourses and power, with the ability to self-monitor and self-regulate, and as capable of resistance through producing counterdiscourses.

I believe Foucault's account of the body can accommodate a variety of feminist concerns. His discussion of genealogy and the body includes descent and emergence. Recall that descent refers to group affiliations, sustained by bloodlines, traditions, or social class. Marxist and socialist feminists would surely agree with Foucault that class is constitutive of identity and shapes the body in particular ways through one's work as well as access to nutrition and health care. Multicultural and global feminists would concur that bloodlines and traditions are a significant aspect of bodily experience and social identity. The notion of descent and the idea of group affiliations provide a way to acknowledge the differences in our histories and our bodies without essentializing that difference. Foucault's notion of emergence is useful as well. If bodies emerge as the result of conflicting forces and the play of dominations, then both the commonalities of women's bodies and the differences can be accounted for. For example, all women are affected by the general representation of women's bodies as passive, weak, inferior; and all women are affected when medical research on new drugs includes only men. But women are not all affected in the same way by medical practices such as forced sterilization, which is inflicted disproportionately on poor women and women of color. Emergence concerns the body as the site of contestation and struggle, an idea with which most feminists would agree. Not just the idea of the body, but the treatment of the body and of various types of bodies, emerges out of concrete political struggles. The good news is that emergence is dynamic, not static. The struggles that formed our bodies and the practices and institutions that continue to shape them continue to be fought. For feminists, this may be most clear around reproductive issues.

Foucault's view of the body as material, yet interpreted through particular discourses and disciplines, is also valuable to feminists. Feminists who wish to produce social and political change need to address the material circumstances of women; the body is central to issues of production as well as reproduction. Workplace health issues are a significant concern for many women, especially poor women and women in developing countries. For instance, in Colombia the flower-picking industry is primarily staffed by women. Strong pesticides that adversely affect the women's health are used on the flowers. Many of these flowers are exported to the United States, where, ironically, the harmful pesticides are banned. Foucault's analysis of the ways that bodies are materially affected by power relations helps to articulate the connection between political power and these types of practical effects on bodies. Often, discursive struggles themselves have practical effects. For example, discursive struggles in legal discourse around the meaning of gender and women's representation influence policies and laws about sex discrimination and sexual harassment. Issues of the representation of the body contribute to women's devaluation, and struggles have taken place and must continue to take place around the objectification of women as merely sex objects. Foucault's idea that the body is shaped by a variety of heterogeneous disciplines, discourses, and practices through power relations accounts for a multilevel, multilayered social reality. Feminists have produced and should continue to produce counterdiscourses, subversive practices, and collective resistance to combat women's oppression.

Foucault's nondualistic conception of the body-as-subject contributes to feminist thinking as well. Many feminists have taken issue with dualism and with the idea that subjectivity is disembodied. Often feminists have offered an embodied conception of subjectivity that takes sex/gender difference as fundamental. This approach produces problems of its own, as I shall discuss in the next chapter. Foucault does not take sex/gender difference as fundamental, although it can be accounted for in his theory. He does, however, offer a theory of embodied subjectivity that avoids reductive materialism. That is, he does not posit the body as simply physical states. Moreover, bodies as constituted through power relations are constituted intersubjectively. Resistance comes from the struggle and contestation of competing claims of power, rather than the ability to get outside of power. Resistances may be counterdisciplines that challenge normalizing power and produce transformation in individual bodies or the social body. Foucault's account of the body as the locus of resistance can be seen as simply the logical conclusion of an argument that locates subjectivity squarely in the body. What besides bodies can resist? It is my body that marches in demonstrations, my body that goes to the polls, my body that attends rallies, my body that boycotts, my body that strikes, my body that participates in work slowdowns, my body that engages in civil disobedience. Individual bodies are requisite for collective political action. Whether engaging in the macropolitics of collective struggle, or in the micropolitics of individual resistance, it is bodies that resist. And this resistance, like power, comes from everywhere—from social movements, from alternative discourses, from accidents and contingencies, from gaps between various ways of thinking, from gross material inequality, and from recognizable asymmetries of power.

Chapter 5

▶•◀

IDENTITY POLITICS: SEX, GENDER, AND SEXUALITY

Feminists disagree about whether or not a unified conception of identity is necessary for an effective feminist politics.[1] Those who advocate a unified concept of identity argue that it is necessary to make political demands on behalf of women. They claim that without appealing to the category "women," one cannot make claims for the group. Not only feminism, but also other new social movements share this idea of the importance of group identity for making political claims.[2] This identity politics has been challenged, especially within feminism. Opponents of identity politics argue that identity categories subsume differences among the group in their attempt at general representation. While representing women, for instance, gender is emphasized at the expense of other factors such as race, class, sexual orientation, and ability. Those who argue against identity politics claim that the demand for a unified category, such as women, implicitly assumes a norm—generally, white, middle class, heterosexual—and that this assumption of a norm excludes some from the category and occludes diversity within the category. This attempt to impose universal categories, they claim, is an exclusionary practice that feminists should avoid. The identity politics debate in feminism seems intractable, with both sides claiming that their position yields the most effective politics. Feminist critics of identity politics are often associated with a postmodernist position. Feminists who believe that the category "women" needs to be retained for an emancipatory politics come from a wide range of positions, including radical feminism, liberal feminism, Marxist feminism, and critical social theory.[3] Part of the intractability of the identity politics debate results from its misconstrual as essentialism vs. social constructionism. Advocates of identity politics are accused of being essentialists, whereas the social constructionist critics of identity politics are accused of undermining the possibility for an effective feminist politics. This characterization is misleading for a number of reasons that I address in the next section.

The social constructionist position is identified with Foucault. His thorough-going historicism reveals the contingency of social categories. And he explicitly argues against the notion of identity, viewing it as part of the insidious operation of power and subjection. Like feminist critics of identity politics, Foucault sees identity categories as normative and exclusionary. Identity categories are exclusionary because of their failure to fully represent the diversity of group members. And because they focus on a particular aspect of identity, they inadvertently operate normatively as well. Furthermore, identity categories often become reified and naturalized. This hides the contingency of identity categories as socially and historically produced. Thus, taking identity categories as a point of departure for politics may reinscribe the very identity categories that are problematic in the first place.

Foucault's reservations about identity as a source for effective politics are related to his general skepticism discussed in chapter 2 and his view of the subject discussed in chapter 3. His concerns about identity categories come out of his idea that they are one of the effects of power. Feminists mobilizing around the category "women" implicitly support a binary heterosexist sex/gender system. If identity categories are one of the effects of power, then using them as the basis for a politics consolidates that power. Yet feminists have a vested interest in dismantling the sex/gender system because it perpetuates women's oppression. In this chapter, I look at both the limitations and the strengths of an identity politics model. Using the examples of intersexuality and bisexuality, I demonstrate the normalizing power of identity categories. And I show that this normalizing power has real social and political effects. In spite of his suspicion of identity categories, Foucault does not reject identity as politically irrelevant. He thinks the most significant thing about identity is that it is historically, socially, and culturally produced. Examining the production of social identities can help to reveal the historical and political struggles waged in its production. I suggest that a feminist politics conscious of the politics of identity production would not uncritically or exclusively employ identity politics, but would also aim to dismantle the structures—institutions, laws, and social practices—that produce and reinforce the current binary regime of sex/gender identity.

IDENTITY POLITICS

Identity politics forms the basis of new social movements from the women's movement to the gay and lesbian movement to some aspects of the civil rights movement. In "Identity and Politics in a 'Postmodern' Gay Culture: Some Historical and Conceptual Notes," Steven Seidman claims that, "[b]y the mid-1970's, the left was socially, ideologically and politically decentered . . . composed of a plurality of movements, each focused on its own particular project of building an autonomous community, evolving its own language of social analysis, and forging an oppositional politic."[4] Identity politics begins from the assumption that the most radical politics is based upon the identities of members of a marginalized group. Following models of ethnic identity, models of sexual identity make the following claims: that individual identity is significantly related to group membership; that group membership relies on a particular shared feature; that shared traditions, histories, and communities are important to the maintaining of individual identity; and that group membership results in a shared experience. The Combahee River Collective, a Black feminist collective from the 1970s, explains identity politics this way: "This focusing on our own oppression is embodied in the concept of identity politics. We believe that the most profound and potentially radical politics come directly out of our own identity as opposed to working to end someone else's oppression."[5] In the women's movement in the United States, identity politics may be most closely associated with the radical feminist position. Radical feminists looked at the ways that systems of patriarchal oppression affected the experiences of women. Employment practices that privileged men, a legal system that did not protect women from discrimination, and cultural norms that devalued women's experiences all contributed to women's exclusion from public life. Identity politics mobilizes oppressed groups to demand equal rights and representation. Making claims for inclusion on behalf of the oppressed group has been a fairly effective political strategy. In addition to its political effectiveness, identity politics can be psychologically empowering for members of oppressed groups. Structural oppression such as sexism or racism operates at many levels—political, legal, social, cultural, and linguistic. While political and legal remedies can address issues such as inclusion in the political process and discrimination, they cannot address social and cultural issues, such as media images of women. Sharing experiences with members of one's own group can serve to confirm that one's individual experience fits into a larger pattern of oppression. This recognition of the impact of systemic oppression on individual experience can help to consolidate one's identity as a member of an oppressed group and to foster collective action. In spite of these political and psychological benefits, the problems with identity politics are well documented in feminist theory.[6] One of the most significant drawbacks of an identity politics model is the tendency toward group homogeneity; because identity politics focuses on a particular aspect of identity, e.g., sexual orientation, race, ethnicity, or gender, it de-emphasizes the other aspects of identity.

The "ethnic identity model" of lesbian and gay identity gained currency in the 1970s.[7] Steven Epstein argues that a resurgence of ethnic identity among white European ethnic groups in the 1970s corresponded with the consolidation of lesbian and gay identity and the privileging of the erotic and sexual dimension of human life. The ethnic identity model consolidates group identity and mobilizes individuals as part of a political group by focusing on the group members' minority status. This minoritizing logic focuses on achieving rights and securing resources for the oppressed group within the current political structure. Group membership is based on some common feature among members of the group, such as race, ethnicity, sex, sexual orientation, or physical ability. This feature of the individual is thought to constitute her identity. The reasoning goes something like this: this feature, e.g., sex, shapes my experience in fundamental ways in a sexist society; it also shapes the experiences of others who are similarly situated in similar ways, e.g., we are all at risk of sexual harassment, sex discrimination in employment, etc.. So, this shared feature leads to shared experience, which leads to shared identity. Identity politics has been very effective in mobilizing oppressed groups to demand political equality and equal opportunities. However, there are significant problems with this approach. Ironically, in spite of the fact that feminism relies on an identity politics model, criticisms of identity politics come from feminists who have a variety of feminist approaches. First, as mentioned above, the focus on one aspect of identity as salient neglects other aspects of identity; thus some members of an oppressed group may feel misrepresented or excluded. Multicultural, Marxist, and radical feminists argue that feminism's focus on sex often minimizes issues of race, class, and sexual orientation. Second, the categories themselves can be exclusionary, functioning as normative categories.[8] Global feminists sometimes charge that Western feminism employs concepts and language that are imperialist, that is, that the categories of rights, freedom, and equality themselves distort or misrepresent the experience of non-Western women. Third, in spite of "shared oppression," there is no necessary connection between group membership and individual identity insofar as that identity means a shared politics.[9] Some socialist feminists and feminist critical social theorists argue that institutions and social structures, such as the economy and the legal system, should be the target for political change, and that working for social justice has little to do with identity. For different reasons, liberal feminism, too, holds that identity issues are irrelevant to social justice. And fourth, relying on identity to ground a politics reifies the very category that is being appealed to. Some radical feminists have pointed out that feminist approaches that appeal to women as mothers or as caregivers as a justification for their theory may simply be reinforcing stereotypical views of women and valorizing traits that are produced through patriarchal oppression. This reification and naturalizing of identity has resulted in charges of essentialism leveled at those who advocate identity politics.[10]

Characterizing the identity politics debate as essentialism vs. social constructionism misrepresents both sides of the debate—most of those who advocate identity politics are not committed to essentialism of any kind, and the social constructionist position is caricatured as an antirealist position that views objects as fictions. In general, an essentialist view is one that appeals to an unchanging, universal characteristic, an "essence." This essence is thought to be outside of or prior to social, historical factors. Indeed, sometimes it is used as the foundation for social collectivities, for instance, the now contested category of "women." There are several different versions of essentialism, for instance, biological, sociological, and metaphysical. Biological essentialists assert that women are fundamentally different from men based on biological and anatomical differences. Sociological essentialists posit that men and women think differently, not because of biological differences, but because of gender role socialization. An example of this would be Carol Gilligan's view that women are more likely to exhibit a care ethic than men. And metaphysical essentialists believe that women have some ineffable quality that men do not; radical feminist Mary Daly holds this view. While I cannot go into detail here about the differences among these essentialist positions, I wish to point out that in most cases the difference between men and women is thought to be natural, and the assumption is that nature and culture are diametrically opposed.

This opposition between nature and culture carries over into the social constructionist view as well. Social constructionists hold that nothing is prior to history, or outside of the social and cultural. Thus, in some sense everything is seen as socially or historically produced. But this presentation of the position seems to imply that social construction "goes all the way down," that there is no material reality. Ian Hacking's *The Social Construction of What?* goes some way toward clearing up the confusion about the social constructionist position.[11] Social construction is a misleading misnomer. Hacking points out that something can be both socially constructed and real. He distinguishes between ideas and objects, pointing out that most social constructionists are arguing for the social construction of the former, not the latter. He also notes that ideas and objects may interact, notably in the case of the classification of human beings. Hacking calls this interaction between people and their classifications a "looping effect." Classifications of people are embedded in institutions, practices, and language, and maintained through everyday interactions. Foucault is clearly concerned with social construction as it applies to classifications and categories of people, as his interest in the human sciences demonstrates. Some critics, however, wrongly attribute a stronger constructionist view to Foucault. The strong view of social constructionism seems to deny the materiality of things. As I have demonstrated, Foucault's analyses are grounded in real, material practices and institutions. But even the weaker view that restricts social construction to ideas and not objects seems to privilege culture, the social world, and meaning over nature.

The contrast between the essentialist and social constructionist positions on the issue of the body further illuminates this presumed split between nature and culture. Diana Fuss puts it this way: "For the essentialist, the body occupies a pure, pre-social, pre-discursive space. The body is 'real,' accessible, and transparent; it is always there and directly interpretable through the senses. For the constructionist, the body is never simply there, rather it is composed of a network of effects continually subject to sociopolitical determination."[12] As I have argued in chapter 4, for Foucault the body is both "real and there" and "continually subject to sociopolitical determination." The contrast between an essentialist view and a social constructionist view is often overdrawn, and usually elides differences between varieties of essentialism and varying degrees of social constructionism. Furthermore, it may be a mistake to see essentialism as undergirding identity politics, and to see social constructionism as a threat to identity politics. As Ladelle McWhorter points out in *Bodies & Pleasures*, socially constructed identities may serve as the basis for groups coming together and even for engaging in collective political action. She uses the example of Christianity as an unquestionably socially constructed identity that nonetheless serves as a basis for group solidarity and political action. McWhorter unravels some of the assumed connections among community, identity, and political action. She argues that social constructionists and essentialists both have accounts of identity, although the accounts differ. Essentialists think that identity precedes and forms the basis for community, while social constructionists think that developing a particular identity requires the support of a community. Thus, holding an identity politics position does not depend on one's being committed to essentialism. However, as I have pointed out above, there are other reasons to be cautious about endorsing an identity politics model.

FOUCAULT ON IDENTITY

Foucault discusses identity in different ways in his work: as sameness, as the result of normative categorization, and as the end of the process of individualization. In each case, he views identity as restrictive and limiting. Foucault held little regard for consistency of identity: "To be the same is really boring."[13] In his later writings, he stressed that the point of philosophical writing is self-transformation. Adherence to a particular identity for Foucault inhibits the possibility for change. He warns against this stasis of identity: "But the relationships we have with ourselves are not ones of identity, rather, they must be relationships of differentiation, of creation, of innovation."[14] Foucault's reluctance to advocate identity stems from his view that identity is formed through the regulatory apparatus that defines and subjects individuals. Identity categories create new types of persons: the homosexual, the criminal, the madman. Social science discourses attach new meaning to acts and behavior and seek the "truth" about them in the individual. The individual becomes describable, analyzable through innovations in social science, such as statistical analysis, and she is documented as a case through writing. As discussed earlier, the procedure of confession, too, serves to individualize, "The truthful confession was inscribed at the heart of procedures of individualization by power."[15] Individualization through documentation describes the objectification of the individual through external third-party classifications and statistical categorization in relation to the general population. This objectification through documentation is evident in life insurance actuary tables, which calculate one's average life expectancy and assess the costs and benefits to the company of providing the life insurance policy, and in health care through doctor's records, medical charts, and family history. The consequences of documentation may be good; for instance, the documentation of an individual as a medical case may allow the early detection of a disease. On the other hand, the consequences of this documentation may serve to penalize certain individuals, for instance, barring smokers from some life insurance plans. In confession, the confessor is complicit in the process of individualization. The person gives an account of herself that serves to locate her in the social structure. In spite of the differences in the procedure of confession, which emanates from the individual and is touted as a liberatory practice, and the process of documentation, which comes from outside the individual, Foucault believes that the process of becoming a subject through confession and of individualization through documentation both increasingly tie one to one's identity.

Categories of identity are formed through exclusionary practices, which Foucault calls dividing practices, that divide the normal from the abnormal. Because normal refers to the majority or dominant group, those who deviate from this norm are marginalized. Marginalization has effects at the material level, e.g., less economic power and access to resources, and at cultural levels, e.g., less cultural authority to speak. Normative categories produce psychological effects, such as internalized oppression, or low self-esteem. They also have material effects through their power to define and to exclude, for example, sex categories. Foucault argues that the discourse of sexuality is pervasive, organizing social relations and influencing our understanding of ourselves. The discourse of sexuality (like discipline) operates primarily on bodies. Part of Foucault's point in *The History of Sexuality Volume One* is that what we take to be "natural" biological facts are themselves the product of cultural understandings and interpretations.[16] Normative categories have real effects. As we shall see, normative assumptions about male and female bodies result in harm to the individuals who do not fit these categories. Foucault's notion of social norms and the way they operate illuminates the practical, material effects and political implications of normative categories. He provides a link among laws, institutions, and individuals that is helpful for understanding the relationship between social structures and social groups. Recognizing the relationships among institutions, social practices, social norms and categories, and group and individual identity is important for feminists who need to work on multiple fronts to overcome sex/gender oppression.

POSTMODERN CRITICISMS OF IDENTITY POLITICS

Feminist critics of identity politics agree with Foucault that identity categories tie one to one's identity. They argue that using group identity as a political category is dangerous in at least four ways. First, using identity as a category can reify the category, that is, it may serve to reinforce and naturalize differences that are the social and historical result of oppression. Second, using identity categories as political categories preempts questions about the political and social conditions under which that identity was formed, and who the identity might exclude. In feminist theory, it is often put this way, "Who is the 'we' in whose name these demands are being made?"[17] The "we" question is related to the normalizing function of categories; identity categories usually pick out one feature of an individual shared by the group, such as sex. But in doing so, implicit criteria are relied upon. For instance, in the case of sex, whether or not male-to-female transsexuals count as women is a matter of heated debate in some lesbian separatist communities.[18] Assuming that identity categories are or can be the basis of political solidarity leaves such basic questions as "Who counts and why?" out of the scope of the political. Third, using identity categories as the basis for political solidarity not only preempts questions of who belongs to the group, but also serves to fragment one oppressed group from another, and to fracture those who belong to more than one oppressed group.[19] Oppressed groups may divide on issues of who is more oppressed, or whose political claims are currently most urgent. Individuals belonging to more than one oppressed group may feel that their allegiance is pulled in more than one direction. Finally, as previously mentioned, identity politics models assume a false connection between identity and politics.

Foucault's wariness of normative categories is apparent throughout his work. Normative categories are in large part a result of "advances" in social scientific knowledge. But Foucault's genealogies reveal the contingency of events that led up to our current understandings, thus undermining this notion of progress. Using identity as a political category without questioning its formation works against his attempt to undermine the givenness of such categories. With regard to the question of the "we," Foucault says: "But the problem is, precisely, to decide if it's actually suitable to place oneself within a 'we' in order to assert the principles one recognizes and the values one accepts; or if it is not, rather, necessary to make the future formation of a 'we' possible, by elaborating the question. Because it seems to me that the 'we' must not be previous to the question; it can only be the result—and the necessarily temporary result—of the question as it is posed in the new terms in which one formulates it."[20] Butler echoes this concern specifically with respect to feminism, "Through what exclusions has the feminist subject been constructed, and how do those excluded domains return to haunt the 'integrity' and 'unity' of a feminist 'we'? And how is it that the very category, the subject, the 'we,' that is supposed to be presumed for the purpose of solidarity, produces the very factionalization it is supposed to quell? Do women want to become subjects on the model which requires and produces an anterior region of abjection, or must feminism become a process which is self-critical about the processes that produce and destabilize identity categories?"[21]

A Foucauldian feminist approach such as Butler's does not simply advocate abolishing all categories, but mandates attention to the effects of normative categories as part of the operation of power. Butler views identity as a useful fiction that may be deployed strategically for political purposes. In fact, Foucault himself allows for a variety of different political strategies. Although Foucault is critical of the normalizing function of identity categories, he does not reject the possibility of their political usefulness altogether. He says, "Well, if identity is only a game, if it is only a procedure to have relations, social and sexual-pleasure relationships that create new friendships, it is useful. . . . We must not exclude identity if people find their pleasure through this identity, but we must not think of this identity as an ethical universal rule."[22] For Foucault, strategic appeals to identity are acceptable, so long as identity does not function as a universal rule or category. Political tactics and strategies depend on the situation or context. Foucault's strategic view of politics allows for appeals to both rights and identity while taking neither as foundational. His primary concern about appealing to categories such as identity, freedom, and rights is that they have been and may be used to limit freedom. Foucault cautions, "What we call humanism has been used by Marxists, liberals, Nazis, Catholics. This does not mean that we have to get rid of what we call human rights or freedom, but we can't say that freedom or human rights has to be limited at certain frontiers."[23] In spite of his reservations about the use of such categories as human rights, Foucault recognizes that sometimes it is politically efficacious to adopt them. He supports gay and lesbian efforts to work for civil rights, saying "[h]uman rights regarding sexuality are important and are still not respected in many places. We shouldn't consider that such problems are solved now."[24] Sexual politics must appeal to both rights and identity to be effective. Members of marginalized groups need equal protection under the law. At the same time, the impact of identity on one's experience must also be taken into account.[25]

Identity can be an important source of empowerment. Shared group identity can help individuals from oppressed groups see their experiences not as psychological failures, as was often the case for women before the women's movement, but as social and political issues. Liberal strategies work well to garner legal rights and political representation for oppressed groups, but as the old saying goes, "You can't legislate consciousness." Social theorists from Marx to Foucault make a compelling case that social, environmental, and cultural factors strongly influence our consciousness. Because of this influence, issues of representation become political issues. For example, depictions of women on billboards and album covers became a political issue for feminists in the United States in the 1970s. Degrading depictions of women contribute to their devaluation in society.[26] Cultural myths and stereotypes work against full political equality. They reinforce and perpetuate prejudice and discrimination, and they may affect individuals' own assessment of their capabilities, life possibilities, and choices. Identity is an important category politically because of these kinds of cultural and social effects. Feminists, for example, have documented the parallels between women's lack of cultural authority and lack of political representation. But in spite of the political significance of identity, it can function in harmful and limiting ways.

I offer two extended examples of the limitations of an identity politics model.[27] Both hermaphroditism and bisexuality raise troubling questions about the categories of sex, gender, and sexual orientation. Neither hermaphrodites nor bisexuals fall within normative sex categories. Furthermore, both seem to confound the very binary structure of normative sexual categories themselves. Alternately, hermaphrodites are neither or both male and female; bisexuals are neither or both heterosexual and homosexual. Sex categories are significant not simply as a point around which to mobilize politics, but in every aspect of one's daily life. One's sex prescribes certain behaviors, the horizons of personal aspirations are affected by sex, and social and political rights and responsibilities are sex related.[28] Sex and gender regulation takes place at all levels, institutional and interpersonal, through the medical establishment, the legal systems, the educational system, and in daily life through such things as single-sex toilets, gift giving, and styles of dress. An assumed sexual dimorphism makes us read bodies as male or female. But not all bodies are clearly unambiguously male or female. In fact, a significant percentage of persons are born with both male and female traits.[29] Persons with a combination of male and female traits are commonly called hermaphrodites or, more recently, intersexuals. Historically, the treatment of those whose anatomies combine male and female traits has varied. Before the nineteenth century hermaphrodites were allowed to choose their sex, and the legal designation of male or female with all its attendant rights and obligations followed from that choice. Beginning in the nineteenth century, the issue of a "true sex" became a medical issue;

the sex of the hermaphrodite was to be decided by a team of medical experts, judiciaries, and religious authorities. Foucault's *Herculine Barbin* documents this shift from individual choice to the adjudication of sex through medical, legal, and religious institutions. The interest in a "true sex" for each individual persists in the twentieth century. In *Hermaphrodites and the Medical Invention of Sex*, Alice Dreger refers to this as the "one body, one sex" rule.[30] The "one body, one sex" rule is still in place today, now enforced primarily by the medical establishment. Enforcing this rule involves what is euphemistically termed the medical management of intersexed infants or what intersexual activists refer to as genital mutilation.

HERCULINE BARBIN AND THE SEXED BODY

As discussed in chapter 4, the sex/gender distinction has been important to feminists; it allowed for biological differences between men and women without prescribing social differences. The separation between sex and gender meant that sex could be viewed as relatively stable, while gender roles and norms could be seen as historically and culturally variable. The introduction of the sex/gender distinction in feminist theory coincides with the early work of psychologist John Money on gender identity. In 1972, he and colleague Anke Ehrhardt popularized the idea that sex and gender were separate categories. Parallel to the sex/gender distinction in feminist theory, sex refers to one's anatomy and physiology, while gender was viewed as psychological and behavioral. Consequently, gender was seen as relying on socialization, while sex was given at birth. But what if sex is not "given" at birth? As we shall see, Money's research created a medical paradigm that has turned out to be damaging to intersexuals. The assumption that gender is learned, combined with the assumption that there are only two sexes, paved the way for the "medical management of intersexed infants," which involves genital surgery. Theories of gender and sex have practical implications.

Currently, many feminists claim there is no rigid distinction between sex and gender. The breakdown of the sex/gender distinction results both from the recognition that biological sex and sexed bodies are tremendously diverse and from the recognition that we always interpret the sexed body through cultural and linguistic categories. Thus, it is not simply gender that results from socially imposed categories, but sex itself. As discussed in chapter 4, Butler's influential theory of gender as performance challenges the standard view, which holds that gender is the expression or cultural meaning of sex. Instead, she argues that the performance of gender helps to construct sex. Other feminists, for instance, Sarah Hoagland and Marilyn Frye, focus on the role that normative gender roles play in perpetuating sexism and heterosexism. They argue that gender roles both result from and perpetuate compulsory heterosexuality.[31] Sex, too, plays a role in perpetuating compulsory heterosexuality because "appropriate," that is, normative gender roles derive from one's sex.

A long-term historical view provides some evidence for the historical and cultural specificity of sex and gender categories, as do some anthropological studies. In terms of sex, our understanding of who counts as male and who counts as female has changed historically.[32] Alice Dreger's *Hermaphrodites and the Medical Invention of Sex* chronicles the change in criteria from anatomy (external physical characteristics) to gonads (internal physical characteristics, i.e., ovaries or testes) used to determine sex. Even the priority of sex for self-understanding and social organization has shifted historically. In volumes 2 and 3 of *The History of Sexuality*, Foucault examines a time before the discourse of sex was dominant. He shows that other aspects of bodily life were privileged and that one's relation to oneself did not depend on establishing the truth in relation to sex. Foucault's *Herculine Barbin* exemplifies the way that the discourse of sexuality works to produce the truth about subjects in relation to sex. From the nineteenth century to the present, the question of "true sex" has remained important.

Nowhere is the power of the social control of normative categories more apparent than in the case of hermaphrodites. Anne Fausto-Sterling provides a Foucauldian analysis of the power that social and cultural categories have not only to shape our perceptions of natural phenomena, but also to actively intervene to pattern natural phenomena after social categories. In her article "The Five Sexes," Anne Fausto-Sterling advocates a sex classification system that allows for more than two sexes.[33] She cites research that shows that in addition to male and female there are three other sexes, each with a mixture of male and female characteristics. These three sexes she calls merms, ferms, and herms. She focuses on the relation between the categories we use to describe the sexes and the phenomena that those categories describe. She argues that in a two-sex system the categories are prescriptive, and this often results in the medical management of those individuals that do not fit neatly into the category of male or female.

Foucault himself was concerned with the issue of hermaphroditism as exemplifying the damage that normative categories can do. He brought attention to the case of Herculine Barbin, a nineteenth-century hermaphrodite, by publishing a collection of documents relating to her/his case, including Herculine's memoirs.[34] The case of Herculine is significant for Foucault because it shows the way in which knowledge, norms, and self-constitution interact: "[i]t is [also] these three axes and the play between types of understanding [*savoir*], forms of normality, and modes of relation to oneself and others which seemed to me to give individual cases the status of significant experiences—cases like Pierre Riviere or Alexina B. [Herculine] . . ."[35] Herculine's case is exceptional, not because hermaphroditism was rare in the nineteenth century, but because it is the only known case from the period where there is a first-person account.[36] This is significant for Foucault in two ways—theoretically his third axis of investigation focuses on the modes of relation to oneself, and more generally in his work he attributes importance to the ability of the oppressed to speak for themselves.[37]

Foucault raises the question of a "true sex" in the introduction to *Herculine Barbin*.[38] Technically, Foucault is the editor rather than the author of this text. The book consists of three parts: the memoir of Herculine Barbin; a section that includes excerpts of medical reports, copies of court documents, and selected newspaper articles relevant to the case of Herculine Barbin; and a short story based on her life. Foucault provides a brief introduction to these texts and a few explanatory notes regarding the documents collected in the second section. According to Foucault, the theme of the hermaphrodite was prominent in the nineteenth century. Foucault cites a few reasons why the case of Herculine Barbin merits our attention. Herculine was brought up in the single-sex environment of convents, she provides a first-person account of her life before and after her reidentification as a man, and her life is chronicled in the short story "The Scandal at the Convent," written by a psychiatrist who died in an asylum.

The problem that the nineteenth century poses with regard to hermaphroditism is the demand for a true sex. Foucault claims that before she was reclassified as a man, Herculine enjoyed "the happy limbo of a non-identity."[39] But the drive to categorize, and to discover the "truth" of subjectivity, made it impossible to remain in that limbo of nonidentity; "they [western societies] have obstinately brought into play this question of a true sex in an order of things where one might have imagined that all that counted was the reality of the body and the intensity of its pleasures."[40] Note that Foucault again appeals to bodies and pleasures as a point of resistance to the deployment of sexuality, as he does in *The History of Sexuality Volume One*. As I argued in chapter 4, his appeal to the body as a point of resistance does not entail that the body transcend description, only that it is not exhausted by any one description or categorization. *Herculine Barbin* can be seen as part of Foucault's larger project of criticizing the processes of subjection that take questions about the truth of one's sex to be at the heart of subjectivity.

Using the case of Herculine Barbin, Foucault illustrates the increasing control of juridical and medical institutions on identity. This increased control resulted in a demand for each person to have one true sex. In *Herculine Barbin*, Foucault focuses on the epistemological questions surrounding this shift toward demanding a "true sex" that appeared as a theme in the mid-nineteenth century. He emphasizes that hermaphroditism itself was not, of course, a new phenomenon, but the way it was dealt with changed at this time. In the Middle Ages, hermaphrodites were considered to have two sexes, and at the time of baptism the

father or godfather decided which sex the child would be raised as; then at adulthood, the hermaphrodite was able to decide whether to continue on with this sex
designation or switch to the other. This decision was to take place before marriage,
and once the decision was made it could not be changed without penalties and social sanctions. Even in the case of sexually ambiguous bodies, the social pressures
to be "heterosexual" persist. By the eighteenth century, the idea that one individual could have two sexes was displaced; each person was allowed to have one and
only one sex. Foucault argues that this epistemological shift corresponded with
changes in the laws, and perhaps most importantly, with medicine's interest in rendering sex unambiguous. Whereas before hermaphrodites were able upon adulthood to decide their sex, now medical experts were accorded the authority to
determine a hermaphrodite's "true" sex. Moreover, because of the shifts in "biological theories of sexuality, juridical conceptions of the individual, [and] forms of
administrative control in modern nations" the conceptual framework had changed;
hermaphrodites were no longer considered of indeterminate sex and allowed to
choose which sex to live as; instead doctors were supposed to discover the "true
sex" of the (now pseudo) hermaphrodite.[41]

Questions of sex are clearly linked to sexual orientation in a society that imposes compulsory heterosexuality as normal. Foucault recognizes this connection,
yet he leaves it undeveloped in his introduction to *Herculine Barbin*. He alludes to
the moral interest that inheres in the medical diagnosis of a "true" sex, specifically
its interest in restricting homosexual relationships.[42] And he notes, ". . . individuals might also very well be suspected of dissembling their inmost [sic] knowledge
of their true sex and of profiting from certain anatomical oddities in order to
make use of their bodies *as if they belonged to the other sex* (emphasis added)."[43]

The texts that Foucault has brought together raise a number of questions.
The epistemological question of a true sex is inextricably tied to moral and sociopolitical questions of sexuality and sexual identity. One of the questions that
the text raises is the role that Herculine's sexuality played in the determination of
her "true" sex. Herculine, raised as a girl, had sexual relationships with women.
One can only wonder what Herculine's case would have been like had she desired
men. Would she have been reclassified as a man? Although the answer is specula-
tive, I highly doubt it. In what follows, I examine the complex interplay of sex,
gender, and sexual orientation.[44] The medical, scientific interest in rendering sex
unambiguous clearly has a covert moral and political agenda.

Foucault remarks that the case of Herculine Barbin did not attract much interest during her lifetime, yet it was significant enough to be the subject of a short
story, as well as of several medical articles.[45] The short version of Herculine's life
is as follows. Born in 1838, she was designated female, raised in convents, and
trained as a teacher. She lived as a woman until she was redesignated male at the

age of twenty-two. Unable to adjust to living as a man, at the age of thirty, Herculine committed suicide. The events that led to Herculine's redesignation as male were facilitated by religious authorities and medical experts working in concert with judiciaries. Inadvertently, Herculine began the series of events that ultimately resulted in her reassignment from female to male. Plagued by poor health throughout her adolescence, in her early twenties Herculine experienced such sharp pains in her abdomen that she required medical attention. She was examined by a doctor who was disturbed and surprised by his findings. He kept the nature of his findings to himself, although he did recommend that Herculine be expelled from the school where she lived and taught. Herculine continued to have health problems, and she was acutely aware that she was in some sense different from other women. Seeking advice she went to the Monseigneur, a highly respected religious authority. She confessed to the Monseigneur all that had happened, including the intimate sexual nature of her relationship with Sara, and the doctor's reaction when he examined her. The Monseigneur recommended that Herculine be examined by his doctor to help to determine the best course of action. Upon examination, the doctor determined that a mistake had been made and that, indeed, Herculine was a man. The legal apparatus was set into motion, the doctor examined Herculine once more to be sure, and then her civil status was "rectified" from female to male.

From the medical reports, we learn that Herculine was a "true hermaphrodite," possessing the genitalia of both a male and a female; "in fact, it is difficult, as will be seen later on, to discover a more extreme mixture of the two sexes, as concerns everything relating to the external genital organs."[46] As discussed above, in the Middle Ages, Herculine would have been considered as having two sexes and at this juncture allowed to choose which sex she wished to live as. But under the "one body, one sex" rule adopted in the eighteenth century, the authority to choose was no longer her own but rested with the medical establishment. Given that Herculine was an intersexual with ambiguous genitalia, one might ask; "What were the factors that determined her reassignment from female to male?" In what follows, I provide a reading of *Herculine Barbin* that demonstrates the power of normative conceptions of femininity and masculinity and I show how these normative conceptions of gender inform the procedure of sex assignment and are linked to heterosexism.

Feminist theory presents strong arguments for the role that normative constructs of femininity and masculinity play in reproducing themselves, thus perpetuating sexism through the continuation of stereotypical, normative gender categories. One significant way in which normative gender categories are employed relates to physical appearance, the range of what is acceptable for a woman or a man. Both masculinity and femininity are prescriptive rather than simply descriptive categories.

The effect of normative gender categories regarding appearance can be seen in the life of Herculine. When Herculine was a woman, she was too strong, too awkward, too gawky, too tall, too masculine. But when she was a man, she was too soft, too weak, too feminine. But her body and appearance were the same. The normative categories of gender are dichotomous; what women are, men are not and *vice versa*. There is little or no room for gender ambiguity. In what follows, I show how this intolerance for gender ambiguity led to the sex reassignment of Herculine, and ultimately to her death.

In her article "Sexism," Marilyn Frye illuminates the sex-marking that goes on all the time in daily life—the clothes one wears, the length and style of one's hair, one's gestures and movements. She points out that this sex-marking has twofold consequences; it marks individuals as either male or female and it serves to perpetuate masculine and feminine gender roles and normative heterosexuality. Frye argues that sex-marking is pervasive and socially obligatory. So long as one's sex determines the roles and opportunities available to one, then flagrant displays of sex-marking serve to mark out one's place in the social world.

In her memoirs, Herculine noted that her physical appearance was different from that of her peers:

> At that age when a women's graces unfold, I had neither that free and easy bearing nor the well-rounded limbs that reveal youth in full bloom. My complexion with its sickly pallor denoted a condition of chronic ill health. My features had a certain hardness that one could not help noticing. My upper lip and a part of my cheeks were covered by a light down that increased as the days passed. Understandably, this peculiarity often drew to me joking remarks that I tried to avoid by making frequent use of scissors in place of a razor. As was bound to happen, I only succeeded in making it even thicker and more noticeable still. My body was literally covered with it, and so, unlike my companions, I carefully avoided exposing my arms, even in the warmest weather. As for my figure it remained ridiculously thin. That all struck the eye, as I realized everyday.[47]

This difference in Herculine's physical appearance from the other teenage girls at the convent is echoed in Oscar Panizza's short story. "In appearance, Alexina [Herculine] was certainly odd and different. She was tall and slender, with a rapid long stride that kept her skirts in ungainly motion."[48] These physical descriptions of lean angular body type, graceless awkward gestures, and hairy face and body are interspersed throughout the memoirs and short story. These descriptions of masculine appearance may not be surprising in light of the fact that Herculine, living as a woman, was later reclassified as a man. But what are we to make of a competing set of physical descriptions, attributed to Herculine after her re-classification? When

Herculine sought work as a servant in Paris, his potential employer said to him, "[Y]ou look weak, delicate to me and not at all cut out for work of that sort."[49] Keep in mind that Herculine had not undergone a physical change of any kind; her body, her face, her gestures were exactly as before, the only change being that formerly she was read as (an inadequate) woman, and after her sex reassignment she was read as a man, although still clearly falling short of the normative requirements of masculinity. Normative categories structure and shape the way we view things. Furthermore, they have the power to define what should fall inside a particular category and what should fall outside of it.

In "'Femininity,' Resistance, and Sabotage," Sarah Hoagland persuasively argues that definitions prescribe what counts in a particular category. She claims that femininity is not an empirical concept, but a metaphysical category used by those in power to determine perception of facts.[50] Her discussion illuminates how normative femininity functions, excluding those who do not fit into its rigid boundaries, while reinscribing the category itself. Stereotypical conceptions of femininity help to enforce male domination and to fortify the institution of heterosexuality. Her argument demonstrates the element of social control and power that resides in definitions and their application within social contexts. It is just this insidious power that is at work in the case of Herculine Barbin.

Herculine defied definition and normative categorization. Herculine was neither a man nor a woman, or if you like both a man and a woman. Herculine had both male and female genitalia:

> Is [Herculine] a woman? She has a vulva, labia majora, and a feminine urethra, independent of a sort of imperforate penis, which might be a monstrously developed clitoris. She has a vagina. True, it is very short, very narrow; but after all, what is it if not a vagina? *These are completely feminine attributes.* Yes, but [Herculine] has never menstruated; the whole outer part of her body is that of a man, and my explorations did not enable me to find a womb. *Her tastes, her inclinations draw her toward women.* At night she has voluptuous sensations that are followed by a discharge of sperm, her linen is stained and starched with it. Finally, to sum up the matter, *ovoid bodies and spermatic cords* are found by touch in a divided scrotum. These are the *real proofs of sex.* We can now conclude and say: [Herculine] is a man, hermaphroditic, no doubt, but with an obvious predominance of masculine sex characteristics (emphasis added).[51]

In this excerpt from the medical report by Dr. Chesnut, who examined Herculine when she was twenty-two (in 1860), the testes are the real proof of sex in spite of the fact that anatomically her genitalia are clearly a mixture of the two sexes. This substantiates Dreger's and Foucault's claims that medical authorities had the last word on determining sex, and that the criteria for sex determination changed over time. It is also interesting to note that Herculine's sexual desire for women is listed among the criteria in the doctor's report as proof of her masculinity. In a framework that views sex, gender, and sexual orientation as dichotomous, and heterosexuality as normal, sexual desire becomes a criterion for determining sex. Although the system of compulsory heterosexuality was a contributing factor in determining Herculine's sex, as is indicated by the medical report, her memoirs indicate that before her sex reassignment, she had successful and satisfying lesbian relationships, whereas after she was reclassified as a man, he did not have any intimate relationships. Foucault does not pursue this in his brief analysis of Herculine's case, although he is well aware that the moral interest in rendering sex unambiguous is to deter homosexuality. Herculine refers to herself both as a man and as a woman in her memoirs. Foucault notes that although the memoir was written after Herculine had been reclassified as a man, it is not written from a male point of view. As mentioned earlier, in his introduction to the text, Foucault says that Herculine enjoyed the "happy limbo of non-identity" before her sex reassignment as a man. But this claim obscures the fact that Herculine thought of herself as a woman and her peers, teachers, students, and female lovers thought of her as a woman before her sex reassignment. One might say that Herculine is a victim of the compulsory heterosexuality that renders lesbian existence invisible or impossible (both in her historical context and to Foucault).[52]

The case of Herculine reveals the contingency of the categories of sex, gender, and sexual orientation and the complexity of relations among them. The categories of sex are no more natural than the categories of gender and sexual orientation. Dreger points out that by the eighteenth century, in spite of little agreement about which traits were necessary to malehood and femalehood, there did seem to be agreement that there were only two sexes, and that these sexes were mutually exclusive. But the change in the criteria for sex over time reveals the contingency of sex categories. Moreover, cases of doubtful sex like Herculine's underscore the arbitrariness of sex classification. This doubt undermines the whole enterprise. As Dreger puts it, ". . . the doubt extended far beyond any individual case to the endeavor [of sex classification] as a whole."[53] While historical investigation demonstrates the contingency of sex categories, new scientific research calls for the recognition of a multiplicity of sexes, as well as genders. There are a number of hormonal and chromosomal conditions that result in ambiguous genitalia: Klinefelter syndrome, androgen insensitivity syndrome, congenital adrenal hyperplasia, partial or mixed gonadal dysgenesis, hypospadias. Why then, one might ask, the insistence on two sexes? As Foucault aptly pointed out, there is a moral interest in the scientific quest to render sex unambiguous; unambiguous sex categories are necessary to enforce heterosexuality. There is a connection between normative gender roles and sexism, and between sexism and homophobia.[54] The case of Herculine Barbin makes apparent the damage that can be done by accepting rigid gender distinctions and compulsory heterosexuality and imposing them onto a sexually ambiguous body. The case of Herculine Barbin can be more than a history lesson for feminists. The ambiguity of an intersexed body challenges strict divisions into male and female. Currently intersexual activists lobby against surgery on infants to make their genitals conform to standard male or female appearance. Moreover, transgender activists challenge standard assumptions about gender, such as the correspondence between masculinity and men and femininity and women. The issues surrounding sex, gender, and sexual orientation are complex. A feminism that seeks to be inclusive must negotiate these complexities, rather than rely on standard categories.

BISEXUALITY: IDENTITY AND POLITICS

Bisexual politics is perhaps the newest of the new social movements that emerged in the 1970s in the United States from the leftist politics of the 1960s. Bisexual politics emerged out of the women's movement and the gay and lesbian movement.[55] Bisexuals want to be recognized as a sexual minority distinct from lesbians and gays. Their claim to sexual minority group status relies on an identity politics model. But a bisexual identity politics is inherently problematic. Bisexuality presents a special case for identity politics because, in addition to the many limitations of identity politics discussed earlier, bisexual identity politics seems paradoxical. Bisexuals rely on an identity politics model to justify their demands for recognition from the dominant heterosexual culture, as well as within lesbian and gay groups. However, bisexuality also shows the limits of identity politics. Bisexuality functions ambivalently as a category; on the one hand, the insistence on claiming a bisexual identity as opposed to heterosexual or lesbian or gay identity reifies bisexuality as a third category of sexuality; on the other hand, the shifting fluidity of bisexual identity creates a postmodern challenge to the categories of sexuality, and thus to an identity politics based on sexuality.[56] To complicate matters further, bisexuality is sometimes viewed as a norm expressing the full potential of human sexuality, and at other times as a specific marginalized identity.

Bisexual organizations and visibility first surfaced in the United States in the 1970s, emerging out of the women's liberation, gay liberation, and civil rights movements.[57] Bisexuals as a specific social group articulating demands for recognition and rights underwent a renaissance in the early 1990s with a flurry of political activity and the publication of several books: *Bi Any Other Name: Bisexual*

People Speak Out; Closer to Home: Bisexuality & Feminism; Bisexual Politics: Theo-ries, Queries & Visions; and *Vice Versa: Bisexuality and the Eroticism of Everyday Life.*[58] Local bisexual groups have organized support networks and local political actions, while at the national level activists fought for the inclusion of the category "bisexual" in the name of the 1993 March on Washington for Lesbian, Gay, and Bi Equal Rights and Liberation (the first March on Washington for lesbian and gay rights in 1987 did not name bisexuals). Issues of representation, visibility, and combating stigma and derogatory stereotypes are significant political issues that depend on some recognition of group identity. Yet given the limitations of the identity politics model, I suggest that bisexual politics may be most effective under the general rubric "queer," as a coalition with lesbian, gay, transgender, and trans-sexual people.

Although bisexual activists, scholars, and writers hold a variety of positions, most begin from the assumption that it is important to name and claim the cate-gory of bisexuality. Themes of voice, invisibility, representation, marginalization, community, and homelessness recur throughout the essays in the various antholo-gies. Bisexuals claim they are rendered invisible not only in the dominant hetero-sexual community, but also within the lesbian and gay community. Much of the work on bisexuality is testimonial, the personal stories of the authors coming to terms with their own sexuality.[59] Several authors bemoan the inadequacies of lan-guage and the existing categories of homosexual and heterosexual to capture their experience; "I want to be able to express the truths of my life, and my sexuality, in a language that does not obscure. The word choices available now restrict me. . . . I want some place to belong, a name to be called."[60] Still others see labeling or nam-ing as limiting. Elizabeth Reba Weise, editor of *Closer to Home: Bisexuality & Fem-inism*, discusses the variety of names that the authors, self-identified bisexual women, choose to describe themselves; "[t]he plurality of names, and the combina-tions used, are all attempts, in our clumsy and women-wordless language to create this identity, to make ourselves recognizable."[61] And in reviewing significant issues for bisexuals, Marjorie Garber notes, "Labels and labelling are a big issue for many people who, for lack of a better term, call themselves bisexual. The word 'label' turns up over and over again in bi publications."[62] Naming oneself as bisexual can be empowering, as well as an important step to forming bisexual community and strengthening one's bisexual identity. Feminists have long recognized the power of naming oneself and one's experience. Naming combats invisibility and often pro-vides labels and language to articulate experiences in a new way. And naming con-solidates group identity because it allows others to find people "like them."

Along with naming oneself comes claiming bisexuals from the past. Garber argues that many individuals currently claimed by historians to be gay or lesbian are actually bisexual—Eleanor Roosevelt, Djuna Barnes, Virginia Woolf—to name only a few. She points out two drawbacks of reclaiming historical figures as bisexual. First, as has been well documented, the categories of sexuality are culturally and historically specific.[63] Second, claiming famous bisexuals from the past sets up bisexual interests as oppositional to gay and lesbian interests. In spite of this second concern, many bisexuals feel their legitimacy and visibility in history relies on such a reclaiming.[64] But given the cultural and historical specificity of the categories of homosexual and bisexual, and the more recent emergence of bisexual as a category, the project of reclaiming historical figures remains problematic.

The category of bisexuality reveals the complexity of the connections among sex, gender, and sexuality. Bisexuality functions as a sliding signifier, sometimes referring to a person's desires, sometimes referring to her or his sexual practice, sometimes referring to an individual's sexual history, sometimes referring to aspects of an individual, and sometimes referring to a person's potential sexual orientation. In this sense, bisexuality functions ambivalently, alternately referring to the gender of the person who is bisexual, positioning them as equally masculine and feminine (androgynous), or sometimes referring to the objects of her or his desire.

A classic example of the ambiguous categorization of bisexuals occurs in Freud's work. In his *Introductory Lectures on Psychoanalysis,* he says of homosexuals: "They represent themselves as a special variety of the human species—a third sex which has a right to stand on equal footing beside the other two."[65] Here Freud conflates sexuality and sex, and this conflation applies to bisexuals as well. For Freud, bisexuals are simply a special kind of homosexual (or as he says "inverts"), "amphigenic inverts, that is psychosexual hermaphrodites. In that case their sexual objects may equally well be of their own or of the opposite sex."[66] This classification reinforces the notion of the invert being a particular kind of person, and the bisexual as a particular kind of invert. I cannot go into more detail here about Freud's extensive discussions of sexuality. But his classification of homosexuals as a third sex, and his mention of bisexuals as psychosexual hermaphrodites reveals the slide between sex and sexual orientation prevalent in discussions of bisexuality and homosexuality. Freud's discussion contributed to a shift in thinking in the nineteenth century that began to see sexual desires and actions as indicative of a type of person. As Foucault points out, this categorization was itself an exercise of power, and he believed that the categories of sexuality entailed a major shift in the constitution of subjectivity.

The social constructionist view holds that categories of sexuality are historically and culturally specific. That is, although homosexual behavior has existed throughout history and across cultures, the homosexual as a type of person is a fairly new idea, emerging only in the late nineteenth century. Bisexuality as an identity shares this shift with gay and lesbian identity; all depend on the interiorization of sexual behavior and practices to sexual identities. According to

Foucault, "Homosexuality appeared as one of the forms of sexuality when it was transposed from the practice of sodomy onto a kind of interior androgyny, a hermaphrodism of the soul. The sodomite had been a temporary aberration; the homosexual was now a species."[67] This shift in understanding sexuality as a category and an identity carries over to bisexuality as well. Yet "bisexuality" as a category seems to be uniquely positioned in the essentialist/social constructionist debate about sexuality. On the one hand, to invoke bisexuality as a category invokes an essentialist notion of a specific sexuality that is ahistorical and stable, while on the other hand, bisexuality challenges the idea that sexuality is fixed and static, and undermines current categories of sexuality. The most subversive potential of bisexuality may lie in challenging the categories of sexuality altogether. Part of what is at issue is how sexuality is conceived; because bisexuality destabilizes the dualism of heterosexuality and homosexuality, it reinforces a social constructionist view of desire and identity.

As a category, bisexuality must remain vague; despite the presumed commonality among bisexuals of an attraction to both sexes, there is infinite variation. There are as many kinds of bisexuals as there are bisexuals; some experience dual attraction and maintain more than one sexual relationship. Others practice serial monogamy, sometimes with a partner of the same sex and sometimes with an opposite-sex partner. The issue of the instability of categories is especially acute in the case of the bisexual serial monogamist; without "bisexual" as a possible identity category, her sexual identity changes with the sex of her partner (or even more perplexing, in the absence of a long-term partner, each time she has sex). Bisexuals understand their own sexuality in diverse ways, sometimes as a combination of heterosexual and homosexual and sometimes as beyond categorization altogether. For example, Loraine Hutchins, co-editor of *Bi Any Other Name*, claims she is 70 percent straight and 30 percent lesbian. Others call for a change in the binary thinking that categorizes sexuality as either homo or hetero. Rebecca Kaplan makes the point this way: "A limited binary paradigm describes bisexuals as constantly changing their identity with the sex of their lovers. Only by changing the paradigm can we depict what may be a constant direction of our desires."[68]

In contrast to the view that bisexuals are a specific group different from both heterosexuals and homosexuals, gay liberationists in the 1970s argued that bisexuality was the norm, that everyone was bisexual. This assumption of universal bisexuality may be partially explained by the historical context; gay liberation takes place alongside a general sexual liberation movement.[69] And categories of sexuality are undergirded by the Kinsey scale, which assigns the labels of homosexual and heterosexual only to those at either extreme of the scale and assigns the label of bisexual to those who occupy the entire spectrum of positions in between. One goal of early gay liberation was to overcome gender roles and the "sex/gender system that privileges heterosexuality and men."[70] The assumption that bisexuality is the norm for human sexuality and represents a fuller range of human sexual potential is echoed by current theorists who claim that bisexuality is a vanguard sexual identity because bisexuals can live their polymorphous perversity and enjoy a diffuse eroticism not limited by gender. Marjorie Garber claims in *Vice Versa* that "[bisexuality] is about eroticism, which in many of its most powerful manifestations, today and over time, has been determinedly politically incorrect, depending upon scenarios of inequality, power, denial, demand and desire."[71]

On a Foucauldian reading, bisexuality could be interpreted as part of the proliferation of discourses about sexuality and sexual identity. Although bisexuality emerged as a psychological category in the late 1800s, it did not emerge as a political category until the 1970s. As a political category, bisexuality empowers those who identify as bisexual and enables them to make claims on behalf of the group. However, one reservation about the adoption of bisexuality as a political category is the increased potential for institutional control. For example, the United States Armed Forces' ban on homosexuals includes bisexuals.[72] And bisexuals were named as a separate group in Colorado's constitutional amendment that prohibits laws to protect homosexuals from discrimination and in military policy specifying possible reasons for dishonorable discharge.[73] The increased specification makes it possible to legislate and medicalize bisexuals as a specific group. Foucault warns us against just this sort of social control when he says, "it [the power of nineteenth century bourgeois society] acted by multiplication of singular sexualities. It did not set boundaries for sexuality; it extended the various forms of sexuality, pursuing them according to lines of indefinite penetration. It did not exclude sexuality, but included it in the body as a mode of specification of individuals."[74] Yet categorization can also give rise to counterdiscourses, or what Foucault calls reverse discourses: "There is no question that the appearance in nineteenth-century psychiatry, jurisprudence, and literature of a whole series of discourses on the species and subspecies of homosexuality, inversion, pederasty, and 'psychic hermaphrodism' made possible a strong advance of social controls into this area of 'perversity'; but it also made possible the formation of a 'reverse' discourse: homosexuality began to speak in its own behalf, to demand that its legitimacy or 'naturality' be acknowledged, often in the same vocabulary, using the same categories by which it was medically disqualified."[75] Within lesbian and gay communities, bisexuals vie for recognition and inclusion in events such as the March on Washington and local gay and lesbian pride parades. Recognition is a social good, the withholding of which can be injurious to individual dignity and collective empowerment.[76] Identity politics has been a powerful form of "reverse discourse" in the contemporary United States.

Although radical politics can be in part based on identifications with a so-cial group, they are not necessarily so. That is, an identity as an oppressed group member is neither a necessary nor a sufficient condition for a radical politics. One of the earliest expressions of identity politics recognizes the interlocking of op-pressions not just within a particular social group but across social groups: "The inclusiveness of our politics makes us concerned with any situation that impinges upon the lives of women, Third World and working people."[77] The structural analysis became deemphasized over time, and the focus of identity politics nar-rowed to one's particular group. Without the structural analysis, identity politics runs the risk of losing its radical potential by simply representing one con-stituency within interest group pluralism. This relates to the second major draw-back of identity politics: the factionalization into different groups, and, some argue, an excessive emphasis on the psychological at the expense of the political. Often times, sexuality issues such as sex, gender, and sexual desire are viewed as psychological or cultural issues that are not properly political.[78] I believe that Foucault offers a framework for understanding the interconnectedness of struc-tural institutions, like the economy and the law, and their effects on social groups and individuals. And, as I argue below, sometimes psychological issues are also political issues.

In spite of the many problems previously noted with identity politics, it the-orizes the connection between individual identity and social group membership. Because identity politics emphasizes the connection between individual identity and social group membership, it politicizes issues of representation and internal-ized oppression. Feminist politics that rely on the category "women" ascribe to an identity politics model. Feminist analyses can provide a framework for under-standing the importance of cultural representations and their possibly deleterious effect on an individual. In her essay, "On Psychological Oppression," Sandra Bartky lays out three main categories of psychological oppression: stereotyping, cultural domination, and sexual objectification.[79] The first two are particularly sig-nificant for bisexual politics.

One way in which a bisexual politics can be uncontroversially effective is by combating derogatory images and stereotypes of bisexuals. The mythology sur-rounding bisexuals is rife with derogatory images: bisexuals as promiscuous, bisex-uals as fence-sitters, bisexuals as contaminated (as AIDS carriers), bisexuals as confused. Bisexuals are targeted and stigmatized by the dominant culture like other minority groups, but they have the double jeopardy of being stigmatized within many lesbian and gay communities as well.[80] Some stereotypes of bisexuals are specific to gay/lesbian communities, such as: "bisexuals are unreliable, are not really gay, are really gay but too afraid to come out, and will retreat into hetero-sexual privilege when the going gets tough, etc."

In addition to these stereotypes, the increasing visibility of bisexuals has made them a target for derogatory cultural images and media representations. Bisexual, lesbian, and gay groups protested outside theaters showing *Basic Instinct*, which featured Sharon Stone playing a bisexual alleged serial murderer. In fact, all the villainous women in the movie were lesbian or bisexual.[81] Cultural images help to shape our perceptions of particular groups and it is no accident that just as bisexuals became more visible, they were represented in the mainstream media as psychotic killers. Perhaps more significant than the movie images of bisexuals are the media images regarding AIDS; bisexuals were stigmatized as carriers of AIDS without regard to particular sexual histories or sexual practices. Along with gay men, intravenous drug users, and prostitutes, bisexuals were singled out as a high-risk group. In some sense, bisexuals represented a different sort of threat because they transgressed the boundary between "safe" heterosexuality and "unsafe" homosexuality. Traversing this boundary meant that bisexuals could "contaminate" heterosexuals. Representing bisexuals in this way relies on homophobia, but also creates bisexuals as a special category with a special risk. The internalization of these derogatory images and stereotypes can lead to self-loathing and the loss of an effective political voice. Like feminists and gay activists before them, bisexuals combat the disempowering effect of negative stereotypes by reclaiming and revaluing them. For instance, playing on the stereotype of promiscuity, one bisexual newsletter is titled, "Anything that Moves." Combating stigma and stereotypes is a significant sociopolitical task that is largely unaccounted for within traditional political frameworks. Foucault's recognition that power operates through knowledge, discourses, and institutions can account for the influence of derogatory cultural representations and stereotypes.

Some bisexuals challenge the notion of identity and the static conception of sexuality. This deconstructive model challenges the very foundations of identity politics. The ambivalence of many bisexuals with labeling and naming stems from the fluidity of bisexuality. Marjorie Garber notes, "At stake are questions of 'identity politics' and group solidarity, cultural visibility now and in the past, and the vexed question of bisexuality's fluid nature."[82] She claims that bisexuality is the exception that proves the rule; the fluid nature of bisexuality challenges the categories of sexuality as fixed. She suggests that bisexuality is best conceived as a narrative, a story that relates the sexual self in all its complexity and contradictoriness. I agree with Garber that a diachronic view of sexuality provides a richer account of identity, and that a narrative captures this richness of identity better than a label. However, there are risks involved in taking bisexuality as the paradigm for sexuality. Garber claims, "The question of whether someone was 'really' straight or 'really' gay misrecognizes the nature of sexuality, which is fluid, not fixed, a narrative that changes over time rather than a fixed identity, however complex. The erotic discovery of bisexuality is the fact that it reveals sexuality to be a process of growth, transformation, and surprise, not a stable and knowable state of being."[83] If bisexual politics and theory hopes to provide a framework in which a multiplicity of desires and sexualities are honored, it must avoid the trap of normalizing bisexuality as the paradigm. Some people's desires and attractions remain relatively fixed over their lifetime, and a narrative description would reveal this stability. Bisexuality raises certain problems for an identity politics based on sexuality, as some theorists claim it undermines the notion of a stable identity. Additionally, like homosexuality, it challenges the notion of heterosexual as the norm. These challenges to the binary system of sexual identity and desire in turn challenge the sex/gender system and compulsory heterosexuality. Feminists undoubtedly have a stake in undermining this system as well.

CONCLUSION

Feminist challenges to the sex/gender distinction raise important questions about the body. As I argue in chapter 4, Foucault's notion of the body allows for social and cultural domination and resistance to domination. As I demonstrate in this chapter, Foucault's ideas about the body and identity challenge our uncritical use of normative categories. Postmodern feminism urges us to critically examine the category "women." While some feminists argue that without the category "women," feminism loses its emancipatory potential, I show that there are political stakes involved in adhering to a model that accepts "sex" as a natural fact or given category. Things and interpretations are inseparable. As Foucault says, "there is never an *interpretandum* which is not already an *interpretans*."[84]

Foucault's theoretical framework offers a powerful tool for feminist analysis and social criticism. His conception of power expands the domain of the political beyond traditional ideas of power that relegate it to legal, political, and economic domains. His idea that power operates on the body through discourses, practices, and institutions plays an important role in feminist analysis. Discursive and disciplinary power covers a wide range of social phenomenon, from "naming"—the power to define through language—to physical force, including mutilation, restraint, and incarceration. Feminist discussions of naming talk about the power that comes from defining one's own experience through language. Often this is made possible with the introduction of new words and concepts into discourse and language.[85] Foucault's emphasis on identity categories underscores this feminist insight. He focuses on the converse, the power of naming when someone else is doing the naming. This type of discursive power of words, definitions, and categories cannot be separated from other forms of institutional power. For example, at present the United States immigration policy prohibits "known homosexuals" from immigrating to the United States. And until 1973, homosexuality was listed as a disease in the *Minnesota Multi-phasic Personality Inventory II*, the standard reference book for diagnosing mental disorders. So long as laws and social policies exist that treat men and women, heterosexuals, and homosexuals differently, sexual categories will continue to have real, practical social and political consequences. Currently, in the United States the "medical management" of intersexed infants results in daily genital mutilation. As Foucault demonstrates, scientific and medical categories and discourses are not immune to social and political pressures and implications. Indeed, as he argues, social and political power is constitutive of knowledge and *vice versa*. Since at least the eighteenth century, scientific and medical discourse has occupied a privileged place in the West. Because of its cultural authority, its power of definition, and its presumed objectivity, it is especially important to examine the ways it operates. With regard to the issue of intersexed individuals, the institution of medicine operates to reinforce cultural and social norms without regard for individual autonomy. In fact, the practice of surgical intervention in the case of intersexed infants often puts individuals at greater risk of health problems later in life. And it sometimes limits individuals' possibilities for a satisfying sex life. Treatment of intersexuals goes against many of the accepted protocols of medical ethics, particularly informed consent.[86]

What we take to be "natural facts" have real social and political effects. If we take sexual dimorphism to be a natural fact (in spite of the natural fact of the diversity of real bodies), then our institutions and practices will reflect this, cutting, snipping, and suturing bodies to fit those categories.[87] Identity categories, even sexual identity categories, are historically contingent and culturally relative. To see them as natural, inevitable, or the cause of social inequality contributes to their inviolability. Foucault's work, through his focus on genealogy, the inseparability of power and knowledge, his view of truth, and his redefinition of power, provides powerful tools for social criticism. He encourages us to question the givenness of natural categories and the social arrangements that (seem to) follow from them.

As we have seen, normative sex and gender categories have political and practical implications. Making identity central to politics may have the unwelcome result of perpetuating oppressive practices. It may also unwittingly result in excluding those who do not fit normative categories. Queer theory and political activism move away from an identity politics strategy and toward a strategy of resistance to dominating structures. Queer politics operates at the level of the symbolic and the structural as a "resistance to regimes of the normal."[88] "Queer" operates as an identity and as the umbrella term for a coalition of those resisting heterosexualism. Queer theory and activism models a politics that works against oppression, but without positing an essential identity. Thus, it is not surprising that Foucault's work has been foundational to queer theory. Resisting the regimes of the normal may work well for an inclusive feminist politics as well. Oppositional politics demands not so much a shared identity as a shared commitment to struggling against oppression. For feminists to effectively struggle against sex/gender oppression will entail not merely achieving equal rights and opportunities within this system, but undermining the whole system of sexuality.

Chapter 6

▶•◀

PRACTICES OF THE SELF:
FROM SELF-TRANSFORMATION TO SOCIAL TRANSFORMATION

Foucault's later work has much to offer feminists, not only because it extends his notion of embodied subjectivity, but also because it elaborates a connection between ethical subjectivity and ethical and political context. The politics of the body and the practices of the self do not begin and end with the individual. They are social, cultural, and historical. Recognizing techniques of the self as political does not reduce politics to the personal, or preclude collective action or structural change. Instead, it broadens the political arena to include social and cultural factors that have political implications.

Foucault's later works focus on the process of subjectification or on the self's relation to self. Foucault's discussion of the technologies of the self can be found in *The History of Sexuality Volumes Two* and *Three,* and essays and interviews.[1] Foucault characterizes techniques of the self as "the procedures, which no doubt exist in every civilization, suggested or prescribed to individuals in order to determine their identity, maintain it and transform it in terms of a certain number of ends, through relations of self-mastery or self-knowledge."[2] These techniques of the self vary according to the historical period. In ancient times, these techniques included practices of dream interpretation, the notebooks (*hupomnêmata*) kept by the ancients, correspondence between friends, and the relation to the self through the regulation of the body, including diet, exercise, and sexual austerity.

Foucault does not spend much time discussing contemporary techniques of the self. He does mention autobiography as a type of self-writing. And he discusses writing and doing philosophy as vehicles for critique and self-transformation. I suggest Foucault's notion of practices of the self can be fruitfully applied to some contemporary feminist practices. I explore consciousness-raising as the practice of truth telling or *parrhesia*. I argue that understanding consciousness-raising as a practice of the self illuminates a connection between individual experience and social transformation. This connection is important both to Foucault and to feminists. I also suggest that autobiography and a specific type of therapy, narrative therapy, can function as feminist practices of the self. This is obviously an extension of Foucault's work, as he never discussed consciousness-raising and he had serious objections to therapy and psychoanalysis. But these practices fit his characterization of techniques of the self as procedures that help to determine, maintain, and transform identity with respect to a particular end or goal. Technologies of the self aim at self-transformation. Self-transformation is to become other than what one is, to realize "the possibility of no longer being, doing, or thinking what we are, do or think"; it is the creation of new possibilities, new forms of life achieved through technologies of the self.[3]

FOUCAULT'S TECHNOLOGIES OF THE SELF

In one sense, Foucault's technologies of the self can be viewed as the obverse of his concern with the individualization of the subject through writing and documentation. Recall that individualization occurs in part through the process of objectification of the individual. The individual becomes an analyzable object through the compilation of facts procured by institutions such as educational systems, medical institutions, and social scientific studies. Individuals become cases, their subjectivity inscribed and circumscribed by social norms. Often these norms are imposed mainly by forces outside the individual's control, such as where she falls in the statistical average of, for example, height, weight, intelligence. In other cases, norms are both imposed on and taken up by the individual, as in the procedure of confession. Confession, Foucault says, involves a double sense of subjection; one is compelled to tell the truth about oneself by institutionalized religious norms, but at the same time the speaking subject constitutes herself through this articulation. This differs from the instance where one becomes a case through the careful compilation of deviation from the norm. Confession is at least in part about the subject's participation in her own self-construction. The construction of subjectivity through confession involves an interplay among the speaking subject, the one who listens, and the institutional norms that compel speech. Confession serves as a link between Foucault's discussion of the practices of domination that result in the objectification of individuals and the practices of subjectification that signal self-constitution. Confessional narratives take many forms: traditional religious confession, autobiography, and, later, therapy. Confession, the articulation of one's desires and thoughts, ties one to one's identity. Insofar as confession is coerced and takes place within normative institutions and practices, it reinforces one's domination. But the process of telling the truth does not necessarily result in domination. In his later work, Foucault discusses narrative practices that contribute to the formation of the self in a nonnormalizing way. These practices of the self contribute to the formation of the ethical subject. Practices of the self include care of the self, truth telling (*parrhesia*), and self-writing. All of these practices concern the self's relation to self, or subjectification.

Foucault distinguishes techniques of the self from techniques of production, techniques of signification/communication, and techniques of domination. He elaborates on his definition of techniques of the self, describing them as: "techniques that permit individuals to effect, by their own means, a certain number of operations on their own bodies, their own souls, their own thoughts, their own conduct, and this in a manner so as to transform themselves, and to attain a certain state of perfection, happiness, purity, supernatural power."[4] In the essay "Technologies of the Self," published posthumously, Foucault provides a slightly modified definition of the technologies of the self; they "permit individuals to effect by their own means *or with the help of others* a certain number of operations on their own bodies and souls, thoughts, conduct, and way of being, so as to transform themselves in order to attain a certain state of happiness, purity, wisdom, perfection or immortality (emphasis added)."[5] Technologies of the self do not replace technologies of domination, as some of Foucault's critics seem to imply when they charge that Foucault belatedly introduces a notion of an active and individualist self. All four technologies—of the self, of domination, of production, and of signification—are present simultaneously. However, the importance of a particular type of technology may depend on the historical period. During Antiquity, technologies of the self were the primary form of self-relation. Through changes in the economy, political structure, language, and the development of specialized areas of knowledge, technologies of production, signification, and domination began to play a larger role. According to Foucault, technologies of the self regained importance at the end of the eighteenth century. Prior to the eighteenth century, he says that philosophy entertained a broad array of questions concerning the nature of reality, of knowledge, of truth, and of man, but at the end of the eighteenth century, questions about the self and subjectivity became a central focus for European philosophers. He connects the emergence of the importance of the technologies of the self with Kant's question, "What are we in our actuality?"[6] This Kantian attention to the present is taken up by Foucault in his essay on Kant's "What is Enlightenment?" Foucault credits Kant as the progenitor of the philosophical approach concerned with the historical reflection on ourselves. This historical reflection on ourselves leads to an interrogation of the present and to an examination of the historical and social conditions that led up to the present.[7] While Foucault's genealogical texts dealt with the "history of the present" in terms of institutions, discourses, disciplines, and practices, they focused on the technologies of domination. In his work on the technologies of the self, he is concerned with the question: "How did we directly constitute our identity through some ethical techniques of the self which developed through antiquity down to now?"[8] Foucault's studies of the self of antiquity, *The Use of Pleasure* and *The Care of the Self,* examine practices of the self before the rise of the discourse of sexuality. Foucault argues that sexuality became the privileged site for subjectivity, and for the exercise of normalizing, disciplinary power. In order to examine the ways that identity was constituted before the rise of Christianity and later developments in the human sciences, Foucault goes back to Antiquity. He believes that the imperative of self-knowledge governs our current practices of the self, and that this is at least in part due to the philosophical influence of Descartes, as well as the influences of religion and science.[9] But the imperative to know oneself is by no means a contemporary or even modern phenomenon; it was present even in ancient Greek thought. Foucault points out that the Greek principle that has been handed down to us, "Know yourself," replaced an earlier principle, "Care for yourself." How would a philosophy of the subject or the practice of self-constitution differ if the principle of care of the self had prevailed?

Care of the self included self-knowledge, but was also concerned with bodily practices. In his studies of Antiquity, Foucault points out that the practices of the self concern the body. Dietetics involves close attention to what one eats, when one eats, and how it affects one's body. Medicine also involves close attention to one's body, a vigilance for symptoms of illness, and a detailed regimen of exercise and diet to maintain health. Marital relations and erotic relations are both concerned with sexual activity, though in different ways. Marriage is centrally concerned with monogamy and reproduction, whereas erotic relationships between men and boys are centrally concerned with the issue of proper pleasure. Almost all of these regimens concerning diet, health, sexual activity, and household management required a careful record of activity. In order for these practices of the self concerning the body to become an art of existence, they should include some reflection on oneself set down in writing; "[t]o become an art of existence, good management of the body ought to include a setting down in writing carried out by the subject concerning himself."[10]

SELF-WRITING

Self-writing is a practice of the self that contributes to the self's active constitution. Recall that Foucault discusses the process of individualization of the self as a "describable, analyzable object." The process of individualization occurs through medical discourse with the introduction of case histories, through examinations that monitor educational progress, and through scientific classification as normal or abnormal, or with respect to sexual categories as a pervert or nonpervert. The primary form that this individualization takes is writing, either the individual herself writing or someone writing about the individual. In addition to writing, individualization may also take place through speaking, notably in the case of confession. The process of individualization ties one to one's identity through normalizing discourse. Individualization is one aspect of a larger problematic that Foucault calls a hermeneutic of the self. A hermeneutic of the self refers to the process of self-decipherment, that is, the obligation of individuals to examine their desires, thoughts, and actions. As mentioned earlier, confession positions the subject ambivalently, both as producer of and as produced through her discourse. The subject is both subjected by the dominant discourse that compels her to confess, yet also becomes a subject through this process of speaking. Writing, too, positions the subject ambivalently. The writing of examinations or case histories contributes to the objectification of the subject, whereas self-writing contributes to the subject's own active self-constitution.

Writing has been viewed as one of the quintessential features of modern subjectivity.[11] Foucault, however, traces the importance of self-writing back to Antiquity. Writing as a technology of the self has a long history: "The self is something to write about, a theme or object (subject) of writing activity. That is not a modern trait born of the Reformation or Romanticism; it is one of the most ancient Western traditions."[12] Self-writing is one aspect of the relation between truth and the subject.[13] For the Greeks, self-writing or personal writing served as an *askêsis* of truth, a practice of the self important for ethical subjectivity. The notebooks (*hupomnêmata*) of the ancient Greeks served as guides for one's ethical behavior. The notebooks consisted of significant quotes, records of events, and self-reflections. The *hupomnêmata* served as an aid for memory, as an aid to self-examination, self-reflection, and self-regulation. They played an important role in self-governance. The notebooks were meant to be reread and consulted; they provided a framework for meditation, reflection, and conversation. Foucault distinguishes the early notebooks (*hupomnêmata*) from the journals found in later Christian literature. The Christian journals have a confessional quality, where the author seeks to tell the truth about himself and thus creates a narrative of self. The notebooks of the ancients and early Christians focused on recording the words and deeds of others, rather than oneself. The notebooks were an important first step in the "subjectivation of discourse" because their primary function was to shape the self; the identity of the writer is constituted through his choice of which sayings quotes and events he finds significant.[14] Even though the notebooks are composed of heterogeneous fragments from a variety of sources, they serve to constitute the subjectivity of the writer, who through recording these disparate sources unifies them, and his own particularity is reflected in this unification. In addition to consolidating the writer's identity through his choice of sayings and quotations, the practice of self-writing also served as a type of self-examination and reflection. As an example, Foucault uses the writings of Seneca, where Seneca applauds a nightly accounting of oneself to one's self. Speaking of Sextius, Seneca says, ". . . he would put these questions to his soul: 'What bad habit have you cured today? What fault have you resisted? In what respect are you better? . . ."[15] This nightly accounting helps one to assess and, if necessary, change one's behavior. Writing aids self-examination and reflection on one's actions, whether writing for oneself or to another.

What Foucault calls "cultivation of the self" through writing continues in the practice of letter writing. It is in the early epistolary tradition that Foucault locates the origin of a "narrative of the self." Letters that qualify as narratives of the self are less concerned with external events than with the self's relation to self, for instance, impressions, feelings, how one spends one's leisure time, and the state of one's body. Still, at least in the early Roman epistolary tradition that Foucault examines, letters also aided self-reflection and self-examination. This self-examination often relied on the guidance and advice of a trusted friend. Correspondence serves as a moral compass; "[i]t is something more than a training of oneself by means of writing, through the advice and opinions one gives to the other: it also constitutes a certain way of manifesting oneself to oneself and to others."[16] Letter writing involves, then, a presentation of one's self insofar as it is an examination of and reflection upon one's activities, and also a presentation of oneself to another.

Both the notebooks and letter writing played a role in the cultivation of the self, albeit in different ways. Foucault distinguishes the different aims in different types of self-writing. In the case of the *hupomnêmata*:

> . . . it was a matter of constituting oneself as the subject of rational action through the appropriation, the unification, and the subjectivation of a fragmentary and selected already-said; in the case of the monastic notation of spiritual exercises, it will be a matter of dislodging the most hidden impulses from the inner recesses of the soul, thus enabling oneself to break free of them. In the case of the epistolary account of oneself, it is a matter of bringing into congruence the gaze of the other and that gaze which one aims at oneself when one measures one's everyday actions according to the rules of a technique of living.[17]

Foucault also mentions autobiography as a form of self-writing. Autobiography is one of the forms that confession can take: "[t]he motivations and effects it [confession] is expected to produce have varied, as have the forms it has taken:

interrogations, consultations, autobiographical narratives, letters; they have been recorded, transcribed, assembled into dossiers, published and commented on."[18] Autobiography, then, can function ambivalently as confession or self-writing. Confessional autobiographical narrative produces the subject in terms of her desires and positions subjectivity within the discourse of sexuality. But as mentioned earlier, Foucault points out in *The History of Sexuality Volumes Two* and *Three* that the discourse of sexuality and desire was not always the dominant discourse. He describes Antiquity as a time when individuals were more concerned with the regimes of diet, running a household, and exercise than sexuality. Autobiography as self-writing could function in a similar way to the journals and letters discussed above; it constitutes the subjectivity of the writer as an act of self-fashioning. It presents the self both to the self and to an other, like a letter. And autobiographical narrative provides unity to the heterogeneous and disparate aspects of one's life.

Different types of writing have different ends or goals, but self-writing is an important element in the cultivation of the self. It must be understood in the larger framework of practices of the self. These practices can be found in all cultures, but are historically and culturally specific; "techniques of the self, I believe, can be found in all cultures in different forms."[19] Philosophical writing may be one contemporary example of a practice of the self; "[t]he displacement and transformation of frameworks of thinking, the changing of received values and all the work that has to be done to think otherwise, to do something else, to become other than what one is—that, too, is philosophy."[20] Foucault even speaks of his own philosophical writing as a process of self-transformation: "I also reminded myself that it would probably not be worth the trouble of making books if they failed to teach the author something he had not known before, and if they did not disperse one toward a strange and new relation with himself."[21] Practices of the self aim at transformation. Because our self-understandings and identities always develop in cultural and historical contexts, self-transformation involves a critique of historical, as well as current, social conditions and norms.

A second contemporary example of self-writing as a practice of the self concerns women and writing. Although obviously not what Foucault had in mind, journal writing and women's autobiography can be thought of as feminist practices of the self. Journalling and diaries assumed an important place for women in the wake of the feminist movement. Women were encouraged to write about their own experiences. (This differs, of course, from the *hupomnêmata*, which was not about personal experience.) Journaling serves a variety of purposes, from a simple record of experience to a therapeutic function. Some journals include daily quotes for guidance and inspiration (these are closer to the *hupomnêmata*).

Since the 1970s, there has been an explosion of women's autobiography. Women's autobiography has a special place in the feminist canon. It is significant for at least two reasons; it allows the woman to speak for herself, and it draws on her own experience. Autobiography is a form of self-writing that demonstrates the self's active self-constitution. The writer both produces and presents herself through the process of telling her life story. Women's autobiographies give voice to subjugated knowledge because women's perspectives and experiences have until recently been excluded from mainstream history and literature. Autobiographical narratives usually construct identity as multifaceted and complex, and as dynamic, not static. Because of this, autobiography can challenge fixed identity categories. Yet autobiographical production of the self draws upon identity and social group categories. Multiple aspects of identity can be articulated, come into conflict, and coexist in the same narrative. Writers of autobiographies construct themselves as subjects. But like other practices, autobiographical writing takes place within specific historical and cultural conditions. Thus, the freedom of the writer to represent herself is constrained by those conditions. Women's autobiography can be viewed as a feminist technology of the self because the subject plays an active role in her own self-constitution. Yet autobiography can also be confessional. Confessional autobiography reiterates normalizing discourses and ties one to one's identity. Autobiography, then, can be either an exercise in subjection, if it produces the required truth about oneself, or it can be a process of subjectification, if one critically examines how one came to be as one is with reference to normalizing discourses.[22] Autobiographies as projects of self-constitution are perilously poised between being an exercise of subjection and an exercise of subjectification. There are no guarantees that an autobiography will be an exercise of freedom. Nonetheless, autobiography clearly contributes to the individualization and the self-constitution of the subject.

PARRHESIA (TRUTH TELLING)

Foucault discussed *parrhesia* in his last lecture courses at Berkeley and at the Collège de France. Speaking the truth, or *parrhesia*, is a political practice and also a practice of the self. An examination of *parrhesia* may serve to further illustrate the connections in Foucault's work between the individual and the political, between practices of self-transformation and possibilities for social transformation. Foucault remarks that the Greeks were interested in the "art of life" (*tekhnê tou bio*) and he explicitly says that in fourth and fifth century Greece the art of life involved taking care of the city and one's companions.[23] One of the ways that one took care of the city and one's friends was through truth telling, or *parrhesia*. When Foucault speaks of the art of existence or the art of life, he is referring to the Greek notion of *tekhnê tou bio*, which is concerned with the question of how to live. Practices of the self are the specific techniques that one employs to improve oneself with respect to particular goals. Historically, these goals have shifted, as Foucault's genealogy of subjectivity demonstrates. In his study of Antiquity, he links the aesthetic (the art of life) to the political, noting that the beautiful life is, for the Greeks, one profoundly concerned with one's place in the community, in the *polis*. Foucault explicitly makes this connection regarding the art of existence in Antiquity, stating that the "aesthetic and political . . . were directly linked."[24] The practice of *parrhesia* is necessary to a democracy and telling the truth to one's friends is necessary if one is to provide true moral guidance. *Parrhesia* has both a moral and a political aspect. Morally, the *parrhesiast* speaks the truth, regardless of the consequences. Politically, *parrhesiasts* are concerned with the affairs of the city, and the practice of truth telling is indispensable to a democracy. In fact, Foucault says that "*parrhesia* is a directly political act."[25]

There are four relevant questions one must ask with regard to the practice of truth telling: (1) Who is able to tell the truth? (2) About what can he tell the truth? (3) What are the consequences? (4) What are the relations between the activity of truth telling and relations of power? These questions situate the practice of truth telling within specific social and historical conditions. *Parrhesia* involves a relationship to one's self, a relationship between the truth teller and the listener, and a relationship between the truth teller and a community of citizens. In his examination of the emergence of *parrhesia* as a practice of the self in ancient Greece, Foucault notes that democracy is a historical condition for truth telling and that truth telling is a central practice in maintaining democracy. The practice of truth telling arises within a democracy among citizens. *Parrhesia* required certain political conditions, such as individual liberty.[26] Foucault says that *parrhesia* exists within relations of power; who could be a *parrhesiast* depended on politics and the government. He notes that in ancient Greek texts, those without political or legal power, the weak, were the *parrhesiasts*. However, one could not be totally without political or legal standing and be a *parrhesiast*; Foucault says that the political structure of ancient Greece did not permit women to be truth tellers. *Parrhesiasts* had the political standing of citizens, but not the wealth or good breeding of the politically powerful. *Parrhesia* is agonistic, that is, it challenges injustice in the name of truth. The Cynic is an example of one who leads a true life through challenging social conventions and telling the truth regardless of the consequences. The practice of *parrhesia* provided a way for ordinary citizens to challenge the *status quo*. It promoted democracy and equality among citizens. *Parrhesia* as a political practice enabled fuller (although not complete) participation in the affairs of the city, and provided an important check on unlimited political power. Thus *parrhesia* is an important political virtue.

Truth telling is an important moral virtue as well. *Parrhesia* as a practice of self is a practice of *askēsis*, "the progressive consideration of self, or mastery over oneself, obtained not through renunciation of reality but through the acquisition and assimilation of truth."[27] Foucault discusses the Stoic and early Roman practices of self-examination aimed at self-mastery. He contrasts the notion of *askêsis* with Christian asceticism, noting that while Christian asceticism aims at self-renunciation and detachment from the world, the ancient practice of *askêsis* aimed to develop one's relationship to one's self and to prepare one to confront the world. Often these ancient practices relied on guides, masters, or teachers. The master or teacher aided the disciple or student in his quest to develop self-mastery by leading him through a series of exercises or meditations. The role that truth played in this self-examination was twofold; the individual must tell the truth about himself and be able to tell the truth to others. The relationship to the self that self-examination fostered was not judgmental or juridical, but that of a craftsman or artist who from time to time stops working and examines what he has been doing. This is the crucial difference between Christian confession and Stoic self-examination. Foucault mentions that for Seneca, for instance, self-examination is not an act of judgment to establish responsibility or blame, but an administrative act that allows one to live more fully. In terms of telling the truth to oneself, *parrhesia* is similar to, but not the same as, conscience; it is a virtue, a quality, a technique. In terms of telling the truth to others, Foucault says we need *parrhesiasts* in our lives to overcome self-flattery, and that friendship is the root of *parrhesia*. He even compares *parrhesia* to a medical consultation; you tell the truth in order to be cured, in this case to become more ethical. The bonds of friendship and teacher-student relationships played an essential role in ethical life. To become ethical, one not only needs to tell the truth, but also to have close relations with others who will tell you the truth about yourself. Thus, the practice of *parrhesia* was essential to moral and ethical life.[28]

Parrhesia as a practice of self comprises an important aspect of the aesthetics of existence. The aesthetics of existence for Foucault involves ethical and political considerations; it joins the issue of the production of truth with the constitution of the moral subject. *Parrhesia* is a practice of the self that constitutes the self with the help of at least one other, the listener, in a political context. Although *parrhesia* contributes to the self's self-constitution, questions of power do not drop out. Indeed, the issue of power frames the questions Foucault suggests we ask with regard to truth telling. Who can speak? About what? What will happen? And what relations of power are operating with regard to the practice of truth telling? Feminists began to raise similar questions in the wake of the women's liberation movement. How can women speak so they will be heard? About which topics can we break the silence? Will there be repercussions? And what happens when patriarchy is challenged? One of the main venues for these questions was consciousness-raising groups.

CONSCIOUSNESS-RAISING

In this section, I show that consciousness-raising can be thought of as a feminist practice of the self. Moreover, I argue that consciousness-raising is a practice of the self that involves not only self-transformation, but also social and political transformation. Thus, it illustrates the link between the self and ethics and politics that is crucial to both feminism and Foucault. Consciousness-raising was a contested practice within the women's liberation movement. In a certain way, the debate over consciousness-raising mirrors the debate among feminists about the political utility of Foucault's work. Feminist critics of consciousness-raising claimed that it was not political; and, in fact, they claimed that it detracted from the political focus of the movement. Feminist proponents of consciousness-raising claimed that women sharing their experiences in small groups led to the realization that the problems women faced as individuals were not personal pathologies, but reflected a larger pattern of social and political discrimination. They claimed that this recognition of sexism as a social problem prompted action aimed at social and institutional change.

Consciousness-raising is often viewed as the cornerstone of the women's liberation movement in the United States. Consciousness-raising originated with the second wave of the women's liberation movement in the late 1960s. According to histories of the movement and primary documents from the period, it was developed in 1968 by members of New York Radical Women (NYRW). Kathie Sarachild, a founding member of NYRW, is credited with helping to formulate and popularize the practice. Consciousness-raising begins from women's experience; it involves weekly small-group discussions where women discuss "the politics of their lives."[29] The women's liberation movement in the United States emerged out of the civil rights movement and leftist politics. It was, in part, the sexual division of labor and sexist attitudes within leftist groups that spurred women to form their own groups. Women who participated in early leftist political groups reported that they were based on a Marxist politics with little or no gender analysis. Even when there was a gender analysis of the sexual division of labor in society, it did not always apply to the group itself. So, women began forming their own groups and radical feminism emerged.[30] In the early women's movement, there was a split between women who wanted to continue to work within the Left, and women who felt that they needed to form autonomous women's groups. In *Daring to Be Bad*, Alice Echols refers to the women who argued for staying within the larger leftist movement as "politicos"; she distinguishes "politicos" from the group she calls "feminists," who advocated for separate women's groups. Her designation of politicos refers to the positions I have labeled Marxist and socialist feminists, and her designation of feminists refers to the position I have called radical feminists. Radical

feminists spearheaded consciousness-raising. For those who advocated consciousness-raising, it was a political tool. Women sharing their experiences was not an
end in itself; the goal was political and social transformation.

Consciousness-raising provided a forum for women to discuss their experiences and articulate the ways that sexism affected their daily lives. Discussing topics often seen as trivial or "silly female stuff," such as housework, childbirth, child
rearing, orgasm, fear of aging, and beauty, women discovered some commonalities
in their experiences.[31] Even more important, sharing their experiences enabled
women to see their problems not as individual pathology, but as social and political issues. "Sisters who thought themselves abnormal or neurotic because they
were unhappy with the feminine role discover the normalcy of their discontent.
Consciousness-raising fosters self-confidence among its participants. Often self-
confidence leads to action—action against the institutions that oppress women,
action against the individuals who act in the name of these institutions."[32] As previously discussed, women's experience has often been pathologized, including their
sexuality and their psychological development. Viewing women's experience as
pathological, abnormal, or neurotic contributes to their devaluation in the larger
culture and to individual disempowerment. As Foucault points out, it is primarily
through social norms and disciplinary practices that individuals are divided into
normal and healthy, as opposed to abnormal, neurotic, and pathological. Exposing
the social norms and disciplinary practices that create these divisions as operations
of normalizing power helps to empower those who are disenfranchised and opens
up possibilities for resistance. Social norms provide this connection between self-
transformation and political and social change. Consciousness-raising helps to illuminate this connection, while Foucault's work provides a social theory that
recognizes the way that social norms operate politically and serve to link the individual to the social.

Consciousness-raising as a practice of the self involved self-transformation
with the goal of social transformation. Some derided consciousness-raising as
"hen parties," "coffee klatches," and "bitch sessions"; they charged that consciousness-raising was merely therapeutic and individualistic.[33] The emphasis on self,
they said, detracted from the political action necessary for the women's movement.
Defenders of consciousness-raising disagreed: "Consciousness-raising is one of
the most political acts in which one can engage. In consciousness-raising, women
learn what economics, politics, and sociology mean on the most direct level: as
they affect their lives."[34] Directly addressing the criticism that consciousness-raising is therapy, one author states, "Consciousness-raising is many things, but one
thing it is not is psychotherapy, or any other kind of therapy. Therapeutic
processes have been employed mostly to encourage participants to adjust to the
social order. Consciousness-raising seeks to invite rebellion."[35]

Consciousness-raising was not simply group discussion, but adhered to a specific set of guidelines. Although there was some variation in the guidelines and procedures, there was an attempt to codify both the purpose and the procedures of consciousness-raising. Most consciousness-raising groups saw their work as both personal and political; "slowly we came to see that both approaches [personal and political] were necessary, interdependent, and doomed to failure if attempted alone."[36] This connection between the personal and the political is not left to chance; many consciousness-raising guidelines discuss the different stages of the process.[37] In one of the early books on consciousness-raising, *Free Space*, Pamela Allen divides the stages of discussion in a consciousness-raising group into opening up, sharing, analyzing, and abstracting. While the first two stages focus on women's personal experience and feelings, the second two require that personal experience be explicitly connected to systems of political oppression. Thus, "[t]he total group process is not therapy because we try to find the social causes for our experiences and the possible programs for changing these."[38] Consciousness-raising in feminist groups explicitly linked personal experience to social and political structures and institutions. Moreover, the goal was to motivate women to confront and change sexist institutions. As one set of guidelines to consciousness-raising unequivocally puts it: "political awareness is the purpose of consciousness-raising; personal growth is the gravy; if the focus shifts so that these are reversed, the group is not doing feminist political consciousness-raising."[39] Because political action is the hoped-for outcome of consciousness-raising, some guidelines suggest that each consciousness-raising session should end with an action session where the women think together about collective, social solutions to change the oppressive structures that circumscribe their experience. *The Guidelines to Feminist Consciousness-Raising* even suggests that after the series of consciousness-raising sessions are over, the group may want to form an action squad that would work together to achieve social and political change. This focus on action is seen as consistent with the aims of feminist consciousness-raising; "feminist activism is one of CR's primary goals."[40]

Thus far I have focused on the positive contribution that consciousness-raising can make to social and political change. However, the practice of consciousness-raising was not without its problems. Consciousness-raising was susceptible to some of the criticisms raised against identity politics, for instance, that the focus on the shared experience of women obscured the differences among them. During its early phases, consciousness-raising was controversial, even among radical feminist groups. For instance, Redstockings and NYRW felt consciousness-raising was essential to the women's movement, while Cell 16 and The Feminists had some reservations about it.[41] One of the originators of consciousness-raising, Kathie Sarachild, "maintained that consciousness-raising was crucial in developing a sense of 'class consciousness' and class solidarity, or 'sisterhood' among women."[42] This assumed commonality among women was, of course, problematic because it viewed sex/gender as the primary oppression and minimized other types of oppression, such as those based on class, race, and sexual orientation. Even when proponents of consciousness-raising advocated that consciousness-raising groups be heterogeneous and diverse, it was assumed that they would discover commonalities in their experience. They would "discover that all women suffer and have problems in a sexist society; the problems may vary in specifics from group to group, but their general nature is essentially the same for everyone . . . all women are sisters under the skin."[43] This assumption of commonality and viewing sex as the primary form of oppression ultimately served to undermine the very unity that the women's movement hoped to achieve. Although consciousness-raising topics included race, class, and sexual orientation, the focus on a shared experience of women, and the assumption that sexism affected all women in the same way regardless of differences, were obvious limitations of consciousness-raising.

Radical feminists were not the only feminists using consciousness-raising; by 1968, consciousness-raising had become a regular activity of the National Organization for Women (NOW), a group associated with a liberal feminist perspective.[44] NOW and many radical feminist groups used consciousness-raising as an organizing tool, recruiting new members to their organizations through the consciousness-raising groups. For many feminist groups, especially the radical feminist groups that emerged in and after 1967, consciousness-raising was fundamental to women's liberation. The Redstockings Manifesto states, "[o]ur chief task at present is to develop female class consciousness through sharing experience and publicly exposing the sexist foundation of all our institutions. Consciousness-raising is not 'therapy,' which implies the existence of individual solutions and falsely assumes that the male-female relationship is purely personal, but the only method by which we can ensure that our program for liberation is based on the concrete realities of our lives."[45] Based on personal experience, the aim of consciousness-raising was to analyze this experience, to generalize from it, and to develop strategies for political action.

Consciousness-raising assumes a relationship between the personal and the political. As discussed above, its advocates felt that the link between women's experience and sexist oppression was best articulated through consciousness-raising. Detractors of consciousness-raising, however, felt that consciousness-raising's strategy of self-transformation shifted the focus from the political to the personal. Critics of consciousness-raising felt that it focused too much on the personal and individual and devolved into an issue of lifestyle rather than revolutionary social action. The well-known feminist slogan "the personal is political" can be read in this way. Assuming that personal choices have political implications prompted some radical feminist groups to set a limit on the number of women living with men who could be among their members. The idea that personal choices have

political import justifies close scrutiny of individuals' lives and can result in a stultifying political correctness. The emphasis on the personal can also minimize and
displace the political. This displacement of the political by the personal may lead
to a merely individualistic concern with lifestyle. However, this collapse of the political into the personal is only one possible interpretation and outcome of the
phrase "the personal is political." As discussed above, many radical feminists
viewed the connection between personal and political not in terms of individual
choices or lifestyle, but in the ways that political and social institutions and structural oppression affected individuals' lives. They hoped that awareness of the impact of oppression on one's life would motivate women to change oppressive social
and political structures. This reverses the sense of the phrase; the point is not to
collapse the political into the personal or to make personal choices the end point
of politics.[46] Rather, the point is to understand the relationship between an individual's experience of oppression and oppressive political and social structures,
with the aim of transforming them. This is clearly stated in one set of consciousness-raising guidelines that changes the wording of the phrase, "a basic part of the
feminist consciousness-raising philosophy is the phrase *from* the personal *to* the
political (emphasis added).'"[47] The point of consciousness-raising was not to collapse the distinction between political and personal, nor to valorize individual
lifestyle choices as political. Rather, the goal of consciousness-raising was to make
women aware of the connection between their personal experience, especially with
regard to their dissatisfaction with traditional social roles, and the sexist political
and social institutions that perpetuate these traditional roles. The ultimate target
of change was social institutions, not the individual. And yet, awareness of one's
own situation as the result of oppressive conditions and not personal failure can
foster self-confidence and empowerment in individuals that may help them
achieve political action to promote social change. Thus, self-transformation can be
an important step toward social and political transformation.

Consciousness-raising exemplifies the type of self-transformation that Foucault refers to in his discussion of practices of the self. One engages in practices
of the self to produce self-transformation within a social context. Practices of the
self draw upon the rules, methods, and customs of one's culture, but are also practices of freedom, that is, they create new nonnormalizing modes of existence and
relationships. Practices of freedom are ethical practices requiring the work of oneself on oneself. Work on oneself occurs within social and historical contexts, but
with the aim of understanding how that context has shaped us, and with an eye
toward social and political change. Foucault reinterprets the Kantian critical tradition to accommodate our contemporary circumstances; he redefines criticism as
"a historical investigation into the events that have led us to constitute ourselves
and to recognize ourselves as subjects of what we are doing, thinking, saying."[48]
According to Foucault, criticism and analysis can be used as tools for social

change. "Among the cultural inventions of mankind there is a treasury of devices, techniques, procedures and so on, that cannot exactly be reactivated but at least constitute, or help to constitute, a certain point of view which can be very useful as a tool for analyzing what's going on now—and to change it."[49]

I suggest that consciousness-raising, as articulated by radical feminist groups in the late 1960s, is both a technology of the self and a practice of freedom. Consciousness-raising is a technology of the self because it involves work on the self that results in self-transformation. And it is a practice of freedom insofar as it aims toward not simply understanding the social and historical conditions that constitute us as subjects, but at changing those conditions. Indeed, Foucault links together self-mastery, care of the self, and freedom, and connects them to the critical task of philosophy: ". . . To a certain extent, this critical function of philosophy [calling domination into question] derives from the Socratic injunction 'Take care of yourself,' in other words, 'Make freedom your foundation, through the mastery of yourself.' "[50]

Consciousness-raising is a practice of freedom in Foucault's sense insofar as it involves the self's relationship to self, and it aims at self-transformation. Although consciousness-raising draws on the rules and conventions of the culture, and follows specified guidelines, its aim is to be a nonnormalizing practice. Indeed, its power lies in exposing oppressive, sexist social norms and the ways that they affect individual experience. It is this link between the normalizing practices of subjection and the process of individualization that Foucault makes explicit in his genealogical analyses. One of the ways we resist this normalization is through engaging in practices of freedom that explore new ways of self-constitution. Thus, self-transformation can lead to social transformation as individuals create new nonnormalizing, noninstitutionalized ways of living with and relating to one another. For instance, Foucault proposes that rather than introducing homosexuality into existing relational social norms, such as marriage, we should create new types of relationships: "Let's escape as much as possible from the types of relations that society proposes for us and try to create in the empty space where we are new relational possibilities. . . . we should try to imagine and create a new relational right that permits all possible types of relations to exist and not be prevented, blocked, or annulled by impoverished relational institutions."[51] In addition to creating new types of relationships, Foucault also sees possibilities for creating nonnormalized ways of being in "a culture that invents ways of relating, types of existence, types of values, types of exchanges between individuals which are really new and are neither the same as, nor superimposed on, existing cultural forms."[52] These nonnormalizing relationships and ways of being may originate from marginalized groups, such as homosexuals, and they can also be taken up by nonhomosexuals. The creation of culture includes "the creation of new forms of life, relationships, friendships in

society, art, culture and so on through our sexual, ethical, political choices."⁵³ This
sounds surprisingly similar to some radical feminists' call for an alternative women's
culture. Yet Foucault is not advocating separatism, but a proliferation of ways of
being, some of which resist the normalizing force of the dominant culture. These
creations and innovations are not limited to individual lifestyles, but may provide
nonnormalized institutions, such as domestic partnerships. These new nonnormalized institutions would provide new ways of recognizing a relationship for both
homosexual and heterosexual partners. The invention, creativity, transformation,
and innovation that Foucault advocates pertains to both individual and collective
endeavors. Indeed, given his conception of the subject as embodied and as constituted in and through social practices, it is hard to see how self-transformation could
be separated from social and political transformation.

One final example may help to illustrate the way that Foucault's work can be
helpful in thinking about the relationship between the self and social change. Although it may seem odd given Foucault's reservations about psychoanalysis, his
work has profoundly influenced contemporary therapeutic practice. Postmodern
thought in general has influenced the discipline of psychology, notably with respect to a constructivist understanding of the self and knowledge. Within the discipline of psychology, the narrative therapy approach owes a specific debt to the
influence of Foucault's work. Narrative therapy focuses on the ways in which personal experience is organized into stories. The stories reveal the ways that people
assign meaning to their lives. In narrative therapy, the goal is not to reveal historical truth, but to produce narrative intelligibility. Narrative therapy seeks to exter-
nalize problems, seeing them not as individual problems, or even as located within
the family structure, but as an aspect of the dominant social structure. The founder
of narrative therapy, Australian Michael White, was profoundly influenced by
Foucault's work. From Foucault's genealogical work, White gleaned that dominant discourses dehumanize, objectify, and marginalize individuals and social
groups through what Foucault calls "dividing practices"—the separation of the
normal from the abnormal. White sees these dominant discourses as disempowering and oppressive. The aim of narrative therapy, then, is to deconstruct these oppressive dominant discourses. Narrative therapists "view problems through a
political lens"; and they look at the effects of "toxic social narratives such as misog-
yny, racism, class bias, and heterosexism" as well as ordinary cultural assumptions
such as the definition of success.⁵⁴ Narrative therapy, like feminism, is committed
to analyzing and overcoming the various axes of oppression that stratify our social
world. Moreover, narrative therapy draws on feminism to inform both its theory
and practice.

The political orientation of narrative therapy encourages clients to view
their problems in relation to the dominant discourses of the social, political

context. Recognizing that individual problems are connected to the larger social, political milieu means that at least sometimes the solution to individual problems lies in social and political change. This emphasis on the political carries over to the therapists as well as the clients; narrative therapists are encouraged to examine the influence of dominant cultural narratives on their own experience. Furthermore, narrative therapists are often drawn to the narrative therapy approach because of its political orientation. Some are political activists who see their work in therapy as an extension of the pursuit of social justice. Self-described 1960s activists Jill Freedman and Gene Combs say this about their initial attraction to narrative therapy: "[h]e [Michael White] was citing Michel Foucault who wrote about the objectification and subjugation of persons, and talking about helping people stand up to 'the gaze' of the dominant culture. Now middle-aged '60s activists, we had no idea what these ideas would look like when applied to therapy, but we sure wanted to find out!"[55] Narrative therapy applies Foucault's ideas as an antidomination strategy. Narrative therapists help clients deconstruct the dominant social and cultural messages that serve to oppress them. Narrative therapy is thus situated between the political and the personal. Because individual problems are assumed to be rooted in an oppressive social system, rather than in the individual, as is the case with traditional psychoanalysis, individual change is linked to political change in the narrative therapy approach. The narrative therapy approach may be particularly well suited for women and other members of oppressed groups because it does not focus on adjustment, like traditional therapies, but analyzes and questions social and cultural narratives of domination. This questioning of domination is consistent with feminist aims. Thus, narrative therapy can be seen as a feminist practice of the self insofar as it aims at self-transformation and aims toward a particular goal, resisting the dominant discourse.

CONCLUSION

Recently feminists have begun to explicitly explore the connection between ethics and politics implicit in much feminist theorizing. In their introduction to *Daring to Be Good*, Ann Ferguson and Bat-Ami Bar On discuss the split between ethics and politics since Modernity.[56] They note that the rise of the nation state and the development of classical liberal political thought consolidated the split between what previously had been the distinct, but overlapping, areas of ethics and politics. When politics and ethics are viewed as separate, politics is associated with government, state power, and public policy. Ethics, on the other hand, is associated with individual actions and relationships and seen as relevant to private life. Feminists have offered criticisms of the liberal state and its practices, for instance, the marginalization of women and racial minorities from decision-making processes, the split between public and private that excludes the family and domestic life from adhering to principles of justice, and the focus on sameness at the expense of the recognition of difference. Feminists have also offered alternative visions of ethics based on women's ethical practices such as mothering and caring, for instance, Gilligan's care ethics discussed in chapter 3. Still other feminists offer communitarian alternative ethical visions based on feminist practices and oppositional communities. Each of these feminist approaches is important if we are to radically transform the existing political institutions, economic structures, social practices, and cultural ideals that support the current military industrial capitalist heterosexist white supremacist patriarchal system. Yet to some extent these feminist approaches recapitulate the split between ethics and politics: "One camp (those reacting to and correcting liberal political discourses) is engaged in rethinking politics, while another camp (those reacting to the limitations of mainstream ethical theory) is engaged in rethinking and producing oppositional feminist values."[57] But feminism, with its dual focus on both systemic and interpersonal change, clearly needs to rethink the relationship between ethics and politics, as well as challenging the traditional theories and concepts in each. On some accounts, feminist ethics requires a politics. Alison Jaggar proposes a practical agenda for feminist ethics that includes articulating a moral critique of the actions and practices that perpetuate women's subordination, and that prescribes ways of resisting such actions and practices.[58] Because women's subordination is perpetuated by systemic forces such as the economic system, the legal system, and the political system, resistance to that subordination must include collective political action aimed at changing those structures. But women's subordination is also perpetuated through a variety of institutions such as educational institutions, religious institutions, and the traditional nuclear family. And women's subordination is enforced through the representation of women as inferior in the media, in scientific discourse, and in medical discourse. Interpersonal relationships, insofar as they recapitulate the power dynamics of the dominant culture, can also play a role in women's subordination. Given the multifaceted sources of women's subordination and the reality that sex and gender oppression is linked in complex ways to class oppression, racial oppression, and the oppression of homosexuals, to name only the most obvious, feminists need a social theory that conceives of power as a complex web of relations that operates not only through the law and the economy, but also through social norms and cultural practices.

I have argued that Foucault's work provides such a theory. Acknowledging that there are multiple sources of oppression and that all social relations are power relations can account for feminist insights about the interconnection of oppressions and the ways that individuals who are members of one oppressed group, for instance, white women, may also be oppressors. But contrary to some feminist criticism that Foucault's analyses of power and domination leave us without hope for social and

political change, I have suggested that his analyses are a necessary prerequisite for social and political action. Foucault's project of the genealogy of subjectivity provides
some insight into practices and techniques of domination, which is helpful for those
engaged in the struggle against domination. And he also provides some alternative
ways to think about self-constitution through his discussion of techniques or practices of the self. Foucault looks to Antiquity, where the problematic of the self and
the relation between self and society were conceived very differently than they are
today. Foucault says he is not advocating a return to Greek ideals, and that it is not
possible to import solutions to current problems from other historical and cultural
periods. But he does note that there is a similarity between the contemporary problem of constructing an ethics and the situation of the ancient Greeks. The Greeks
elaborated an ethics that was not based on religion, and that was not primarily enforced through the law. In contemporary society, religious pluralism and the recognition of a diversity of moral values likewise require an ethics not based on religion
or imposed through the law. Foucault notes, "Recent liberation movements suffer
from the fact that they cannot find any principle on which to base the elaboration
of a new ethics."[59] For reasons articulated in his genealogical work, he does not think
that the scientific paradigm offers much hope for this new ethics because it contributes to the process of domination and objectification of the individual. The aesthetic paradigm, however, does not pose the same risks. In this view, the relationship
to one's self is characterized not by judgment, but by creative management. Ethical
action is determined not by the imposition of universal rules, but by individualized
procedures, techniques of the self. Yet these techniques of the self often require the
assistance or guidance of others, and are always related to the social and political
context. Foucault sees his own work as bridging the separation between ethical and
political that has been so pronounced since Modernity.[60] As I have discussed above,
feminists have a stake in bridging this gap as well because radical social change requires shifts in both ethical and political thinking. Foucault's discussion of techniques of the self offers a way to think about self-constitution as dependent on
relations with others and as historically and culturally situated. Some techniques of
the self, such as care of the self, are concerned with the body. Other techniques of
the self, such as self-writing, enable an individual to develop an ethical relationship
with herself based on self-reflection rather than universal rules; still other techniques, such as *parrhesia*, are directed toward the community and political life. Thus,
the idea of techniques of the self implies that the body, self-reflection, and political
activity are all important components of an individual's life. What I have called feminist practices of the self, consciousness-raising and critical autobiography, have
played a dual role in transforming both individuals and society.

▶•◀

CONCLUSION

I have addressed feminist objections to Foucault's work, and demonstrated the ways that his work has been and can be useful to feminists. I have focused on feminist criticisms of Foucault's account of subjectivity, countering objections that it is incapable of resistance. I have explicated Foucault's analytics of power, showing that it can account for asymmetries of power, reversals of power, and resistance. Foucault's criticism of humanistic universal norms as excluding difference resonates with feminist criticisms of the humanistic subject as implicitly white, male, and European. Moreover, Foucault's account of social norms is also useful to feminists. Foucault demonstrates that social norms are imposed upon and taken up by subjects through a variety of social practices and institutions, that these norms are incorporated bodily, and that it is through norms that subjectivity is constituted. His account is especially apropos to explain gender norms that are reinforced in almost all institutions and social practices, are primarily bodily, and are central to subjectivity. At the same time as his account of social norms explains their ability to constitute subjectivity, his attention to the historical contingency of these norms indicates their historical and cultural variability and the possibility for change in the future. Foucault's commitment to antidomination, implicit in his genealogies, becomes more explicit in his later work, where he advocates the positive values of innovation, creativity, freedom, self-transformation, and social transformation. In spite of these commitments, Foucault does not offer a blueprint for social change or political action. In fact, much of his work seems to warn us away from setting general agendas for social change because of the risk that these agendas may in fact reproduce the relations of domination they are intended to overcome. He even hesitated to impose his views on readers, saying, "I think it is always a little pretentious to present in a more or less prophetic way what people have to think. I prefer to let them draw their own conclusions or infer general ideas from the interrogations I try to raise in analyzing historical and specific material. I think it's much more respectful for everyone's freedom and that's my manner."[1] I have inferred general ideas from Foucault's historical studies that I think are particularly useful for feminism. To conclude, I apply some of these ideas to a current situation in feminist politics.

In his work, Foucault discusses both the subjection and the subjectivation of the individual. While subjection results from the ways that dominating disciplines and practices constitute the subject, subjectivation refers to the individual's active constitution of the self through work on the self. Foucault focuses on these two aspects of self-constitution in different texts. This leads some to suspect that Foucault drastically changes his notion of the subject from a passive, determined subject in *Discipline and Punish* and *The History of Sexuality Volume One*, to an active and autonomous subject in *The History of Sexuality Volumes Two* and *Three*, and in his essays and interviews on practices of the self and ethics. I suggest that Foucault's conception of the subject is not contradictory, that is, he does not conceive of the subject as totally determined (as I argue in chapters 3 and 4), and then as completely free and autonomous (as I demonstrate in chapters 3 and 6). Rather, both of these aspects are present, even when his discussion highlights one aspect at the expense of the other. Furthermore, I submit that this tension in Foucault's conception of the subject is endemic to the problem of attempting to think of subjectivity in a nonreductive, nondualistic way. A conception of the subject that begins from the materiality of the body, but does not end there, must articulate a new conception of freedom as well. In my view, Foucault provides the theoretical resources to think through issues of constraint, domination, agency, and collective action as embodied practices. Even in his genealogical texts, where he emphasizes the domination and subjection of the individual through normalizing discourses and practices, a space for freedom and resistance can be found. Of course, freedom is reconceptualized as a practice, not an end or an ultimately attainable state. Techniques of the self are the flip side of techniques of domination; both exist simultaneously in tension with one another. To the extent that one engages in what Foucault calls "a critical ontology of ourselves"—that is, examining how we came to think, do, and be what we are with the possible goal of no longer doing, thinking, and being in the same way—one engages in a practice of freedom.[2] Practices of freedom do not take place outside of normalizing discourse or social practices, but they may reveal their contingent character and, in turn, allow for new possibilities.

As I argue in chapter 2, questioning domination is one of the aims of genealogy as critique. Domination occurs when relations of power ossify, lock together, and become fixed. Foucault's understanding of domination can account for asymmetrical relations of power. Feminist theory requires such an understanding of unequal notions of power in order to analyze sex/gender domination. But there is an even more significant way in which Foucault's notion of power contributes to feminist theory. As discussed earlier, Foucault's notion of power is not limited to political power, but exists in social relations. Power is a relationship that can direct or determine behavior, Foucault calls these relations of power and the techniques that allow them to be exercised "governmentality."[3] Governmentality can apply to a society, a group, a community, a family, a person. It refers to the multifarious ways that nonsovereign power operates to govern individuals and groups, "[t]he ensemble formed by the institutions, procedures, analyses and reflections, the calculations and tactics that allow the exercise of this very specific albeit complex form of power. . . ."[4] Governmentality does not operate through the law; rather it is tactical and strategic. Its aim is to manage populations from within, unlike state power, which imposes control from above. Governmentality targets the interests, needs, aspirations, and consciousness of individuals, as well as of the population as a whole.[5]

Analyzing the ways that patriarchal power manifests itself not only in the laws and through economic inequalities, but also in social relations, is important for feminism. The unequal, sexist division of labor in the home or in leftist political organizations could not fully and adequately be addressed through the law or the economy. Early radical feminists did call for political change with respect to the law. But they also called for change in a wide array of extralegal institutions and social relations. Although they did not articulate it in Foucault's terms, early feminists clearly realized that power operates in a variety of social and political institutions including, but not limited to, the law. In workplaces, in political organizations, in the home, the sexual division of labor persisted; feminists argued for legal redress and social and cultural change. Some of the changes focused on language and representation; feminists pushed for the use of nonsexist language, introduced the title Ms. to parallel the male moniker Mr., and urged married women to retain their own surnames. Feminists also addressed the issue of representation through images and discourses. Feminists objected to images of women in stereotypical domestic roles, as well as images that depicted women as merely sexual objects. Feminists also objected to discourses and knowledges that devalued women or reinforced cultural stereotypes of women as passive, weak, and emotional. These representations of women not only perpetuated sexist attitudes, but had practical implications for the treatment of women.

These practical implications are especially clear in the area of women's health. Historically, scientific and medical discourses have marginalized women's experience. Often, medical discourse pathologized women's experience, for instance, in the diagnoses of hysteria so prevalent in the nineteenth century. Even when not explicitly pathologized, the explanations of women's bodies and bodily processes often reflect cultural bias. For instance, feminists have discussed the cultural bias inherent in accounts of reproduction.[6] One classic example is the way that women's role in re-production has been represented; eggs are passive, while sperm are active. This view of reproduction recapitulates the stereotypical idea that women are passive, while men are active. In reality, both the egg and the sperm play an active role in repro-duction. In addition to reproduction, sexuality is another obvious site to look for the cultural bias of medical discourse. As many feminists have pointed out, women's sex-uality has been pathologized at least since Freud. His account of women's mature sexuality as based on vaginal orgasm reflects little knowledge of women's sexual anatomy. Nonetheless, it became prescriptive. Women judged themselves, and were judged by others, according to Freud's misguided standards. Radical feminists, such as Anne Koedt, directly challenged Freud's interpretation of women's sexuality. Her article "The Myth of the Vaginal Orgasm," discussed in chapter 4, challenged the prevailing medical and psychological model of women's sexuality by challeng-ing the sexist and heterosexist bias embedded in Freud's discussion of women's sexuality. Scientific, medical, and psychological discourses influence women's self-understanding; when models that incorrectly represent women's experience are taken as the norm, women may view themselves and be viewed as pathological. More im-portantly, scientific, medical, and psychological discourses have concrete, material ef-fects. For instance, surgery was performed on women to move their clitorises closer to their vaginas so they could achieve Freud's vaginal orgasm during intercourse, and, as discussed in chapter 5, intersex infants undergo surgical mutilation to "correct" their ambiguous genitalia to conform to our binary notion of sex categories. Scien-tific discourses have real effects on individuals and on groups of individuals.[7] Femi-nists have recognized the political significance of scientific discourse. Yet the political effects of scientific discourse cannot be remedied through the law; alterna-tive discourses must be produced.[8] Feminists and Foucault share this view that issues of interpretation and representation through scientific discourse are political.[9] In a discussion about the relationship between progressive politics and the study of dis-course, Foucault says: "There exists at present a problem which is not without im-portance for political practice: that of the status, of the conditions of exercise, functioning and institutionalization of scientific discourses."[10] The study of dis-course, both the ways that it is produced and the way that it produces its objects (and subjects), is obviously important for feminists who wish to address issues of oppres-sion in social and cultural institutions.

While attention to the ways that discourse produces subjects (and objects) in the dominant discourse is important for challenging sexist norms, it serves a valuable function within feminism, too. In chapter 1, I set out a variety of feminist approaches. In some ways, the approaches I discuss chart the historical develop-ment of feminism in the United States. If the various feminist approaches are viewed as the development of feminist theory and politics, then each subsequent approach can be seen as correcting the shortcomings of the previous approach and supplanting it. Liberal feminism's focus on equality and similarity of women and men was challenged by radical feminism's focus on sexual difference. Marxist feminism challenged both liberal and radical feminist perspectives for thinking that social change could come about simply from changes in the legal system (liberal feminism) or changes in cultural and social institutions (radical feminism); Marxist feminists argued that the economic system was the linchpin of social organization and thus should be the focus of social and political change. Socialist feminists acknowledged the fundamental role of the economy in social organization, but maintained that the sexual division of labor and gender issues were just as important. Feminist critical theorists added an emphasis on the legal system, cultural institutions, and the political process to the dual focus on the economy and sex/gender issues. Multicultural feminists argued that issues of race, ethnicity, and culture must be integrated into any feminist analysis. Global feminists pointed out that issues of nationalism, colonialism, cultural imperialism, and religion were also important for a broad-based feminist theory and politics. Postmodern feminists argued that the identity "woman" imposed by the oppressive dominant patriarchal system serves to perpetuate sex/gender oppression, and that therefore feminists should be wary of using the category of "women" as a basis for politics.

In actuality, the history and development of feminist theory and politics has not been so clear-cut. In the United States, feminist theory and politics emerged out of the women's liberation movement, which in turn emerged out of other social movements such as the Black civil rights movement, the antiwar movement, and Marxist political groups.[11] These movements overlapped historically, with membership in the various groups also overlapping. The fact that autonomous women's groups emerged out of other social movements means that concerns about race and class arose prior to concerns about gender, and were present even in the early stages of radical feminism. To make things more complicated, liberal feminist political strategies such as working to pass the Equal Rights Amendment became more prevalent in the 1970s, displacing the direct activism of radical feminism and other leftist political movements popular during the 1960s. So, historically, there is overlap and interaction among various feminist political approaches and perspectives, rather than a developmental trajectory. Moreover, as indicated by my discussion of representatives from each of the feminist approaches in chapter 1, these perspectives still coexist simultaneously. Indeed, these days there seems to be little agreement about the future direction for feminist theory and politics. This is in part because we are in a different historical moment. On the one hand, the concrete legal and economic gains made by the women's movement make it appear to younger generations that we are no longer in need of a women's movement. On the other hand, the conservative religious and political backlash against feminism since the 1980s makes fighting for women's causes less attractive, even as it makes it more necessary. And, finally, dynamics within the feminist movement itself have discouraged some younger women from joining the feminist movement. These dynamics include schisms within feminism and the perception that feminism requires a stultifying political correctness about what to believe, what to wear, and how to act.

Contemporary feminism is characterized by conflict and dissent. Along with the various feminist approaches I have laid out come a variety of feminist positions on particular issues. One of the decisive moments for feminism in the United States was the heated debate in the 1980s around issues of sexuality, such as prostitution, pornography, butch-femme roles in lesbian relationships, and lesbian sadomasochism (hereafter S/M). Usually termed the "sex wars," this period was characterized by a vigorous debate in academic and popular journals and a proliferation of feminist groups. Feminists were divided over what the "proper" feminist position should be on these issues. Some radical feminists maintained that pornography and prostitution exploited the women who participated in them and contributed to the sexual objectification and consequent devaluation of women in general. Some radical feminists also opposed lesbian S/M and butch-femme roles, saying that the idea of dominating another woman contravened basic feminist principles of power sharing and nondomination. Some Marxist and socialist feminists focused on the aspect of economic coercion involved in sex work, such as prostitution and pornography. They pointed out that the women workers were being exploited because they often earned very little compared to the others (usually male) involved in the process, such as producers and sellers of pornography and pimps. Furthermore, they argued that the lack of decent-paying jobs for women coerced them into sex work. Liberal feminists were more likely to take a laissez-faire attitude to the issues of pornography, prostitution, butch-femme roles, and lesbian S/M because they construed these practices as choices and were committed to protecting women's choices and autonomy. From a different perspective, so-called "sex-radicals" also defended the right of women to engage in the practices and institutions of pornography, prostitution, butch-femme roles, and lesbian S/M. While sex radicals did not share liberal feminists' commitments to viewing participation in all these practices simply as free choice, they were against the regulation of sexuality and worried about the conservative impact such regulation would have. Feminist groups such as the Feminist Anti-Censorship Taskforce (FACT) worked to keep pornography legal, while other feminist groups such as Women Against Pornography worked to pass restrictive legislation to limit the distribution and sale of pornography. Sex workers organized, forming groups such as COYOTE (Call Off Your Old Tired Ethics) to assert their right to self-determination. The "sex wars" that raged during the 1980s

created strange bedfellows, with radical feminists and right-wing religious funda-
mentalists both preaching the evils of pornography and prostitution, while liberal
feminists, sex radicals, and sex workers defended these enterprises.

No one really won the sex wars. Antipornography ordinances were passed in
Minneapolis and Indianapolis, but were later found to be unconstitutional. Prostitution was not legalized in states other than Nevada, where it was already legal.
Lesbian communities continue to debate if S/M is violence and if butch-femme
roles simply imitate the patriarchy and heterosexuality. In the 1990s, the sex wars
were replaced by the gender wars. While the sex wars were characterized by a lack
of agreement among feminists about issues that affected women, the gender wars
are characterized by disagreement over the categories of "woman" and "women."
The challenge to sex and gender as stable, natural categories is not simply an abstract, theoretical issue put forth by postmodern feminist theorists, but has roots
in concrete social and political struggles. Gender became a contested category
within feminist communities. The definition of the category "woman" was challenged by individuals who identified as transgender or transsexual. Transgender
individuals challenge conventional normative conceptions of sex and gender that
assume that gender somehow follows from or depends upon sex. Transgender and
transsexual issues challenge not only conventional notions of gender, but the stability and naturalness of sex and gender categories themselves. Transgender issues
became increasingly visible in the 1990s with the publication of several books, notably Leslie Feinberg's *Stone Butch Blues* and *Transgender Warriors*, and, more recently Riki Anne Wilchins', *Read My Lips*, and films such as *The Crying Game* and
Boys Don't Cry.[12] As mentioned in chapter 5, the 1990s was a time for increased
visibility for bisexuality as well, and it was in the mid-1990s that intersexual activists began to organize politically. Obviously, political organizing around intersexuality, transgender, and transsexual issues cannot rely on standard sex or gender
categories. In fact, activists point out the damage that normative sex/gender categories perpetuate. These "gender activists" work to counter the legal, political,
medical, economic, and social structures that reinforce the normative notions of
sex and gender, including the idea that sex and gender categories are binary, that
they are or ought to be stable, and that sex and gender have a necessary relationship. If feminism is not to be at odds with other struggles for social justice around
issues of sex, gender, and sexuality, then it cannot uncritically invoke "women" as a
basis for politics. But what practical political strategy is left open to feminists?
Like these newer gender activist groups, we can work against gender oppression.
Working against gender oppression still directs our attention to the structures that
shape gendered experience and so long as those structures continue to produce
subjects and social groups of "women" who are situated differently than "men,"
feminists would still lobby on behalf of women. But simultaneously we would

work to undermine the way the category itself is produced and reproduced through the law, media, medical discourse, and other social institutions. We cannot simply do one or the other; we must do both.

I read Foucault as an activist deeply suspicious of the dominant culture, traditional ways of thinking, and traditional politics. I believe his work is helpful to feminist politics because it articulates a complex notion of power and it accounts for oppression both through larger social structures and in terms of the identities produced by these structures without then taking the identities as static, or as the basis for changing the oppressive structures; in this way, it combines the best insights of socialist feminism, radical feminism, and postmodern feminism. No one category of feminism is adequate for the political task ahead; along with the polyvocality of contemporary feminism we need a multipronged political approach and theories that reflect the complexity of our contemporary situation, rather than reduce it. I think that Foucault's work offers some resources to think through the complexity of experience with the aim of a politics of antidomination. I do not offer it up as the sole answer for feminist politics or the solution to feminist conflict. In fact, as I have thought and rethought the relationship between feminism and Foucault, I have come up with three contradictory ways of understanding it, all of which I think are nonetheless true. First, I think that Foucault's ideas provide a supplement, not a replacement, to some feminist politics, such as liberal feminism. His understanding of power certainly adds to liberal feminism, yet we clearly need to pursue political and social change through existing traditional forms such as legislation. His recognition of the politics of social practices is an important supplement to a focus restricted to legal and economic institutions because it politicizes issues of representation, language, and interpretation often left out of traditional political analysis. Of course, the study of discourse, even in its broader meaning of institutions and practices, need not—indeed should not— replace analyses that focus on political, legal, and economic issues.

Second, I think that Foucault's ideas are compatible with some feminist ideas, such as the radical feminist understanding of power and the emphasis on diversity espoused by multicultural feminists. Both Foucault and radical feminists understand power as present in social relations; both recognize the effect of power on the constitution of identity. And both believe that institutions, practices, discourses, and knowledge are produced and sustained through power relations and are therefore political. Foucault's concern with exclusion and marginalization of nondominant individuals and groups is similar to multicultural feminists' concern with the exclusion and marginalization of women of color. Both Foucault and multicultural feminists worry about the exclusionary effect of normative categories; both recognize that social identity categories carry implicit norms. And both point out that social identity categories, such as "woman," perform a dual function; even as they define and solidify collective group identity, they exclude nondominant members from the group. Moreover, Foucault's account of power is able to account for the complexity of power relations that multicultural feminists articulate. Multicultural feminists argue that women are not simply oppressed, but may also be oppressors with respect to their membership in other dominant groups. Foucault's account of power allows for both the interlocking of oppressions in the construction of identity and the multiple social affiliations that make each of us both oppressor and oppressed in some respect.

Third, Foucault's work challenges feminisms other than postmodern feminism because it challenges the fundamental categories through which feminism makes political claims, such as woman, women, and the natural body. His challenge to identity categories and the body seems to undermine the possibility for a unified politics. I have argued that Foucault's analyses are in part analyses of large-scale institutional and social structures, and the ways that these structures constitute subjectivity. A unified antidomination politics would aim at changing those structures without subscribing to the identities produced by them. Although there is much overlap between Foucault's ideas and postmodern feminism, I think that Foucault pays more attention to material practices and large-scale structural institutions, such as the economy and the law, than most postmodern feminists. So long as women are oppressed, as complicated as that oppression may be, and as contested as the category "women" may be, we need to ground our politics in the various material realities that women inhabit, and I believe Foucault's ideas can help us do that.

▶•◀

NOTES

In citing works in the notes, short titles have generally been used after the initial reference. Works frequently cited have been identified by the following abbreviations:

HS 1   *The History of Sexuality Vol. 1: An Introduction*
         Michel Foucault

GE   "On the Genealogy of Ethics: An Overview of Work in Progress"
         Michel Foucault

NGH   "Nietzsche, Genealogy, History"
         Michel Foucault

EW 1   *The Essential Works of Foucault 1954–1984: Vol. 1: Ethics, Subjectivity and Truth*
         ed. Paul Rabinow

BSH   *Michel Foucault: Beyond Structuralism and Hermeneutics*
         Hubert L. Dreyfus and Paul Rabinow

CHAPTER 1

1. Jana Sawicki makes the most persuasive case for a Foucauldian feminism in *Disciplining Foucault: Feminism, Power and the Body* (New York: Routledge, 1991). Several feminists argue that Foucault's work can be useful for feminism or they use a Foucauldian approach to feminist theorizing, for example, Judith Butler, *Gender Trouble: Feminism and the Subversion of Identity* (New York: Routledge, 1990); Judith Butler, *Bodies That Matter* (New York: Routledge, 1993); Susan Bordo, *Unbearable Weight: Feminism, Western Culture and the Body* (Berkeley: University of California Press, 1993); Susan Hekman, *Gender and Knowledge: Elements of a Postmodern Feminism* (Boston: Northeastern University Press, 1990); and Ladelle McWhorter, *Bodies & Pleasures: Foucault and the Politics of Sexual Normalization* (Bloomington: Indiana University Press, 1999). Among the feminists who see Foucault's ideas as dangerous to feminism or who have expressed reservations about

adopting a feminist Foucauldian approach are Nancy Hartsock, *The Feminist Standpoint Revisited & Other Essays* (Boulder: Westview Press, 1998); Somer Brodribb, *Nothing Mat(t)ers: A Feminist Critique of Postmodernism* (North Melbourne: Spinifex Press, 1992); Toril Moi, "Power, Sex and Subjectivity: Feminist Reflections on Foucault" in *Paragraph: The Journal of the Modern Critical Theory Group*, 5 (1985): 95–102; and Rosi Braidotti, *Nomadic Subjects* (New York: Columbia University Press, 1994). There are many feminists who take a middle position, applying Foucault's work to feminists issues, but expressing reservations, or applying some aspects of Foucault's work while criticizing and rejecting others. Feminists who take this middle position include Sandra Bartky, *Femininity and Domination: Studies in the Phenomenology of Oppression* (New York: Routledge, 1990); Linda Alcoff, "Feminist Politics and Foucault: The Limits to a Collaboration" in *Crises in Continental Philosophy*, eds. Arleen Dallery and Charles Scott (Albany: State University of New York Press, 1990); Linda Alcoff, "Cultural Feminism Versus Poststructuralism: The Identity Crisis in Feminist Theory" in *Signs: Journal of Women in Culture and Society* 13:3 (1988): 405–436; and Nancy Fraser, *Unruly Practices: Power, Discourse and Gender in Contemporary Social Theory* (Minneapolis: University of Minnesota Press, 1989).

2. In much of the literature in this debate, poststructuralism and postmodernism are used interchangeably. Although this practice is somewhat confusing, I will use them as synonyms here. Foucault's relationship to these labels is complicated. His early work has been characterized as structuralist, a label he explicitly denied, and he attempted to distance himself from this approach; see the Foreword to the English edition of *The Order of Things: An Archaeology of the Human Sciences* (New York: Pantheon Books, 1971): xiv. Foucault also denied that he was a postmodernist, and there has been significant debate about whether his work is modern or postmodern. Nonetheless, he is generally seen as one of the most prominent postmodern thinkers.

3. Progressive politics includes a range of positions that advocate social justice, including struggles based on overcoming domination of oppressed groups, working towards economic equality, and working against environmental degradation. Here I am most concerned with political movements that focus on particular marginalized groups of people, such as the gay and lesbian movement, antiracism, and feminism. My focus is on feminism in particular, and I elaborate on a number of feminist positions in this chapter.

4. Barbara Epstein, "Why Poststructuralism is a Dead End for Progressive Thought" in *Socialist Review* 25:2 (1995): 83–119, 84.

5. Ibid., 43.

6. Brodribb, *Nothing Mat(t)ers*, xix.

7. Toril Moi, "Power, sex, and subjectivity," 95.

8. Nancy Hartsock, "Foucault on Power: A Theory for Women?" in *Feminism/Postmodernism*, ed. Linda Nicholson (New York: Routledge, 1990): 157–175, 158.

9. Alcoff, "Feminist Politics and Foucault," 69.

10. As we shall see, the critique of power is widespread among feminist critics of Foucault. For representative arguments, see Nancy Hartsock, "Foucault on Power: A

Theory for Women?" and Linda Alcoff, "Feminist Politics and Foucault: The Limits to a Collaboration."

11. Feminist interest in Foucault in the 1990s can be compared to feminist interest in Marx in the 1970s. Since 1988, three anthologies dealing specifically with the relationship between feminism and Foucault have been published: *Feminism and Foucault: Reflections on Resistance*, eds. Irene Diamond and Lee Quinby (Boston: Northeastern University Press, 1988); *Up Against Foucault: Explorations of Some Tensions Between Foucault and Feminism*, ed. Caroline Ramazanoglu (New York: Routledge, 1993); and *Feminist Interpretations of Michel Foucault*, ed. Susan Hekman (University Park: Pennsylvania State University Press, 1996). Additionally, there have been many recent books that address the issue of the compatibility of postmodern thought and feminist theory; see for instance, *Feminism/Postmodernism*, ed. Linda Nicholson (New York: Routledge, 1990); *Feminist Practice & Poststructuralist Theory*, Chris Weedon (Oxford: Blackwell, 1987); *Gender and Knowledge: Elements of a Postmodern Feminism*, Susan J. Hekman (Boston: Northeastern University Press, 1990). There have been surprisingly few book-length treatments of the relationship between Foucault and feminism or the usefulness of Foucault's work for feminism, this is in contrast to the spate of articles about these issues. Two exceptions to this that explore the usefulness of Foucault's ideas for feminism and the possibility of a Foucauldian feminism are Jana Sawicki, *Disciplining Foucault: Feminism, Power and the Body* (New York: Routledge, 1991), and Lois McNay, *Foucault & Feminism: Power, Gender and the Self* (Cambridge: Polity Press, 1992; Boston: Northeastern University Press, 1993). Until recently it was rare for Foucault's later work to be taken into account in the literature on feminism and Foucault; a notable exception to this is McNay's book, although her reading of this work and the conclusions she draws about its usefulness for feminism, as well as its relationship to Foucault's earlier work, are different from my own. For articles that deal specifically with Foucault's later work and feminism, see Jean Grimshaw, "Practices of Freedom" in *Up Against Foucault*, 51–72; and Jana Sawicki, "Feminism, Foucault, and 'Subjects' of Power and Freedom" in *Feminist Interpretations of Michel Foucault*, 159–78.

12. Irene Diamond and Lee Quinby, Introduction to *Feminism and Foucault*, ix–xx.

13. See, for instance, Sandra Bartky, *Feminity and Domination*, Susan Bordo, *Unbearable Weight*, and Jana Sawicki, *Disciplining Foucault*.

14. The periodization of Foucault's work is a complicated matter; the notion of an early, middle, and late period merely serves as a heuristic device. It may be more helpful to refer to his books in the way that he did, as dealing with three modes of the subject: the speaking subject, the objectified subject, and the subjectified subject. But for my purposes in this text, I will continue to refer to his work as archaeological (early), genealogical (middle), or ethical (late). The texts I will be referring to fall into these categories as follows. Early (archaeological) works include: *Madness and Civilization: A History of Insanity in the Age of Reason*, trans. Richard Howard (New York: Random House, 1965), originally published in a much longer unabridged edition as *Folie et déraison: Histoire de la folie à l'âge classique* (Paris: Plon, 1961); *The Birth of the Clinic*, trans. Alan Sheridan (New York: Vintage, 1973), originally published as *Naissance de la clinique: une archéologie du régard médical* (Paris: PUF, 1963); *The Order of Things*, trans. Alan Sheridan (New York: Random House, 1970), originally published as *Les mots et les choses: une archéologie des sciences humaines* (Paris: Gallimard, 1966); and *The Archaeology of Knowledge*, trans. Alan

Sheridan (New York: Pantheon, 1972), originally published as *L'archéologie du savoir* (Paris: Gallimard, 1969). Middle (genealogical) works include: *Discipline and Punish*, trans. Alan Sheridan (New York: Pantheon, 1977), originally published as *Surveiller et punir: naissance de la prison* (Paris: Gallimard, 1975); *The History of Sexuality: Vol.1: An Introduction*, trans. Robert Hurley (New York: Pantheon, 1978), originally published as *Histoire de la sexualité, Vol. 1: la Volonté de savoir* (Paris: Gallimard, 1976). Late (ethical) works include: *The History of Sexuality: Vol. 2: The Use of Pleasure*, trans. Robert Hurley (New York: Pantheon, 1985), originally published as *L'usage des plaisirs: histoire de la sexualité, Vol. 2* (Paris: Gallimard, 1984); *The History of Sexuality: Vol. 3: The Care of the Self*, trans. Robert Hurley (New York: Pantheon, 1986), originally published as *Le Souci de soi: histoire de la sexualité, Vol. 3* (Paris: Gallimard, 1984). This is not a complete list of Foucault's books; for a more comprehensive bibliography, see *The Cambridge Companion to Foucault*. One reason the chronological categorization does not work well is that although *Madness and Civilization* is his earliest published book and categorized as archaeological, it deals with dividing practices, like the genealogical texts that comprise his middle work. A second, even more compelling reason is that the texts listed comprise only a fraction of Foucault's work; he authored several more books, wrote many essays and articles, and provided many interviews. Indeed, his collected essays and articles in French, *Dits and écrits* (Sayings and Writings), consist of almost 4,000 pages.

15. Michel Foucault, "On the Genealogy of Ethics: An Overview of Work in Progress" (hereafter in notes GE), Afterword in Hubert L. Dreyfus and Paul Rabinow, *Beyond Structuralism and Hermeneutics* (hereafter in notes *BSH*) (Chicago: University of Chicago Press, 1982): 229–52; Michel Foucault, "The Subject and Power," Afterword in *BSH*, 208–26; Michel Foucault, "Technologies of the Self" in *Technologies of the Self*, eds. Luther H. Martin, Huck Gutman, and Patrick H. Hutton (Amherst: University of Massachusetts Press, 1988): 16–49, reprinted in *EW 1* 223–51; Michel Foucault, "The Ethic of Care for the Self as a Practice of Freedom" in *The Final Foucault*, eds. James Bernauer and David Rasmussen (Cambridge: MIT Press, 1988): 1–20. This same interview appears in *The Essential Works of Michel Foucault: Vol. 1: Ethics, Subjectivity and Truth*, ed. Paul Rabinow (New York: New Press, 1997) (hereafter cited as *EW 1* in notes) with a slightly different title, "The Ethics of the Concern for Self as a Practice of Freedom." Because the translations are different, I will be referring to both versions.

16. Foucault, "The Subject and Power" in *BSH*, 208–9. Foucault also discusses this in the preface to his *The Use of Pleasure*.

17. Rosemary Tong, *Feminist Thought: A Comprehensive Introduction* (Boulder: Westview Press, 1989), 1.

18. Here I am following the divisions that Alison Jaggar and Paula Rothenberg make in their text *Feminist Frameworks* (New York: McGraw-Hill, 1993). A quick survey of feminist theory texts will reveal that there are many possibilities for dividing up feminist thought. In spite of this variation, feminist political approaches usually include liberal, radical, Marxist, and socialist feminism as standard categories. For instance, in her comprehensive introduction to feminist thought, Rosemary Tong covers psychoanalytic, existentialist, and postmodern feminism as well as liberal, Marxist, radical, and socialist feminism.

19. See Martha C. Nussbaum, "The Professor of Parody: The Hip Defeatism of Judith Butler" in *New Republic,* 22 February 1999, 37–45. Nussbaum notes Foucault's influence on North American feminism and criticizes Judith Butler's postmodern feminism, especially her appropriation of Foucault and other French theorists.

20. Ibid., 38.

21. Ibid., 41.

22. Not all radical feminists thought this; there are differences of opinion within the radical feminist position. Here I overlook those differences in order to sketch out a general position.

23. Early radical feminists who saw women's reproductive capacity as an impediment to full equality include Shulamith Firestone; see her *The Dialectic of Sex* (New York: Bantam Books, 1970). These feminists focused on technological solutions to liberate women from childbearing. Later radical feminists who celebrated women's reproductive capacities include Dorothy Dinnerstein; see her *The Mermaid and the Minotaur: Sexual Arrangements and Human Malaise* (New York: Harper Colophon Books, 1977).

24. Andrea Dworkin and Catherine MacKinnon are well known for their antipornography work. During the early 1980s, they introduced antipornography legislation in Minneapolis and Indianapolis; the Indianapolis ordinance was signed into law, although it was later ruled unconstitutional. For their arguments against pornography, see Andrea Dworkin, *Pornography: Men Possessing Women* (New York: Perigee Books, 1981); Catherine A. MacKinnon, *Feminism Unmodified: Discourses on Life and the Law* (Cambridge: Harvard University Press, 1977); and Catherine A. MacKinnon, "Feminism, Marxism, Method and the State: Toward Feminist Jurisprudence" in *Signs: Journal of Women in Culture and Society* 8:4 (1983): 635–58.

25. Mary Daly is probably the best known of radical feminists who believe "naming" can be a powerful political experience for women insofar as it redefines reality; see especially her *Gyn/Ecology: The Metaethics of Radical Feminism* (Boston: Beacon Press, 1978) and *Pure Lust: Elemental Feminist Philosophy* (Boston: Beacon Press, 1984). See also Dale Spender, *Man Made Language* (Boston: Routledge and Kegan Paul, 1980); and Adrienne Rich, *On Lies, Secrets and Silences: Selected Prose, 1966–1978* (New York: W. W. Norton, 1979).

26. Gays and lesbians have also adopted this strategy, arguing that gays and lesbians should reclaim the terms "fag," "dyke," and "butch."

27. A version of the debate between the liberal and radical feminist perspective has gone on in feminist legal theory under the rubric of the equality/difference debate. See Joan W. Scott, "Deconstructing Equality-Versus-Difference: Or, the Uses of Poststructuralist Theory for Feminism" in *Conflicts in Feminism,* eds. Marianne Hirsch and Evelyn Fox Keller (New York: Routledge, 1990).

28. See, for example, Barbara Ehrenreich and Deirdre English, *For Her Own Good: 150 Years of the Experts' Advice to Women* (New York: Doubleday, 1978).

29. Brodribb, *Nothing Mat(t)ers,* 50.

30. See, for instance, Evelyn Reed, "Women, Caste, Class or Oppressed Sex" in *Feminist Frameworks*, 170–3.

31. Ibid., 173.

32. As far as I know, Hartsock was the first to develop feminist standpoint theory. Since then, many other feminists have drawn on her work or formulated their own versions of a feminist standpoint. See, for example, Sandra Harding's *The Science Question in Feminism* (Ithaca: Cornell University Press, 1986); Donna Haraway "Situated Knowledges: The Science Question in Feminism and the Privilege of Partial Perspective" in *Feminist Studies* 14:3 (1988): 575–99; and Patricia Hill Collins, *Black Feminist Thought: Knowledge, Consciousness, and the Politics of Empowerment* (New York: Routledge, 1991).

33. Nancy Hartsock, "The Feminist Standpoint: Developing the Ground for a Specifically Feminist Historical Materialism," in *The Feminist Standpoint Revisited & Other Essays*, 107. Originally in *Discovering Reality: Feminist Perspectives on Epistemology, Metaphysics, Methodology and Philosophy of Science*, eds. Sandra Harding and Merrill B. Hintikka (Dordrecht, Holland: D. Reidel Publishing, 1983).

34. Generally, socialist feminism is seen as the combination or integration of Marxist feminism and radical feminism. Rosemary Tong argues that socialist feminism includes insights from psychoanalytic feminism as well.

35. Heidi Hartmann, "The Unhappy Marriage of Marxism and Feminism: Towards a More Progressive Union" in *Feminist Frameworks*, 191.

36. Ibid., 194.

37. See Iris Marion Young, "Socialist Feminism and the Limits of Dual Systems Theory" in *Socialist Review* 50–51 (1980): 169–88 for an argument that these two systems are intertwined.

38. I will use the term sexual orientation throughout this book to refer to sexual desire or identity, for example, gay, lesbian, bisexual, heterosexual, except in chapter 4, where I use sexual desire as synonymous with sexual orientation, and in chapter 5, where I use sexuality as a synonym for sexual orientation. I prefer the term sexuality because it does not connote whether one's desires are fixed or a matter of choice, the way that sexual orientation and sexual preference do. But because Foucault uses the term sexuality in a general way to refer to a whole range of discourses and practices, I will use it in a more general sense in this book as well, with the above noted exception.

39. Seyla Benhabib, "Feminism and Postmodernism: An Uneasy Alliance" in Seyla Benhabib et al., *Feminist Contentions: A Philosophical Exchange* (New York: Routledge, 1995), 20.

40. Seyla Benhabib, *Situating the Self: Gender, Community and Postmodernism in Contemporary Ethics* (New York: Routledge, 1992), 222.

41. Barbara Christian, "The Race for Theory" in *Radically Speaking: Feminism Reclaimed*, eds. Diane Bell and Renate Klein (North Melbourne, Australia: Spinifex Press, 1996), 316; originally in *Cultural Critique* 6 (Spring 1987): 335–45.

42. Currently, the term used in international, multinational contexts for non-Western countries is "newly industrialized countries" (acronym NICs). This replaces the earlier "third world" and the more recent "developing countries."

43. Just as postmodernism is a broad category, postmodern feminism is an extremely loose generalization that includes feminists who are significantly influenced by or draw upon postmodern thinkers such as Lyotard, Derrida, or Foucault.

44. Foucault uses three terms to refer to the self—self, subject, and individual. In general, he uses subjectivity, individualization, and individuality to refer to normalized subjectivity; he uses self and individual to refer to pre-Modern (nonnormalized) conceptions of the self. For the most part, his usage correlates with the time period he is discussing, for example, when talking about the Ancient period he uses self, when discussing the Classical Age (modernity) he uses subject. However, he does use subject and subjectivity when talking about the formation of the ethical subject of Antiquity. He uses individual mostly in the context of his discussions of Antiquity, but uses individualization and individuality throughout his genealogical texts. I discuss this further in chapter 3.

45. Staunch critics include Nancy Hartsock, Toril Moi, and Barbara Epstein. Moderate critics include Nancy Fraser and Linda Alcoff. Extenders include Sandra Bartky and Susan Bordo. And feminist Foucauldians include Jana Sawicki, Judith Butler, and Susan Hekman.

46. See note 11 above. It is notable that no other postmodern philosopher has drawn this much attention from feminists.

47. Susan Hekman claims this is one reason why Foucault has been of such interest to feminists.

48. Ramazanoglu, *Up Against Foucault*, 3.

49. Hekman, *Feminist Interpretations of Michel Foucault*, 10.

CHAPTER 2

1. See Nancy Fraser, "Michel Foucault, A 'Young Conservative'?" originally in *Ethics* 96: 1 (1985): 165–84. And see, Charles Taylor, "Foucault on Freedom and Truth"; Michael Walzer, "The Politics of Michel Foucault"; Richard Rorty, "Foucault and Epistemology"; and Jürgen Habermas, "Taking Aim at the Heart of the Present"; all in *Foucault: A Critical Reader*, ed. David Couzens Hoy (Oxford: Basil Blackwell, 1986). See also Jürgen Habermas, *The Philosophical Discourse of Modernity*, chs. IX, X, trans. Frederick G. Lawrence (Cambridge: MIT Press, 1987).

2. Many feminists who engage with Foucault make this criticism. Some of the most compelling criticisms are made by Nancy Hartsock, "Foucault on Power: A Theory for Women?" in *Feminism/Postmodernism*, ed. Linda Nicholson (New York: Routledge, 1990) and "Postmodernism and Political Change: Issues for Feminist Theory" in *Feminist Interpretations of Michel Foucault*, ed. Susan Hekman, (University Park: Pennsylvania State University Press, 1996); Nancy Fraser, "Foucault on Modern Power: Empirical Insights and

Normative Confusions," and "Michel Foucault: A 'Young Conservative'?" in *Unruly Practices* (Minneapolis: University of Minnesota Press, 1989); Rosi Braidotti, especially chapter 7 in her *Nomadic Subjects* (New York: Columbia University Press, 1994); and Lois McNay, "The Foucauldian Body and the Exclusion of Experience" in *Hypatia* 6 (1991):125–37 and her *Foucault & Feminism.*

3. See Jane Flax, "Postmodernism and Gender Relations in Feminist Theory" in *Feminism/Postmodernism*, 39–62, especially 41.

4. See Charles Taylor, "Foucault on Freedom and Truth"; Michael Walzer, "The Politics of Michel Foucault"; and Jürgen Habermas, "Taking Aim at the Heart of the Present"; all in *Foucault: A Critical Reader,* ed. David Couzens Hoy (Oxford: Basil Blackwell, 1986). See also Jürgen Habermas, *The Philosophical Discourse of Modernity*, chs. IX, X, trans. Frederick G. Lawrence (Cambridge: MIT Press, 1987).

5. Michel Foucault, "Truth and Power," in *The Foucault Reader,* ed. Paul Rabinow (New York: Pantheon Books, 1984), 51–75, 72–3.

6. Foucault, *Discipline and Punish,* 27.

7. Sawicki, *Disciplining Foucault,* 100–1.

8. Foucault repeatedly stresses that power is everywhere. See, for instance, Michel Foucault, *The History of Sexuality: Vol. 1 : An Introduction,* trans. Robert Hurley (New York: Vintage Books, 1980), 92–6. (Hereafter in notes this text will be cited as *HS 1*.) See also Michel Foucault, "Two Lectures," 78–108, and "Truth and Power," 109–133 in *Power/Knowledge: Selected Interviews and Other Writings 1972–1977*, ed. Colin Gordon (New York: Pantheon Books, 1980).

9. Originally published in the mid-1980s, their articles continue to set the tone for feminist engagement with Foucault. Here I will be referring to three of Nancy Hartsock's articles: "Foucault on Power: A Theory for Women?" in *Feminism/Postmodernism*, "Postmodernism and Political Change: Issues for Feminist Theory" in *Feminist Interpretations of Michel Foucault,* and "Postmodernism and Political Change" in *The Feminist Standpoint Revisited & Other Essays.* There is considerable overlap between these last two essays, but there are differences that are significant for my argument. I will also be referring to three of Nancy Fraser's essays: "Foucault on Modern Power: Empirical Insights and Normative Confusions," originally in *Praxis International* 1: 3 (October 1981): 272–87; "Foucault's Body Language: A Posthumanist Political Rhetoric?" originally in *Salmagundi* 61 (Fall 1983): 55–73; and "Michel Foucault: A 'Young Conservative'?" originally in *Ethics* 96: 1 (October 1985): 165–84; all are reprinted in her *Unruly Practices: Power, Discourse and Gender in Contemporary Social Theory* (Minneapolis: University of Minnesota Press, 1989). Subsequent notes refer to the page numbers in *Unruly Practices*. One indication of their continuing influence is that Fraser's "Michel Foucault: A 'Young Conservative'?" and Hartsock's "Postmodernism and Political Change: Issues for Feminist Theory" have been reprinted in the section exploring the possibility of feminist engagement with Foucault in the most recent anthology on feminism and Foucault, *Feminist Interpretations of Michel Foucault.*

10. Nancy Hartsock, "Foucault on Power: A Theory for Women?" 160.

11. Ibid., 167.

12. Ibid.

13. Ibid., 168.

14. Ibid., 169.

15. See, for example, Foucault, *HS 1*, 122.

16. Hartsock, "Foucault on Power," 169.

17. Ibid., 170.

18. Ibid.

19. Nancy Hartsock, "Postmodernism and Political Change: Issues for Feminist Theory," 46.

20. As mentioned in chapter 1 note 2, there is some debate about whether Foucault can be accurately characterized as a postmodern thinker. Foucault himself rejected this characterization of his work. For a good discussion of the complexities of classifying any thinker as postmodern, see Judith Butler's "Contingent Foundations: Feminism and the Question of Postmodernism" in *Praxis International* 11: 2 (1991).

21. As Hartsock notes, she gets this phrase from Donna Haraway.

22. Nancy Hartsock, "Postmodernism and Political Change: Issues for Feminist Theory," 44.

23. Nancy Hartsock, "Postmodernism and Political Change," 217.

24. Fraser, "Michel Foucault: A 'Young Conservative'?" 41.

25. Ibid., 43.

26. See Michel Foucault, "What Is Enlightenment?" in *The Foucault Reader*, ed. Paul Rabinow (New York: Pantheon Books, 1984).

27. Fraser associates David Hoy with the first interpretation and Hubert Dreyfus and Paul Rabinow with the third.

28. Nancy Fraser and Linda Nicholson, "Social Criticism without Philosophy: An Encounter between Feminism and Postmodernism" in *Feminism/Postmodernism*, 25.

29. Ibid., 34.

30. McWhorter, *Bodies & Pleasures*, see especially 72–3 and 162–92.

31. Todd May, *Between Genealogy and Epistemology: Psychology, Politics, and Knowledge in the Thought of Michel Foucault* (University Park: Pennsylvania State University Press, 1993), 100.

32. See Nancy Fraser, "Foucault's Body Language: A Posthumanist Political Rhetoric?" in *Unruly Practices*.

33. Foucault's genealogical work traces the histories of specific institutions and practices. In the two texts usually considered his genealogical works, *Discipline and Punish* and *The History of Sexuality Vol. 1,* he examines the histories of the penal institution and

sexuality, respectively. In my discussion of genealogy as critique, I include *Madness and Civilization: A History of Insanity in the Age of Reason,* trans. Richard Howard (New York: Vintage Books, 1988), originally published in French unabridged as *Folie et déraison: Histoire de la folie à l'âge classique* (Paris: Plon, 1961), as well because it is obviously critical of the "humanistic reforms" in dealing with madness. Although Foucault wrote it during his archaeological period and it is not usually seen as a genealogical work, he later claims there is a genealogical aspect to it.

34. Hubert Dreyfus and Paul Rabinow call this "interpretive analytics" in their *Michel Foucault: Beyond Structuralism and Hermeneutics.* They also use the term "critical re-description"; this is similar to what I mean here.

35. Foucault, "Two Lectures" in *Power/Knowledge,* 83.

36. Ibid., 82.

37. Foucault, *Discipline and Punish,* 136.

38. Ibid., 31.

39. There is debate over whether or not Foucault is a "proper" historian; some accuse him of being too selective with his sources. See, for example, Gary Gutting, "Foucault and the History of Madness" in *The Cambridge Companion to Foucault,* ed. Gary Gutting (Cambridge: Cambridge University Press, 1994), 47–70.

40. Foucault, *Discipline and Punish,* 19.

41. Foucault, *HS 1,* 43.

42. Foucault, *HS 1,* 159.

43. See Nancy Hartsock, "Postmodernism and Political Change," 45.

44. Foucault, *Discipline and Punish,* 308.

45. Michel Foucault, "Clarifications on the Question of Power," in *Foucault Live: Collected Interviews, 1961–1984,* ed. Sylvere Lotringer, trans. Lysa Hochroth and John Johnston (New York: Semiotext(e), 1989), 255–63, 261.

46. See, for example, Nancy Fraser, "Michel Foucault: A 'Young Conservative'?"

47. See, for example, Nancy Hartsock, "Postmodernism and Political Change" and Jean Grimshaw "Practices of Freedom," in *Up Against Foucault.*

48. See, for instance, Habermas, "Taking Aim at the Heart of the Present," and Taylor "Foucault on Freedom and Truth" in *Foucault: A Critical Reader.*

49. Foucault, "Truth and Power" in *The Foucault Reader,* 64.

50. Foucault discusses this in "Two Lectures" in *Power/Knowledge,* see especially 108.

51. See Foucault, *HS 1,* 123–7.

52. Ibid., 124.

53. See Dreyfus and Rabinow, *BSH,* 184, 188.

54. Ibid., 184

55. This is because feminism is based on the idea that there is an inequality of power between men and women. See Jaggar's and Rothenberg's introduction to *Feminist Frameworks* for an overview of this issue. See also Amy Allen, *The Power of Feminist Theory: Domination, Resistance, Solidarity* (Boulder: Westview Press, 1999).

56. Foucault, *HS 1*, 83.

57. For Foucault's most extensive discussions of power, see *HS 1*, 88–96; "Truth and Power," "Two Lectures," "The Eye of Power," "Power and Strategies," and "Body/Power," all in *Power/Knowledge*; "Intellectuals and Power," "Power Affects the Body," and "Clarifications on the Question of Power" in *Foucault Live*; and "The Subject and Power," in *BSH*.

58. Foucault, *HS 1*, 92.

59. Ibid., 93.

60. The points I have enumerated come mainly from his discussion of power in *HS 1*, 92–4.

61. See Dreyfus and Rabinow, *BSH*, 187.

62. For a discussion of this, see *BSH*, 187, where Dreyfus and Rabinow quote Foucault, "People know what they do; they frequently know why they do what they do; but what they don't know is what what they do does." [Michel Foucault, personal communication]

63. Here I focus on the political-ethical consequences of this claim, although they are related to the epistemic consequences regarding justification. See Ladelle McWhorter's *Bodies & Pleasures*, 43–49, for a clear and concise argument against the idea that Foucault's position results in epistemic relativism. See also Todd May, *Between Genealogy and Epistemology*, especially chapter 6.

64. For instance, the arguments made by Habermas, Rorty, Taylor, Walzer, Hartsock, and Fraser noted earlier.

65. Foucault explicitly says this is a misunderstanding of his concept of power. See *HS 1*, 95, "Should it be said that one is always 'inside' power, there is no 'escaping' it, there is no absolute outside where it is concerned, because one is subject to the law in any case? Or that history being the ruse of reason, power is the ruse of history, always emerging the winner? *This would be to misunderstand the strictly relational character of power relationships.*" (emphasis added).

66. Michel Foucault, "The Subject and Power," 226.

67. Ibid.

68. See Foucault, "Two Lectures," 99; Foucault, "Interview with Lucette Finas," in *Michel Foucault: Power, Truth, Strategy,* eds. Meaghan Morris and Paul Patton (Sydney: Feral Publications, 1979), 67–75, 72; Foucault "The Subject and Power," 217–18, and especially 223; Foucault, "The Ethic of Care for the Self as a Practice of Freedom," 3, 12.

69. Foucault, "Two Lectures," 99.

70. Michel Foucault, "The Ethics of the Concern for Self as a Practice of Freedom" in *EW 1*.

71. Ibid., 293.

72. Ibid., 292.

73. Ibid., 282–3.

74. Michael Hechter and Karl-Deiter Opp, Introduction, in *Social Norms*, eds. Michael Hechter and Karl-Deiter Opp (New York: Russell Sage Foundation, 2001), xi.

75. Ibid.

76. Ibid.

77. See McWhorter, *Bodies & Pleasures*, for an argument that humanism assumes a political neutrality that is a luxury experienced by those with nonmarginalized identities.

78. Foucault, GE, 231.

79. Discussion at Berkeley, April 1983, cassette and manuscript; hereafter Berkeley, April 1983, Mss. This discussion took place among Charles Taylor, Paul Rabinow, Bert Dreyfus, Robert Bellah, Martin Jay, Leo Lowenthal, and Michel Foucault. The cassette tape [#0250 (7)] and transcript are in the Foucault Archives, Paris.

80. Berkeley, April 1983, Mss., 1.

81. Foucault, GE, 231–2.

82. Berkeley, April 1983, Mss., 3, 11, 14.

83. Although published under the pseudonym "Maurice Florence," the entry on Foucault's work is widely believed to be written by Foucault himself.

84. Michel Foucault [Maurice Florence, pseud.], "Foucault, Michel 1926–" in *The Cambridge Companion to Foucault*, 314–319, 317.

85. Michel Foucault, "The Return of Morality," in *Foucault Live*, 465–473, 473.

86. Foucault, "Foucault, Michel 1926–," 314.

87. Foucault, "What is Enlightenment?" 46.

88. Ibid.

89. Foucault, "The Ethics of the Concern for Self as a Practice of Freedom," 300–1.

90. Foucault, "What is Enlightenment?" 46–7.

91. Here I disagree with critics such as Lois McNay who claim that Foucault's later work is a return to Enlightenment concepts of freedom, self-reflexivity, etc. See McNay's *Foucault & Feminism*, especially chapters 4 and 5.

92. For more on Foucault's political activism, see Didier Eribon, *Michel Foucault*, trans. Betsy Wing (Cambridge: Harvard University Press, 1991); David M. Halperin, *Saint=Foucault: Towards a Gay Hagiography* (Oxford: Oxford University Press, 1995); Didier Eribon, *Foucault et ses contemporains* (Paris: Fayard, 1994).

93. Michel Foucault, "What Is An Author?" in *The Foucault Reader*, 104. One may well wonder what to make of Foucault's own authorship in light of his "What Is An Author?"

In this essay, Foucault examines the way that the concept "author" has functioned. He questions how an author's *oeuvre* is determined. Is it only published works? What does that mean for works published posthumously? Using Nietzsche as an example, Foucault includes rough drafts, plans for his aphorisms, deleted passages, and marginal notes as part of his work. But what if one finds among the aphorisms a laundry list, the notation of a meeting? Foucault says that we lack a theory of the work that would provide an answer to this question—"How can one define a work amid the millions of traces left by someone after his death?"

94. For a longer argument that justifies such inclusion, in fact demands it, see Deborah Cook, "Umbrellas, Laundry Bills and Resistance: The Place of Foucault's Interviews in His Corpus" in *The Subject Finds a Voice: Michel Foucault's Subjective Turn* (New York: Peter Lang, 1993), 97–106.

95. Foucault, "Politics and Ethics: An Interview" in *The Foucault Reader*, 373–380, 374.

96. Foucault, GE, 237.

97. This is contrary to some critics who claim that Foucault lapses into aestheticism and individualism in his later work. See, for example, Jean Grimshaw, "Practices of Freedom," and Peter Dews, "The Return of the Subject in the Late Foucault," in *Radical Philosophy* 51 (1989): 37–41. For a more detailed argument against this criticism, see my "Foucault and the Subject of Feminism" in *Social Theory and Practice* 23: 1 (1997): 109–28. I explore this issue further in chapters 3 and 6.

98. This is how Foucault describes his own project; see GE, 236–7.

99. Foucault, *HS 1*, 95.

100. Michel Foucault, "Sexual Choice, Sexual Act," in *EW 1*. Foucault was speaking specifically about gay politics and the gay community here. The omitted sentence reads, "Gays have to work out these matters themselves."

101. Sarah Lucia Hoagland, "Femininity, Resistance and Sabotage," in *Women and Values: Readings in Recent Feminist Philosophy*, ed. Marilyn Pearsall (Belmont, CA: Wadsworth Publishing, 1993).

102. Marguerite Guzman Bouvard, *Revolutionizing Motherhood: The Mothers of the Plaza de Mayo* (Wilmington, DE: Scholarly Resources, 1994) 65.

103. In spite of the traditional gender norms and the ideal of virtuous motherhood prevalent in Argentine society, the Mothers of the Plaza de Mayo were not immune to the violence they sought to end. Several leaders of the group were harassed, threatened with violence, and some were abducted and killed.

CHAPTER 3

1. However, I do not think one should take the modern/postmodern split as definitive. And as I pointed out in chapter 1 note 2, even if one does take it as definitive, it is not clear that Foucault belongs on the postmodern side.

2. See, for instance, Lois McNay, *Foucault & Feminism*, chapter 5, especially 159, 164–5, 172; Jean Grimshaw, "Practices of Freedom," and Jane Flax, "Beyond Equality: Gender, Justice and Difference," in *Beyond Equality & Difference*, eds. Gisela Bock and Susan James (New York: Routledge, 1992), 193–210, see especially 202. Often those who applaud Foucault's version of the self in his later writings as autonomous and capable of freedom simultaneously misinterpret his return to the subject as an endorsement of some version of the liberal subject. As I shall argue, his genealogy of the subject is consistent in viewing the subject as constituted by social practices, located in communities, and acting within institutional constraints, cultural conventions, and historical traditions.

3. Rosi Braidotti, *Nomadic Subjects: Embodiment and Sexual Difference in Contemporary Feminist Theory* (New York: Columbia University Press, 1994), 140–141.

4. Hartsock, "Foucault on Power: A Theory for Women?" 163.

5. Seyla Benhabib raises this question with regard to Judith Butler's "deed without the doer." See Seyla Benhabib, *Situating the Self: Gender, Community and Postmodernism in Contemporary Ethics* (New York: Routledge, 1992), especially chapter 7, 215.

6. Of course, there are epistemological implications to one's concept of subjectivity as well. But here I focus on the ethical and political implications.

7. Gilles Deleuze, *Foucault*, trans. Sean Hand (Minneapolis: University of Minnesota Press, 1988), 90.

8. Lois McNay, "The Foucauldian Body and the Exclusion of Experience" *Hypatia* 6 (1991): 125.

9. See, for instance, Diana T. Meyers, "The Socialized Individual and Individual Autonomy: An Intersection between Philosophy and Psychology," 139–53, and Seyla Benhabib, "The Generalized and the Concrete Other: The Kohlberg-Gilligan Controversy and Moral Theory," 154–77, both in *Women and Moral Theory*, eds. Eva Feder Kittay and Diana T. Meyers (Totowa, NJ: Rowman & Littlefield Publishers, 1987). See also Benhabib's *Situating the Self*.

10. Foucault claims that the subject was always the theme of his research; see "The Subject and Power" in *BSH*, 208–9.

11. Foucault, *The Order of Things*, 385.

12. Ibid., 385, 386.

13. Foucault, *The Archaeology of Knowledge*, 73.

14. Ibid., 54.

15. Foucault, *Discipline and Punish*, 28.

16. Ibid., 136.

17. Ibid.

18. Foucault, *HS 1*, 59.

19. Foucault, *Histoire de la sexualité: Vol. 1: la Volonté de savoir*, 82, translation mine.

20. Honi Fern Haber, "Foucault Pumped: Body Politics and the Muscled Woman," in *Feminist Interpretations of Michel Foucault*, ed. Susan Hekman (University Park: Pennsylvania State University Press, 1996).

21. Sandra Lee Bartky, "Foucault, Femininity, and the Modernization of Patriarchal Power," in her *Femininity and Domination* (New York: Routledge, 1990).

22. For the first claim, see *Discipline and Punish*, 136; for the second claim, see *HS 1*, 58–9; for the third claim, see "Two Lectures," 98 in *Power/Knowledge*.

23. Michel Foucault, "Body/Power" in *Power/Knowledge: Selected Interviews and Other Writings 1972–1977*, ed. Colin Gordon, trans. Colin Gordon et al. (New York: Pantheon Press, 1980), 58.

24. Michel Foucault, "Truth and Power," in *Power/Knowledge*, 117.

25. See for instance, *Madness and Civilization*, 103–110, and *The Order of Things*, 322–328.

26. Michel Foucault, "The Ethic of Care for the Self as a Practice of Freedom," in *The Final Foucault*, 10.

27. Michel Foucault, "Final Interview," *Raritan* 5: 2 (1985): 1–13.

28. Ibid., 11.

29. Ibid., 12.

30. Ibid.

31. Ibid. It is interesting to note that in French the words Foucault uses for subject (*sujet, assujettissement*) throughout *HS 1* have the dual meaning of subject and to subjugate, constrain, and compel. The word that Foucault uses for self (*soi*) in volumes 2 and 3 of *The History of Sexuality*—*The Use of Pleasure* and *The Care of the Self*—has no such double meaning; it is a pronoun that translates as oneself, herself, himself, itself.

32. Foucault refers to the period generally known as the Modern period in philosophy (1600s–1800s) as the Classical Age. Although this practice is somewhat confusing, given that it is common to refer to the period of ancient Greek philosophy as the Classical age, I have retained Foucault's usage. He invariably refers to the ancient Greek and early Roman period as Antiquity; to avoid confusion I do this as well. But I refer to the Enlightenment period (1600s–1800s) as either the Modern period or, following Foucault, the Classical Age. Foucault uses the term subjectivization in his "Final Interview," 12, to refer to "the procedure by which one obtains the constitution of a subject."

33. For Foucault's call to get rid of the subject, see *Power/Knowledge*, 58, 117.

34. Foucault, "Two Lectures," 97.

35. Michel Foucault, *The History of Sexuality: Vol. 2: The Use of Pleasure*, 5, hereafter *The Use of Pleasure*.

36. See Peter Dews, "The Return of the Subject in the Late Foucault," *Radical Philosophy* 51 (1989): 37–41; Jean Grimshaw, "Practices of Freedom" in *Up Against Foucault*; and Linda Alcoff, "Feminist Politics and Foucault."

37. For criticisms of Foucault's later work as focusing on the aesthetic and lapsing into individualism, see Peter Dews, ibid., and Jean Grimshaw, ibid.. See also Terry Eagleton, *The Ideology of the Aesthetic* (Oxford: Basil Blackwell, 1990), especially 384–395; Lois McNay, *Foucault & Feminism* (Boston: Northeastern University Press, 1992), especially 158, 164–5, 172; and Kate Soper, "Productive Contradictions," in *Up Against Foucault*, especially 38.

38. See, for instance, Foucault's introduction to *The Use of Pleasure* and his "The Subject and Power" in *BSH*.

39. See Jana Sawicki, *Disciplining Foucault*, for a similar view of Foucault's subject, especially chapters 3 and 5.

40. Notable exceptions are Jean Grimshaw, "Practices of Freedom"; Jana Sawicki, "Feminism, Foucault, and 'Subjects' of Power and Freedom"; Lois McNay, *Foucault & Feminism;* and Teresa de Lauretis, *Technologies of Gender: Essays on Theory, Film and Fiction* (Bloomington: Indiana University Press, 1987), chapters 1 and 2.

41. Foucault, "The Ethic of Care for the Self as a Practice of Freedom," 11.

42. Michel Foucault, "Interview with Lucette Finas," in *Michel Foucault: Power, Truth and Strategy*, 70.

43. Ibid., 72.

44. Foucault, "The Subject and Power," in *BSH*, 221.

45. Ibid., 226.

46. Foucault, "Two Lectures," 98.

47. Ibid.

48. Admittedly, even Foucault himself said that he may have focused too much on the domination aspect of power in his genealogical work; see Michel Foucault, "Technologies of the Self," in *Technologies of the Self: A Seminar with Michel Foucault*, eds. Luther H. Martin, Huck Gutman, and Patrick Hutton (Amherst: University of Massachusetts Press, 1988), 19.

49. See Peter Dews, "Power and Subjectivity in Foucault," *New Left Review* 144 (March–April 1984): 72–95, and Dews "The Return of the Subject in the Late Foucault," *Radical Philosophy* 51 (1989): 37–41.

50. Foucault, *The Use of Pleasure* , 6.

51. For example, in "Disciplining Women," which deals with the early and middle works of Foucault, Isaac Balbus writes, "We have seen that the Foucault who tries to 'get rid' of the subject is at odds with the Foucault who embraces subjectivity as a vital source of history." Isaac Balbus, "Disciplining Women: Michel Foucault and the Power of Feminist Discourse" in *Feminism as Critique*, eds. Seyla Benhabib and Drucilla Cornell (Minneapolis: University of Minnesota Press, 1988), 124. For Foucault's implicit appeal to norms, see Nancy Fraser, "Foucault on Modern Power: Empirical Insights and Normative Confusions" in *Praxis International* 1: 3 (1981): 272–87; Charles Taylor, "Foucault on Freedom and Truth" in *Foucault: A Critical Reader;* and Terry Eagleton, *The Ideology of the Aesthetic.*

52. Here I follow Kate Soper's suggestion in "Productive Contradictions," in *Up Against Foucault,* 29–50.

53. Foucault, *HS 1,* 66.

54. In addition to the regimen of dietetics, *The Use of Pleasure* also examines economics, erotics, and philosophy in the use of the pleasures and the stylization of sexuality.

55. Foucault, *The Use of Pleasure,* 251.

56. See François Ewald, "A Power Without an Exterior," in *Michel Foucault Philosopher,* ed. Timothy J. Armstrong (New York: Routledge, 1992), 169–75.

57. See Jean Grimshaw, "Practices of Freedom."

58. Flax, "Beyond Equality: Gender, Justice and Difference," 202.

59. McNay, *Foucault & Feminism,* 157.

60. Ibid., 159.

61. Foucault, GE, in *BSH,* 231, 236, 234.

62. Ibid., 236.

63. See Michel Foucault, "The 3rd thing is that this work on the self," manuscript, Berkeley lecture, n.d., Foucault Archives, Paris. Note the similarity between Foucault's claim that the project of constituting one's self as an ethical subject is not complete until the end of one's life and Aristotle's claim that happiness refers to a complete life.

64. Foucault, GE, 237.

65. See *The Gay Science,* no. 290. Friedrich Nietzsche, *The Gay Science,* trans. Walter Kaufmann (New York: Vintage, 1974), 232–3.

66. See Flax, "Beyond Equality: Gender, Justice and Difference," 202; and Foucault, GE, 237.

67. Foucault, "The Ethics of the Concern for Self as a Practice of Freedom," 287.

68. Ibid.

69. Foucault, "Subjectivity and Truth," in *EW 1,* 87–92, 88.

70. Ibid.

71. Foucault, *The Use of Pleasure,* 26.

72. See Foucault, *The Use of Pleasure,* 26–8, and the transcript from Foucault's discussion on 26 April 1983 with Dreyfus and Rabinow at Berkeley. Manuscript. Foucault Archives, Paris.

73. Foucault, *The Use of Pleasure,* 28.

74. Foucault, "The Ethics of the Concern for Self as a Practice of Freedom," 287.

75. Foucault, *The History of Sexuality: Vol. 3: The Care of the Self,* 45. Hereafter *The Care of the Self.*

76. Foucault, "The Ethic of Care for the Self as a Practice of Freedom," 44.

77. Foucault, *The Care of the Self,* 42.

78. Ibid., 51.

79. Ibid., 71.

80. Others who have made this comparison include Isaac Balbus in "Disciplining Women"; Jean Grimshaw in "Practices of Freedom"; Lois McNay in *Foucault & Feminism;* and Jana Sawicki in *Disciplining Foucault,* especially chapters 3, 4, and 5. Balbus, Grimshaw, and McNay contrast what I am calling the feminist relational self with the active self of the later Foucault. They find Foucault's notion of self in his later works individualistic and androcentric. Sawicki's position is closer to my own, which views Foucault's self as similar to the relational view of self held by object relations theorists.

81. Some representative essays dealing with this issue can be found in *Feminist Challenges: Social and Political Theory*, eds. Carole Pateman and Elizabeth Gross (Boston: Northeastern University Press, 1987); *Feminist Interpretations and Political Theory*, eds. Mary Lyndon Shanley and Carole Pateman (University Park: Pennsylvania State University Press, 1991); *Beyond Equality & Difference: Citizenship, Feminist Politics, Female Subjectivity*, eds. Gisela Bock and Susan James (New York: Routledge, 1992); and *Feminism/Postmodernism*, ed. Linda Nicholson (New York: Routledge, 1990).

82. This is by now a commonplace feminist criticism of liberal political theory. For some specific arguments, see the work of Virginia Held, Susan Moller Okin, Seyla Benhabib, and Eva Feder Kittay. The phrase "people do not spring like mushrooms from the earth" refers to Hobbes' view of autonomy. See Seyla Benhabib, "The Generalized and Concrete Other" for a discussion of problems with this view.

83. See Susan Moller Okin, *Justice, Gender and the Family* (New York: Basic Books, 1989).

84. The ethic of care is, of course, not restricted to women. Gilligan says that the rights ethic and the care ethic are themes found in the moral reasoning of both men and women.

85. Carol Gilligan, *In a Different Voice : Psychological Theory and Women's Development* (Cambridge: Harvard University Press, 1982), 8.

86. Nancy Chodorow, *The Reproduction of Mothering: Psychoanalysis and the Sociology of Gender* (Berkeley: University of California Press, 1978), 76.

87. Gilligan, *In a Different Voice,* 32.

88. See Diana T. Meyers, "The Socialized Individual and Individual Autonomy: An Intersection Between Philosophy and Psychology" in *Women and Moral Theory*, and, more recently, Diana T. Meyers *Subjection and Subjectivity: Psychoanalytic Feminism & Moral Philosophy* (New York: Routledge, 1994).

89. Seyla Benhabib, *Situating the Self,* 189.

90. See for instance, *Women and Moral Theory, Explorations in Feminist Ethics*, eds. Eve Browning Cole and Susan Coultrap-McQuinn (Indianapolis: Indiana University

Press, 1992); *Feminist Ethics*, ed. Claudia Card (Lawrence: University of Kansas Press, 1991); Sarah Lucia Hoagland, *Lesbian Ethics: Toward New Value* (Palo Alto: Institute of Lesbian Studies, 1988); and Elisabeth J. Porter, *Women and Moral Identity* (North Sydney: Allen and Unwin, 1991).

91. Michel Foucault, "Two Lectures," in *Power/Knowledge*, 90.

92. See his discussion of this in "The Ethics of the Concern for the Self as a Practice of Freedom" in *EW 1*, 298–9; "Sex, Power and the Politics of Identity" in *EW1*, 167–70; and "The Subject and Power" in *BSH*, 224–5.

93. For the first, second, and third criticisms, see Claudia Card, "Gender and Moral Luck" in *Identity, Character, and Morality: Essays in Moral Psychology*, eds. Owen Flanagan and Amélie Oksenberg Rorty (Cambridge: MIT Press, 1990); Sarah Lucia Hoagland, *Lesbian Ethics*; and Bill Puka, "The Liberation of Caring: A Different Voice for Gilligan's 'Different Voice'" in *An Ethic of Care*. For criticisms of the false universalism and ahistoricism of the theories of Nancy Chodorow and Carol Gilligan, see Nancy Fraser and Linda Nicholson, "Social Criticism Without Philosophy: An Encounter Between Feminism and Postmodernism" in *Feminism/Postmodernism*, ed. Linda Nicholson (New York: Routledge, 1990); *Inessential Woman: Problems of Exclusion in Feminist Thought*, Elizabeth Spelman (Boston: Beacon Press, 1988); Carol Stack, "The Culture of Gender: Women and Men of Color," and Linda Kerber, "Some Cautionary Words for Historians" both in *An Ethic of Care: Feminist and Interdisciplinary Perspectives*, ed. Mary Jeanne Larrabee (New York: Routledge, 1993).

94. For criticisms of Foucault's androcentrism, see Diamond and Quinby, *Feminism and Foucault*, xiv–xvii; Frances Bartkowski, "Epistemic Drift in Foucault" in *Feminism and Foucault*, 43–58; Meaghan Morris, "The Pirate's Fiancée: Feminists and Philosophers, or Maybe Tonight It'll Happen" in *Feminism and Foucault*, 21–42; and Isaac Balbus, "Disciplining Women" in *Feminism as Critique*, 110–27. For criticisms of Foucault's androcentric bias relating specifically to volumes 2 and 3 of *The History of Sexuality*, see Soper, "Productive Contradictions," 39–42; Grimshaw, "Practices of Freedom," 65; and Lynn Hunt, "Foucault's Subject in the History of Sexuality," in *Discourses of Sexuality: From Aristotle to AIDS*, ed. Domna C. Stanton (Ann Arbor: University of Michigan Press, 1992): 78–93.

CHAPTER 4

1. See, for instance, *Bodies that Matter*, Judith Butler (New York: Routledge, 1993); *Volatile Bodies*, Elizabeth Grosz (Bloomington: Indiana University Press, 1994); *Imaginary Bodies*, Moira Gatens (New York: Routledge, 1996); *The Bodies of Women*, Rosalyn Diprose (New York: Routledge, 1994); and *Body Images*, Gail Weiss (New York: Routledge, 1999). Susan Bordo's work on the body is among the earliest (mid–1980s) of sustained attempts to theorize the body from a feminist philosophical approach; see *Unbearable Weight: Feminism, Western Culture and the Body*, Susan Bordo (Berkeley: University of California Press, 1993), which is a collection of her essays.

2. See, for example, Genevieve Lloyd, *Man of Reason* (London: Methuen, 1984), and Elizabeth Spelman, "Woman as Body: Ancient and Contemporary Views," in *Feminist Studies* 8: 1 (1982).

3. See Irene Diamond and Lee Quinby's introduction to *Feminism and Foucault: Reflections on Resistance;* and Bordo's *Unbearable Weight.*

4. See, for example, David Michael Levin, "The Body Politic: The Embodiment of Praxis in Foucault and Habermas" in *Praxis International* 9:1/2 (1989): 112–132, where he argues that Foucault holds both of these positions on the body; he calls the social inscription view the "historicist view" and the naturalistic view the "biologistic view." Many other critics make similar claims; see, for example, Rudi Visker, "From Foucault to Heidegger: A One Way Ticket?" in *Research in Phenomenology* XXI (1991): 116–140; Rudi Visker, "Can Genealogy be Critical? A Somewhat Unromantic Look at Nietzsche and Foucault" in *Man & World* 23 (1990): 441–452; and Jeffrey Minson, *Genealogies of Morals: Nietzsche, Foucault, Donzelot, and the Eccentricity of Ethics* (New York: St. Martin's Press, 1985), especially 92–97. And, as I shall discuss in detail later in this chapter, Judith Butler makes this criticism; see her "Foucault and the Paradox of Bodily Inscription," in *The Body,* ed. Donn Welton (Oxford: Blackwell Publishers, 1999), originally in *The Journal of Philosophy* 86 (1989); see also Judith Butler, *Gender Trouble; Bodies That Matter,* and *The Psychic Life of Power: Theories in Subjection* (Stanford: Stanford University Press, 1997).

5. Michel Foucault, "Nietzsche, Genealogy, History" in *The Foucault Reader,* ed. Paul Rabinow (New York: Pantheon Books, 1984), 83. Hereafter in notes NGH.

6. Judith Butler, *Gender Trouble,* 130.

7. Lois McNay, "The Foucauldian Body and the Exclusion of Experience," 137.

8. Foucault, *Discipline and Punish,* 29.

9. Ibid.

10. Ibid., 30.

11. Deleuze, *Foucault;* see especially 94–123.

12. Michel Foucault, "Body/Power," 58.

13. Foucault, NGH, 82, 83, 83.

14. Ibid., 38, 85.

15. Ibid., 85.

16. Ibid., 89.

17. Ibid., 87.

18. See *Gay Science* no. 7, where Nietzsche says, "Even a comparative history of law or at least of punishment is so far lacking completely." (*The Gay Science,* Friedrich Nietzsche, trans. Walter Kaufmann [New York: Vintage Books, 1974], 81).

19. Foucault, *Discipline and Punish,* 28.

20. Ibid., 136.

21. Ibid., 137.

22. J.-B. de La Salle, *Conduite des ecoles chretiennes,* 1759, quoted in Foucault, *Discipline and Punish,* 150.

23. Foucault, *Discipline and Punish*, 145.

24. Ibid., 148.

25. Ibid., 167.

26. Discourse is a slightly misleading translation of the French *dispositif,* which is also translated as apparatus, deployment, employment, and operation. Because *dispositif* is most often translated as discourse in Robert Hurley's translation from the French, I will continue to use discourse in this book. However, as I argue later in this chapter, the use of discourse to refer to the variety of concrete, specific material practices and institutions that Foucault discusses can be misleading if one associates it with only words or text, rather than concrete material practices and institutions.

27. Michel Foucault, "Confessions of the Flesh," in *Power/Knowledge*, ed. Colin Gordon, trans. Colin Gordon et al. (New York: Pantheon Books, 1980), 194. Gilles Deleuze refers to Foucault's notion of the *dispositif* as concrete social apparatuses; see Deleuze "What is a *dispositif* ?" in *Michel Foucault Philosopher*, ed. and trans. Timothy J. Armstrong, (New York: Routledge, 1989).

28. Foucault, *HS 1*, 11.

29. Ibid., 100.

30. Ibid., 101.

31. Ibid., 64.

32. Moira Gatens traces the distinction to psychologist Robert Stoller's work on sex and gender identity; see her *Imaginary Bodies,* chapter 1, for a critique of the sex/gender distinction.

33. See for instance, Butler's *Gender Trouble* and Gaten's *Imaginary Bodies.*

34. Braidotti, *Nomadic Subjects,* 103.

35. See Grosz, *Volatile Bodies*, chapter 6, for this criticism. And see Jean Grimshaw, "Practices of Freedom," in *Up Against Foucault* for a more general charge of androcentrism.

36. Bartky, *Femininity and Domination*, 65.

37. Susan Bordo, "Anorexia Nervosa: Psychopathology as the Crystallization of Culture" in *Unbearable Weight;* originally in *Philosophical Forum* 17:2 (1985).

38. See Kathryn Pauly Morgan, "Women and the Knife: Cosmetic Surgery and the Colonization of Women's Bodies," in *Hypatia* 6: 3 (1991): 25–53, for a feminist Foucauldian analysis of cosmetic surgery.

39. See Bartky, *Femininity and Domination*, 67–9, where she cites Iris Young, Marianne Wex, Susan Brownmiller, and Nancy Henley. See Henley's *Body Politics* for a good empirical study on the difference between men's and women's movements and gestures.

40. Iris Marion Young, "Throwing Like A Girl: A Phenomenology of Feminine Bodily Comportment, Motility and Spatiality," in *Throwing Like a Girl and Other Essays in Feminist Philosophy and Social Theory* (Bloomington: Indiana University Press, 1990), 141–59; originally in *Human Studies* 3 (1980): 137–156.

41. Arlie Russell Hochschild, *The Managed Heart: Commercialization of Human Feeling* (Berkeley: University of California Press, 1983).

42. Here I must note my disagreement with Elizabeth Grosz's interpretation of Bartky. Grosz says that Bartky sees the "adherence to and investment in these techniques of body marking" as signaling "women's acceptance of and absorption into prevailing patriarchal paradigms" (*Volatile Bodies*, 144). Bartky includes a discussion of the social, cultural, and political context in which the disciplinary practices of femininity arise; thus her account does not portray women as eager co-conspirators in the patriarchal norms of femininity. Therefore, it is not simply a psychological investigation, as Grosz claims.

43. Given this, it is surprising that Foucault for the most part avoided discussions of gender and sexual difference and women's issues. As mentioned earlier, his discussion of the body is in gender-neutral terms. Perhaps this oversight is intentional, because although sex is fundamentally constitutive of the body and of identity, it does not have to be. I discuss this further in chapter 5. See Foucault's *The History of Sexuality Vol. 1* and *Herculine Barbin* for extended discussions of the historical production of sex through the discourse of sexuality.

44. See Susan Bordo, "Docile Bodies, Rebellious Bodies: A Foucauldian Perspective on Female Psychopathology," in *Writing the Politics of Difference*, ed. Hugh J. Silverman (Albany: State University of New York Press, 1991), hereafter in text and notes "Docile Bodies"; "Feminism and the Politics of the Body," in *Up Against Foucault*; "The Body and the Reproduction of Femininity," in *Gender/Body/Knowledge: Feminist Reconstructions of Being and Knowing*, eds. Alison M. Jaggar and Susan R. Bordo (New Brunswick: Rutgers University Press, 1989); and "Anorexia Nervosa and the Crystallization of Culture," in *Unbearable Weight*, hereafter in text and notes "Anorexia Nervosa."

45. Bordo, "Docile Bodies," 210–1.

46. Bordo, "Anorexia Nervosa," 141.

47. Foucault, "Body/Power," 57.

48. Bartky, *Femininity and Domination*, 81.

49. Foucault, "Body/Power," 56.

50. Foucault, "Technologies of the Self," in *EW 1*, 234.

51. Foucault, *The Use of Pleasure*, 108.

52. Butler, *Gender Trouble*, 25.

53. Ibid., 8.

54. Butler, *Bodies That Matter*, 9; in the original, this phrase is italicized.

55. Ibid., 10.

56. She also deals with race in her discussion of Nella Larson's *Passing*, but her focus is on gender, sex, and sexuality.

57. For example, Martha Nussbaum, "The Professor of Parody," and Seyla Benhabib, "Feminism and Postmodernism: An Uneasy Alliance," in *Feminist Contentions*.

58. See, for example David Michael Levin, "The Body Politic," Rudi Visker, "Can Genealogy Be Critical?" and Jeffrey Minson, *Genealogies of Morals.*

59. See Judith Butler, "Foucault and the Paradox of Bodily Inscription," in *The Body,* ed. Donn Welton (Oxford: Blackwell Publishers, 1999), originally in *The Journal of Philosophy* 86 (1989); and *Gender Trouble,* 128–33.

60. Grosz, *Volatile Bodies,* 155.

61. Foucault, NGH, 83.

62. Butler, *Gender Trouble,* 130.

63. Butler, *Bodies That Matter,* 33.

64. Ibid. 189, 192.

65. Ibid., 6.

66. Butler, *The Psychic Life of Power,* 84.

67. Ibid., 90.

68. Foucault uses both these terms to refer to the operations of power on the body through discourses and disciplines; see, for example *HS 1,* 58–63 and *Discipline and Punish,* 138, where he speaks of subjection, and see *Discipline and Punish* 149, 161, 167, where he speaks of individualization.

69. For Butler's use of J. L. Austin, see *Bodies That Matter* and *Excitable Speech: A Politics of the Performative* (New York: Routledge, 1997); for her use of Althusser, see *Bodies That Matter* and *The Psychic Life of Power.*

70. Susan Bordo, "Postmodern Subjects, Postmodern Bodies, Postmodern Resistance" in *Unbearable Weight,* 277–300, 292.

71. See NGH 85, 87, where Foucault uses marked, engraved, and molded. In *Discipline and Punish,* he uses terms such as shaped, trained, responds, increases its forces.

72. Foucault, *Discipline and Punish,* 136.

73. Ibid., 161, 162.

74. Ibid., 172.

75. Ibid., 176–7.

76. The Panopticon was Jeremy Bentham's plan for a prison that was never built.

77. Elizabeth Grosz uses this inside/outside distinction throughout *Volatile Bodies* to articulate the formation of embodied selves, although the inside and outside are always related—she uses the metaphor of a mobius strip. While Grosz places Foucault's work clearly on the side of social inscription (the outside), and relies on other sources, notably psychoanalytic, for the inside, I suggest that Foucault's "outside" is connected to an inside.

78. Foucault, "Body/Power," 59.

79. See Foucault, *Discipline and Punish,* 136.

80. He also calls the intelligible body the analysable body and the useful body the manipulable body.

81. Foucault, *The Birth of the Clinic,* xix.

82. See Foucault, *The Birth of the Clinic,* 3—disease; 117—mystery; 129—tissues; 138, 162—organic system; 122—tactile object; 31–197, especially 165—visible object; and 60, 84, 111, 167—case history.

83. Foucault, *Discipline and Punish,* 190, 191.

84. Foucault, *HS 1,* 32.

85. See Boston Women's Health Book Collective, *Our Bodies, Ourselves* (New York: Simon and Schuster, 1984); Emily Martin, *The Woman in the Body: A Cultural Analysis of Reproduction* (Boston: Beacon Press, 1989); Anne Fausto-Sterling, *Myths of Gender: Biological Theories About Men and Women* (New York: Basic Books, 1992); and Anne Fausto-Sterling, *Sexing the Body: Gender Politics and the Construction of Sexuality* (New York: Basic Books, 2000).

86. See, for instance, David M. Halperin, *Saint=Foucault: Towards a Gay Hagiography* (Oxford: Oxford University Press, 1995); and McWhorter, *Bodies & Pleasures;* Butler, *Bodies That Matter,* and *Gender Trouble;* and Dews "Power and Subjectivity in Foucault."

87. See Halperin's *Saint=Foucault* for the former and McWhorter's *Bodies & Pleasures* for the latter.

88. Foucault, *HS 1,* 96.

89. Ibid., 96.

90. Ibid., 157.

91. Anne Koedt, "The Myth of the Vaginal Orgasm" in *Radical Feminism: A Documentary Reader,* ed. Barbara A. Crow (New York: New York University Press, 2000) 371–377, 373.

92. Marilyn Frye, "Lesbian 'Sex'," in *Willful Virgin: Essays in Feminism* (Freedom, CA: Crossing Press, 1992): 109–119, 110.

93. Frye, "Lesbian 'Sex'," 115. In this way, it differs from gay male sex, Frye says, which has a fully developed, explicit language.

94. Ibid., 113.

95. One could say that this strategy is a type of Nietzschean transvaluation.

96. Frye, "Lesbian 'Sex'," 117.

97. Ibid., 116.

98. One can only speculate what Foucault's treatment of this topic would have been in his book on the hysterization of women if he had completed his *History of Sexuality* series as originally conceived.

CHAPTER 5

1. See, for instance, *Feminist Contentions*, where Seyla Benhabib supports the notion of identity (and subjectivity and norms) as necessary for liberatory politics, Judith Butler argues that these notions themselves contribute to oppression, and Nancy Fraser takes a middle position; Seyla Benhabib et al., *Feminist Contentions: A Philosophical Exchange* (New York: Routledge, 1995). For feminist criticisms of identity politics, see: Shane Phelan, *Identity Politics: Lesbian Feminism and the Limits of Community* (Philadelphia: Temple University Press, 1989); Elizabeth Spelman, *Inessential Woman: Problems of Exclusion in Feminist Thought* (Boston: Beacon Press, 1988); Jana Sawicki, "Identity Politics and Sexual Freedom" in *Disciplining Foucault;* Judith Butler, *Gender Trouble;* Diana Fuss, *Essentially Speaking;* Denise Riley *"Am I That Name?" Feminism and the Category of 'Women' in History* (Minneapolis: University of Minnesota Press, 1988); and Ann Ferguson, "Is There a Lesbian Culture?" in *Lesbian Philosophies and Cultures,* ed. Jeffner Allen (Albany: State University of New York Press, 1990) and "Patriarchy, Sexual Identity, and the Sexual Revolution," in *Feminist Theory: A Critique of Ideology,* eds. Nannerl O. Keohane et al. (Chicago: University of Chicago Press, 1982). Those who support some version of identity politics or argue that we need to retain the category of identity for an effective feminist politics include: Seyla Benhabib, *Situating the Self,* Nancy Hartsock, *The Feminist Standpoint Revisited,* and Rosi Braidotti, *Nomadic Subjects.*

2. For example, the gay and lesbian movement, and some movements for racial justice.

3. As I have shown in chapter 1, there are significant differences among these positions. However, all assume some version of a unified subject, and each relies on the category "women."

4. Steven Seidman, "Identity and Politics in a 'Postmodern' Gay Culture: Some Historical and Conceptual Notes," in *Fear of a Queer Planet: Queer Politics and Social Theory,* ed. Michael Warner (Minneapolis: University of Minnesota Press, 1993), 107.

5. Combahee River Collective, "A Black Feminist Statement," in *This Bridge Called My Back: Writings by Radical Women of Color,* eds. Cherrie Moraga and Gloria Anzaldua (New York: Kitchen Table Press, 1981), 212.

6. See the feminist critics of identity politics cited in note 1 of this chapter.

7. Steven Seidman uses this term in "Identity and Politics in a 'Postmodern' Gay Culture: Some Historical and Conceptual Notes," noting that an ethnic minority model emphasizes "cultural difference, community building, and identity-based interest-group politics" (117). I will instead use the term identity politics, which I view as synonymous to "ethnic identity model."

8. See Denise Riley for an example of the ways that the concept "woman" functioned to systematically exclude some women, for example, Black women, from the category.

9. See Bat-Ami Bar On, "Marginality and Epistemic Privilege," in *Feminist Epistemologies,* eds. Linda Alcoff and Elizabeth Potter (New York: Routledge, 1993), for a critique of the view that members of a marginalized social group have epistemic privilege simply based on that marginalization.

10. Although essentialism is associated with identity politics and social constructionism with opposition to identity politics, here I wish to steer clear of setting the debate
up as essentialism vs. social constructionism. It seems obvious that advocates of identity
politics do not have to believe in or appeal to some ahistorical essence in order to appeal to
identity. Identity politics advocates could see identity as socially and historically constituted.
The real issue is about whether or not to appeal to identity regardless of its basis. I demonstrate that proponents and opponents of identity politics are closer on this issue than might
first appear.

11. Ian Hacking, *The Social Construction of What?* (Cambridge: Harvard University
Press, 1999). Hacking's discussion clarifies how social construction has been used and to
what it might best apply.

12. Fuss, *Essentially Speaking,* 5.

13. Foucault, "Sex, Power and the Politics of Identity," in *EW 1,* 166.

14. Ibid.

15. Foucault, *HS 1,* 59.

16. I am using natural and cultural here, although Foucault does not see them as
diametrically opposed. Indeed, part of his point is that they are inseparable.

17. Many feminist critics of identity politics hold this position. See, for instance,
Butler, *Gender Trouble,* Riley, *"Am I That Name?",* Fuss, *Essentially Speaking,* and Weedon,
Feminist Practice.

18. This is an especially crucial issue for womyn-only space, such as the Michigan
Womyn's Music Festival.

19. Identity politics often unintentionally pits one oppressed group against another.
A historical example is the polarization of women and Blacks around the issue of the vote
during suffrage. Sandra Harding in *The Science Question in Feminism* uses the term "frac-
tured identities" when she talks about identity politics and hyphenated identities.

20. Michel Foucault, "Polemics, Politics and Problematizations: An Interview with
Michel Foucault," in *The Foucault Reader,* 385.

21. Judith Butler, "Contingent Foundations," in *Feminist Contentions,* 48.

22. Foucault, "Sex, Power and the Politics of Identity," in *EW 1,* 166.

23. Michel Foucault, "Truth, Power, Self: An Interview with Michel Foucault" in
Technologies of the Self, 15.

24. Foucault, "Sex, Power and the Politics of Identity," in *EW 1,* 164.

25. See Charles Taylor, "The Politics of Recognition," in *Multiculturalism,* ed. Amy
Gutman (Princeton: Princeton University Press, 1994), for an argument about the importance of identity as a political category.

26. Feminists have been making this case in different ways for many years. The early
demonstrations during the women's movement against beauty pageants were an attempt to
draw attention to the ways that the pageants contributed to the objectification of women

by focusing on their appearance. The antipornography movement also claims that the representation of women as sexual objects contributes to their devaluation in society. And, more recently, feminists have argued that depictions of women in advertising and the media contribute to women's low status, as well as shaping our self-perception. See Susan Bordo's *Unbearable Weight* for a Foucauldian feminist approach to this issue.

27. See Shane Phelan, *Identity Politics*, for another extended contemporary example, and see Denise Riley, *"Am I That Name?"*, for the historical exclusions perpetuated by identity politics.

28. Some examples of sex-related rights and responsibilities are: single-sex bathrooms, possible careers, marriageable partners, and obligation to defend one's country.

29. Anne Fausto-Sterling estimates that the figure for intersex births is approximately 1.7 percent; see 51-4 in *Sexing the Body: Gender Politics and the Construction of Sexuality* (New York: Basic Books, 2000).

30. Alice Domurat Dreger, *Hermaphrodites and the Medical Invention of Sex* (Cambridge: Harvard University Press, 1998), 109.

31. Adrienne Rich's article "Compulsory Heterosexuality and Lesbian Existence" in *The Signs Reader* (Chicago: University of Chicago Press, 1983), 139–168, is the *locus classicus* of this argument. For related arguments, see Marilyn Frye, "Sexism," and "To See and Be Seen" in *The Politics of Reality: Essays in Feminist Theory* (New York: Crossing Press 1983); Sarah Hoagland, "'Femininity', Resistance and Sabotage," in *Women and Values: Readings in Recent Feminist Philosophy*, ed. Marilyn Pearsall (Belmont, CA: Wadsworth Publishing, 1993); and Suzanne Pharr, *Homophobia: A Weapon of Sexism* (Little Rock, AR: Chardon Press, 1988).

32. See Alice Domurat Dreger, *Hermaphrodites and the Medical Invention of Sex*, and Anne Fausto-Sterling, *Sexing the Body: Gender Politics and the Construction of Sexuality*.

33. Anne Fausto-Sterling, "The Five Sexes" in *The Sciences* (March/April 1993): 20–24, see her more recent "The Five Sexes, Revisited" in *The Sciences* (July/August 2000): 18–23.

34. In the text, Herculine has several different names: her full name, Adelaide Herculine Barbin; her nickname, Alexina; the name in her memoirs, Camille; and the name she went by after being designated a man, Abel. In the interest of clarity, I have called her Herculine throughout this chapter, even in the quotes where she is referred to by another name.

35. Michel Foucault, "Preface to *The History of Sexuality, Volume Two*" in *EW 1*, 202.

36. See Dreger, *Hermaphrodites and the Medical Invention of Sex* for a comprehensive study of hermaphrodites in France and England during this period.

37. This is true, for example, in his work with the *Groupe d'Information sur les Prisons*, where he facilitated the prisoners speaking and writing about their own situation.

38. Michel Foucault, *Herculine Barbin: Being the Recently Discovered Memoirs of a Nineteenth-Century Hermaphrodite*, trans. Richard McDougall (New York: Pantheon Books, 1980).

39. Foucault, *Herculine Barbin*, xiii.

40. Ibid., vii.

41. Ibid., viii.

42. Ibid., ix.

43. Ibid., ix.

44. I am using these terms in the standard way—sex refers to anatomical body, gender to social role, and sexual orientation to the object of one's erotic desire.

45. "A Scandal at the Convent" by Oscar Panizza in *Herculine Barbin*. And the medical articles: Chesnut, "Question d'identité. Vice de conformation des organes génitaux—hypospadias—erreur sur le sexe" in *Annales d'hygiène publique et de médecine légale*, 1860, 206–209. E. Goujon, "Étude d'un cas d'hermaphrodisme bisexuel imparfait chez l'homme" in *Journal de l'anatomie et de la physiologie de l'homme*, 1869, 599–616. A. Tardieu, "Mémoire sur la question médico-légale de l'identité" in *Annales d'hygiène publique et de médecine légale*, 1872, 149–169 and 384–408.

46. Foucault, *Herculine Barbin*, 129.

47. Ibid., 26.

48. Ibid., 160.

49. Ibid., 107.

50. Hoagland, "'Femininity,' Resistance, and Sabotage," 90.

51. Foucault, *Herculine Barbin*, 127–8.

52. These terms come from Adrienne Rich's article, "Compulsory Heterosexuality and Lesbian Existence"; for other arguments claiming that lesbian existence is rendered at least invisible and perhaps impossible by the dominant phallocratic conceptual scheme, see Hoagland, *Lesbian Ethics*, and Frye, *The Politics of Reality*.

53. Dreger, *Hermaphrodites*, 83.

54. See Pharr, *Homophobia*.

55. Although at first the gay liberation movement included lesbians (post Stonewall), by the early 1970s lesbian feminists were organizing as a separate group. See Sidney Abbot and Barbara Love, *Sappho Was a Right-On Woman* (New York: Stein and Day, 1972); *Lesbianism and the Women's Movement*, eds. Charlotte Bunch and Nancy Myron (Baltimore: Diana Press, 1975); and John D'Emilio, *Sexual Politics, Sexual Communities* (Chicago: University of Chicago Press, 1983), especially Part IV.

56. In this section, I use "sexuality" as a synonym for sexual orientation because, as will become clear, bisexuality both claims to be a sexual orientation and challenges the idea of a fixed sexual orientation.

57. See John D' Emilio, *Sexual Politics, Sexual Communities*, for a history of homosexuality in the United States from 1940 to 1970 and the connections among the gay liberation, feminist and civil rights movements.

58. *Bi Any Other Name: Bisexual People Speak Out,* eds. Loraine Hutchins and Lani Ka'ahumanu (Boston: Alyson Publications, 1991); *Closer to Home: Bisexuality & Feminism,* ed. Elizabeth Reba Weise (Seattle: Seal Press, 1992); *Bisexual Politics: Theories, Queries & Visions,* ed. Naomi Tucker (New York: Harrington Park Press, 1995); and Marjorie Garber, *Vice Versa: Bisexuality and the Eroticism of Everyday Life* (New York: Simon and Schuster, 1995).

59. See *Bi Any Other Name, Closer to Home,* and *Bisexual Politics.*

60. Carol A. Queen, "The Queer in Me," in *Bi Any Other Name,* 17.

61. Elizabeth Reba Weise, Introduction, *Closer to Home,* xv.

62. Garber, *Vice Versa,* 47.

63. See, for example, Jonathan Katz, *The Invention of Heterosexuality* (New York: Penguin Books, 1995); David Halperin, *One Hundred Years of Homosexuality and Other Essays on Greek Love* (New York: Routledge, 1990); and Foucault's *HS 1.*

64. See Garber, *Vice Versa,* 69ff, and Dajenya "We Claim Our Own" in *Bisexual Politics.*

65. Sigmund Freud, *Introductory Lectures on Psychoanalysis* (New York: W. W. Norton, 1966), 377.

66. Sigmund Freud, "Three Essays on Sexuality," in *The Complete Psychological Works of Sigmund Freud, Vol. VII* (London: Hogarth Press, 1953), 136.

67. Foucault, *HS 1,* 43.

68. Rebecca Kaplan, "Your Fence Is Sitting on Me: The Hazards of Binary Thinking," in *Bisexual Politics,* 278.

69. Steven Seidman claims that "Gay liberation is a movement of human sexual liberation" and notes that Dennis Altman draws on a Freudian-Marxist framework that assumes "the essentially polymorphous and bisexual needs of the human being." ("Identity and Politics in a 'Postmodern' Gay Culture: Some Historical and Conceptual Notes," 113.)

70. Ibid., 115.

71. Garber, *Vice Versa,* 90.

72. Lani Ka'ahumanu, "It Ain't Over 'Til the Bisexual Speaks," in *Bisexual Politics,* 66.

73. Ibid.. The amendment to article 2 of Colorado's State Constitution prohibits "any law or policy which provides that homosexual, lesbian or bisexual orientation, conduct or relationships constitutes or entitles a person to claim any minority or protected status, quota preferences, or discrimination" (Ibid., 68).

74. Foucault, *HS 1,* 47.

75. Ibid., 101.

76. See Charles Taylor's "The Politics of Recognition" for an elaboration of the claim that recognition is fundamentally social (because intersubjective) and that the withholding of recognition can be a form of oppression.

77. Combahee River Collective, "A Black Feminist Statement," 217.

78. See Judith Butler, "Merely Cultural" in *New Left Review* 227 (1998): 33–44 for an argument against this claim. She argues that the regulation of sexuality is systematically tied to the functioning of the political economy.

79. Sandra Lee Bartky, "On Psychological Oppression," in *Femininity and Domination*.

80. Unfortunately, David Halperin indulges in just this sort of bi-bashing in his otherwise good book, *Saint=Foucault;* see especially 65–6.

81. See Garber, *Vice Versa*, chapter 3, for a more in-depth analysis of this phenomenon.

82. Ibid., 47.

83. Ibid., 66.

84. Michel Foucault, "Nietzsche, Freud, Marx" in *Critical Texts* 3: 2 (1986), quoted in Gatens, *Imaginary Bodies*, 83.

85. One example is the introduction of "sexual harassment" into legal discourse and common usage in the 1970s.

86. For an overview of this issue, see *Intersex in the Age of Ethics*, ed. Alice Domurat Dreger (Hagerstown, MD: University Publishing Group, 1999).

87. Another example of the power of normative categories and their effects on bodies through surgery is women and the beauty ideal. See Kathryn Pauly Morgan, "Women and the Knife" for her discussion of women and cosmetic surgery.

88. Michael Warner, Introduction, *Fear of a Queer Planet*, xxvi.

CHAPTER 6

1. See especially Foucault's contributions in the edited collection *Technologies of the Self.*

2. Michel Foucault, "Subjectivity and Truth," in *EW 1*, 87.

3. Foucault, "What is Enlightenment?" 46.

4. Michel Foucault, "Sexuality and Solitude," in *EW 1*, 177.

5. Michel Foucault, "Technologies of the Self," in *Technologies of the Self*, 18.

6. Michel Foucault, "The Political Technology of Individuals," in *Technologies of the Self*, 145.

7. This is what Foucault refers to as the history of the present in *Discipline and Punish*.

8. Foucault, "The Political Technology of Individuals," 146.

9. See Michel Foucault, "Subjectivity and Truth" in *The Politics of Truth*, eds. Sylvere Lotringer and Lysa Hochroth (New York: Semiotext(e), 1997), 171–198, originally published in *Political Theory*, 21:2 (1993).

10. Foucault, *The Use of Pleasure*, 108.

11. See, for instance, Charles Taylor, *Sources of the Self: The Making of Modern Identity* (Cambridge: Harvard University Press, 1989).

12. Foucault, "Technologies of the Self," 27.

13. Michel Foucault, "The Hermeneutic of the Subject," in *EW 1*, 101.

14. Michel Foucault, "Self Writing," in *EW 1*, 210.

15. Foucault, *The Care of the Self*, 61.

16. Foucault, "Self-Writing," 216.

17. Ibid., 221.

18. Foucault, *HS 1*, 63.

19. Foucault, GE, 250.

20. Michel Foucault, "The Masked Philosopher," in *EW 1*, 327.

21. Michel Foucault, "Preface to *The History of Sexuality, Volume Two*," in *EW 1*, 205.

22. Morwenna Griffiths suggests something like this as a possible model for a feminist self in her *Feminisms and the Self: The Web of Identity* (New York: Routledge, 1995). She refers to it as critical autobiography.

23. Foucault, GE, 235.

24. Ibid., 239.

25. Michel Foucault, Cours du 19/2/83 au Collège de France, "Le gouvernement de soi et des autres," cassette 68 (07), Foucault Archives, Paris.

26. Michel Foucault, Cours du 12/1/83 au Collège de France, "Le gouvernement de soi et des autres," cassette 68 (03), Foucault Archives, Paris.

27. Foucault, "Technologies of the Self" in *Technologies of the Self*, 35.

28. Here I am drawing on Thomas Flynn's analysis of *parrhesia* in his "Foucault as Parrhesiast: his last course at the Collège de France," in *The Final Foucault*, eds. James Bernauer and David Rasmussen (Cambridge: MIT Press, 1988), as well as Foucault's essay "Technologies of the Self" and cassette tapes of Foucault's "Le gouvernment de soi et des autres," his course at the Collège de France, winter 1983.

29. Claudia Dreifus, *Women's Fate: Raps From a Feminist Consciousness-Raising Group* (New York: Bantam Books, 1973), 5.

30. Much of this history is based on the account given in Alice Echols' *Daring to Be Bad: Radical Feminism in America 1967–75* (Minneapolis: University of Minnesota Press, 1989), and from primary documents from the period. See also Sara Evans, *Personal Politics:*

The Roots of Women's Liberation in the Civil Rights Movement & the New Left (New York: Vintage Books, 1980) for a first-person account. And for some of the classic writings in the early period of the women's movement, see *Sisterhood is Powerful: An Anthology of Writings from the Women's Liberation Movement,* ed. Robin Morgan (New York: Vintage Books, 1970), and *Radical Feminism,* eds. Anne Koedt, Ellen Levine, and Anita Rapone (New York: Quadrangle Press, 1973).

31. Of course, the search for a universal common experience was problematic because it ignored salient differences due to racial, class, and sexuality-based oppression.

32. Dreifus, *Women's Fate,* 5.

33. Note that the criticism of individualism parallels the criticism made of the ethical subject in Foucault's later work.

34. Dreifus, *Women's Fate,* 6.

35. Ibid., 7.

36. Pamela Allen, *Free Space: A Perspective on the Small Group in Women's Liberation* (New York: Times Change Press, 1970), 13.

37. See, for instance, Pamela Allen, *Free Space*; Harriet Perl and Gay Abarbanell, *Guidelines to Feminist Consciousness-Raising* (self published, 1979), Femina Collection, Northwestern University Library; L. A. NOW C-R Committee, *Consciousness-Raising Handbook* (Los Angeles, 1974), Femina Collection, Northwestern University Library; and Jane Freeman and Marge Piercy, *Getting Together: How To Start a Women's Liberation Group* (Boston: New England Free Press, n.d.), Femina Collection, Northwestern University Library.

38. Allen, *Free Space,* 30.

39. Perl and Abarbanell, *Guidelines to Feminist Consciousness-Raising,* 24.

40. Ibid., 16.

41. See Alice Echols, *Daring to Be Bad,* for a historical account of the role consciousness-raising played in radical feminism, especially 83–92.

42. Echols, *Daring to Be Bad,* 83.

43. Perl and Abarbanell, *Guidelines to Feminist Consciousness-Raising,* 16.

44. See L. A. NOW C-R Committee, *Consciousness-Raising Handbook,* 4.

45. Redstockings, "Redstockings Manifesto," in *Sisterhood is Powerful,* 535.

46. Although personal choices can certainly be the result of political and moral convictions, for instance, vegetarianism, reduction of energy consumption, composting, recycling, not marrying, buying only organic food, etc. And, of course, there are ways that political actions depend on individual action, as in the case of boycotts.

47. Perl and Abarbanell, *Guidelines to Feminist Consciousness-Raising,* 3.

48. Foucault, "What is Enlightenment?" 46.

49. Foucault, GE, 236.

50. Foucault, "The Ethics of the Concern for Self as a Practice of Freedom," in *EW 1*, 301.

51. Michel Foucault, "Social Triumph of the Sexual Will," in *EW 1*, 160, 158.

52. Ibid., 159–60.

53. Foucault, "Sex. Power and the Politics of Identity," in *EW 1*, 164.

54. Michael P. Nichols and Richard C. Schwartz, *Family Therapy: Concepts and Methods* (Needham Hts., MA: Allyn and Bacon, 1998), 403.

55. Jill Freedman and Gene Combs, *Narrative Therapy: The Social Construction of Preferred Realities* (New York: Norton, 1996), 14, cited in *Family Therapy: Concepts and Methods*, 404.

56. See their introduction to *Daring to Be Good: Essays in Feminist Ethico-Politics*, eds. Bat-Ami Bar On and Ann Ferguson (New York: Routledge, 1998), i–xix.

57. Ibid., xiii.

58. Alison M. Jaggar, "Feminist Ethics: Projects, Problems, Prospects" in *Feminist Ethics*, 78–104.

59. Foucault, GE, in *BSH* 231; see also 234 for his claim that we cannot return to Greek ideals.

60. See, for example, his discussions in "Politics and Ethics: An Interview"; and "Polemics, Politics and Problematizations," both in *The Foucault Reader*, 373–80, 381–90.

CONCLUSION

1. Michel Foucault, "The Political Technology of Individuals," in *Technologies of the Self*, 145–62, 146.

2. Foucault, "What is Enlightenment?" 50.

3. Michel Foucault, "What Our Present Is," in *Foucault Live*, 410.

4. Michel Foucault, "Governmentality," in *The Foucault Effect: Studies in Govern-mentality*, eds. Graham Burchell, Colin Gordon, and Peter Miller (Chicago: University of Chicago Press, 1991), 102.

5. Ibid., 100.

6. See, for instance, Emily Martin, *The Woman in the Body*. Viewing women's role in reproduction as passive has a long history that goes back to Aristotle.

7. The effect of scientific discourse is most evident with respect to the life sciences, such as biology, medicine, physiology, etc., and the human sciences, such as psychology, sociology, political science, etc.

8. In terms of political and social analysis, scientific discourse could be seen as the "means of interpretation." I would argue that for a fuller understanding of our contemporary situation this aspect should be added to the means of production and the means of reproduction.

9. And some feminists, such as Moira Gatens, draw an analogy between representations of the body and political representation; see her *Imaginary Bodies,* especially chapter 2.

10. Michel Foucault, "Politics and the Study of Discourse," in *The Foucault Effect,* 65.

11. For accounts of the women's movement in the United States, see Paula Giddings, *When and Where I Enter: The Impact of Black Women on Race and Sex in America* (New York: Bantam Books, 1984); Alice Echols, *Daring to be Bad;* and Sara Evans, *Personal Politics.*

12. Leslie Feinberg, *Stone Butch Blues* (Ithaca, NY: Firebrand Books, 1993); Leslie Feinberg, *Transgender Warriors: Making History from Joan of Arc to Dennis Rodman* (Boston: Beacon Press, 1996); and Riki Anne Wilchins, *Read My Lips: Sexual Subversion and the End of Gender* (Ithaca, NY: Firebrand Books, 1997).

▶●◀

BIBLIOGRAPHY

Abbot, Sidney, and Barbara Love. *Sappho Was a Right-On Woman*. New York: Stein and Day, 1972.

Alcoff, Linda. "Cultural Feminism Versus Poststructuralism: The Identity Crisis in Feminist Theory." *Signs: Journal of Women in Culture and Society* 13:3 (1988): 405–436.

———. "Feminist Politics and Foucault: The Limits to a Collaboration." In *Crises in Continental Philosophy*. Edited by Arleen Dallery and Charles Scott. Albany: State University of New York Press, 1990.

Alcoff, Linda, and Elizabeth Potter, eds. *Feminist Epistemologies*. New York: Routledge, 1993.

Allen, Amy. *The Power of Feminist Theory: Domination, Resistance, Solidarity*. Boulder: Westview Press, 1999.

Allen, Jeffner, ed. *Lesbian Philosophies and Cultures*. Albany: State University of New York Press, 1990.

Allen, Pamela. *Free Space: A Perspective on the Small Group in Women's Liberation*. New York: Times Change Press, 1970.

Armstrong, Timothy J., ed. and trans. *Michel Foucault Philosopher*. New York: Routledge, 1992.

Balbus, Isaac. "Disciplining Women: Michel Foucault and the Power of Feminist Discourse." In *Feminism as Critique*. Edited by Seyla Benhabib and Drucilla Cornell. Minneapolis : University of Minnesota Press, 1988.

Bar On, Bat-Ami. "Marginality and Epistemic Privilege." In *Feminist Epistemologies*. Edited by Linda Alcoff and Elizabeth Potter. New York: Routledge, 1993.

Bar On, Bat-Ami, and Ann Ferguson, eds. *Daring to Be Good: Essays in Feminist Ethico-Politics*. New York: Routledge, 1998.

Bartkowski, Frances. "Epistemic Drift in Foucault." In *Feminism and Foucault: Reflections on Resistance*. Edited by Irene Diamond and Lee Quinby, 43–58. Boston: Northeastern University Press, 1988.

Bartky, Sandra Lee. *Femininity and Domination: Studies in the Phenomenology of Oppression.* New York: Routledge, 1990.

Bell, Diane, and Renate Klein, eds. *Radically Speaking: Feminism Reclaimed.* North Melbourne: Spinifex Press, 1996.

Benhabib, Seyla. "The Generalized and the Concrete Other: The Kohlberg-Gilligan Controversy and Moral Theory." In *Women and Moral Theory.* Edited by Eva Feder Kittay and Diana T. Meyers. Totowa, NJ: Rowman & Littlefield Publishers, 1987.

———. *Situating the Self: Gender, Community and Postmodernism in Contemporary Ethics.* New York: Routledge, 1992.

Benhabib, Seyla, and Drucilla Cornell, eds. *Feminism as Critique.* Minneapolis: University of Minnesota Press, 1988.

Benhabib, Seyla et al. *Feminist Contentions: A Philosophical Exchange.* New York: Routledge, 1995.

Bernauer, James, and David Rasmussen, eds. *The Final Foucault.* Cambridge: MIT Press, 1988.

Bock, Gisela, and Susan James, eds. *Beyond Equality and Difference: Citizenship, Feminist Politics, Female Subjectivity.* New York: Routledge, 1992.

Bordo, Susan. "The Body and the Reproduction of Femininity." In *Gender/Body/Knowledge: Feminist Reconstructions of Being and Knowing.* Edited by Alison Jaggar and Susan Bordo. New Brunswick: Rutgers University Press, 1989.

———. "Docile Bodies, Rebellious Bodies: Foucauldian Perspectives on Female Psychopathology." In *Writing the Politics of Difference.* Edited by Hugh J. Silverman. Albany: State University of New York Press, 1991.

———. "Anorexia Nervosa: Psychopathology as the Crystallization of Culture." In *Unbearable Weight: Feminism, Western Culture and the Body.* Berkeley: University of California Press, 1993. Originally in *Philosophical Forum* 17:2 (1985).

———. *Unbearable Weight: Feminism, Western Culture and the Body.* Berkeley: University of California Press, 1993.

———. "Postmodern Subjects, Postmodern Bodies, Postmodern Resistance." In *Unbearable Weight: Feminism, Western Culture and the Body.* Berkeley: University of California Press, 1993.

———. "Feminism and the Politics of the Body." In *Up Against Foucault: Explorations of Some Tensions Between Foucault and Feminism.* Edited by Caroline Ramazanoglu. New York: Routledge, 1993.

Boston Women's Health Book Collective. *Our Bodies, Ourselves.* New York: Simon and Schuster, 1984.

Bouchard, Donald F., ed. *Language, Counter-Memory and Practice.* Translated by Donald F. Bouchard and Sherry Simon. Ithaca: Cornell University Press, 1977.

Bouvard, Marguerite Guzman. *Revolutionizing Motherhood: The Mothers of the Plaza de Mayo*. Wilmington, DE: Scholarly Resources, 1994.

Braidotti, Rosi. *Nomadic Subjects: Embodiment and Sexual Difference in Contemporary Feminist Theory*. New York: Columbia University Press, 1994.

Brodribb, Somer. *Nothing Mat(t)ers: A Feminist Critique of Postmodernism*. North Melbourne: Spinifex Press, 1992.

Bunch, Charlotte, and Nancy Myron, eds. *Lesbianism and the Women's Movement*. Baltimore: Diana Press, 1975.

Burchell, Graham, Colin Gordon, and Peter Miller, eds. *The Foucault Effect: Studies in Governmentality*. Chicago: University of Chicago Press, 1991.

Butler, Judith. *Gender Trouble: Feminism and the Subversion of Identity*. New York: Routledge, 1990.

———. "Contingent Foundations: Feminism and the Question of Postmodernism." In *Praxis International* 11:2 (1991).

———. *Bodies That Matter*. New York: Routledge, 1993.

———. *The Psychic Life of Power: Theories in Subjection*. Stanford: Stanford University Press, 1997.

———. *Excitable Speech: A Politics of the Performative*. New York: Routledge, 1997.

———. "Merely Cultural." In *The New Left Review* 227 (1998): 33–44.

———. "Foucault and the Paradox of Bodily Inscription." In *The Body*. Edited by Donn Welton. Oxford: Blackwell Publishers, 1999. Originally in *The Journal of Philosophy* 86 (1989).

Card, Claudia. "Gender and Moral Luck." In *Identity, Character and Morality: Essays in Moral Psychology*. Edited by Owen Flanagan and Amélie Oksenberg Rorty. Cambridge: MIT Press, 1990.

———, ed. *Feminist Ethics*. Lawrence: University of Kansas Press, 1991.

Chesnut. "Question d'identité. Vice de conformation des organes génitaux-hypospadias-erreur sur le sexe." In *Annales d'hygiène publique et de médecine légale* (1860): 206–09.

Chodorow, Nancy. *The Reproduction of Mothering: Psychoanalysis and the Sociology of Gender*. Berkeley: University of California Press, 1978.

Christian, Barbara. "The Race for Theory." In *Radically Speaking: Feminism Reclaimed*. Edited by Diane Bell and Renate Klein. North Melbourne: Spinifex Press, 1996. Originally published in *Cultural Critique* 6 (Spring 1987): 335–45.

Cole, Eve Browning, and Susan Coultrap-McQuinn, eds. *Explorations in Feminist Ethics*. Indianapolis: Indiana University Press, 1992.

Collins, Patricia Hill. *Black Feminist Thought: Knowledge, Consciousness and the Politics of Empowerment*. New York: Routledge, 1991.

Combahee River Collective. "A Black Feminist Statement." In *This Bridge Called My Back: Writings by Radical Women of Color*. Edited by Cherrie Moraga and Gloria Anzaldua. New York: Kitchen Table Press, 1981.

Cook, Deborah. "Umbrellas, Laundry Bills and Resistance: The Place of Foucault's Interviews in His Corpus." In *The Subject Finds a Voice: Michel Foucault's Subjective Turn*, 97–106. New York: Peter Lang, 1993.

Crow, Barbara A., ed. *Radical Feminism: A Documentary Reader*. New York: New York University Press, 2000.

Dajenya. "We Claim Our Own." In *Bisexual Politics: Theories, Queries and Visions*. Edited by Naomi Tucker. New York: Harrington Park Press, 1995.

Daly, Mary. *Gyn/Ecology: The Meta-ethics of Radical Feminism*. Boston: Beacon Press, 1978.

———. *Pure Lust: Elemental Feminist Philosophy*. Boston: Beacon Press, 1984.

De Lauretis, Teresa. *Technologies of Gender: Essays on Theory, Film and Fiction*. Bloomington: Indiana University Press, 1987.

Deleuze, Gilles. *Foucault*. Translated by Sean Hand. Minneapolis: University of Minnesota Press, 1988.

———. "What Is a *Dispositif* ?" In *Michel Foucault Philosopher*. Edited and translated by Timothy J. Armstrong. New York: Routledge, 1992.

D'Emilio, John. *Sexual Politics, Sexual Communities*. Chicago: University of Chicago Press, 1983.

Dews, Peter. "Power and Subjectivity in Foucault." In *New Left Review* 144 (March–April 1984): 72–95.

———. "The Return of the Subject in the Late Foucault." In *Radical Philosophy* 51 (1989): 37–41.

Diamond, Irene, and Lee Quinby, eds. *Feminism and Foucault: Reflections on Resistance*. Boston: Northeastern University Press, 1988.

Dinnerstein, Dorothy. *The Mermaid and the Minotaur: Sexual Arrangements and Human Malaise*. New York: Harper Colophon Books, 1977.

Diprose, Rosalyn. *The Bodies of Women: Ethics, Embodiment and Sexual Difference*. New York: Routledge, 1994.

Dreger, Alice Domurat. *Hermaphrodites and the Medical Invention of Sex*. Cambridge: Harvard University Press, 1998.

———, ed. *Intersex in the Age of Ethics*. Hagerstown, MD: University Publishing Group, 1999.

Dreifus, Claudia. *Women's Fate: Raps from a Feminist Consciousness-Raising Group*. New York: Bantam Books, 1973.

Dreyfus, Hubert, and Paul Rabinow. *Michel Foucault: Beyond Structuralism and Hermeneutics*. Chicago: University of Chicago Press, 1982.

Dworkin, Andrea. *Pornography: Men Possessing Women*. New York: Perigee Books, 1981.

Eagleton, Terry. *The Ideology of the Aesthetic*. Oxford: Basil Blackwell, 1990.

Echols, Alice. *Daring to be Bad: Radical Feminism in America 1967–1975*. Minneapolis: University of Minnesota Press, 1989.

Ehrenreich, Barbara, and Deirdre English. *For Her Own Good: 150 Years of the Experts' Advice to Women*. New York: Doubleday, 1978.

Epstein, Barbara. "Why Poststructuralism Is a Dead End for Progressive Thought." In *Socialist Review* 25:2 (1995): 83–119.

Eribon, Didier. *Michel Foucault*. Translated by Betsy Wing. Cambridge: Harvard University Press, 1991.

———. *Foucault et ses contemporains*. Paris: Fayard, 1994.

Evans, Sara. *Personal Politics: The Roots of Women's Liberation in the Civil Rights Movement and the New Left*. New York: Vintage Books, 1980.

Ewald, François. "A Power Without an Exterior." In *Michel Foucault Philosopher*. Edited by Timothy J. Armstrong. New York: Routledge, 1992.

Fausto-Sterling, Anne. *Myths of Gender: Biological Theories about Men and Women*. New York: Basic Books, 1992.

———. "The Five Sexes." In *The Sciences* (March/April 1993): 20–24.

———. "The Five Sexes, Revisited." In *The Sciences* (July/August 2000): 18–23.

———. *Sexing the Body: Gender Politics and the Construction of Sexuality*. New York: Basic Books, 2000.

Feinberg, Leslie. *Stone Butch Blues*. Ithaca, NY: Firebrand Books, 1993.

———. *Transgender Warriors: Making History from Joan of Arc to Dennis Rodman*. Boston: Beacon Press, 1996.

Ferguson, Ann. "Patriarchy, Sexual Identity, and the Sexual Revolution." In *Feminist Theory: A Critique of Ideology*. Edited by Nannerl O. Keohane, et al. Chicago: University of Chicago Press, 1982.

———. "Is There a Lesbian Culture?" In *Lesbian Philosophies and Cultures*. Edited by Jeffner Allen. Albany: State University of New York Press, 1990.

Flanagan, Owen, and Amélie Oksenberg Rorty, eds. *Identity, Character and Morality: Essays in Moral Psychology*. Cambridge: MIT Press, 1990.

Flax, Jane. "Beyond Equality: Gender, Justice and Difference." In *Beyond Equality and Difference*. Edited by Gisela Bock and Susan James, 193–210. New York: Routledge, 1992.

———. "Postmodernism and Gender Relations in Feminist Theory." In *Feminism/Postmodernism*. Edited by Linda Nicholson. New York: Routledge, 1990.

Firestone, Shulamith. *The Dialectic of Sex*. New York: Bantam Books, 1970.

Flynn, Thomas. "Foucault as Parrhesiast: His Last Course at the Collège de France." In *The Final Foucault*. Edited by James Bernauer and David Rasmussen. Cambridge: MIT Press, 1988.

Foucault, Michel. *Madness and Civilization: A History of Insanity in the Age of Reason*. Translated by Richard Howard. New York: Random House, 1965. Reprint. New York: Vintage Books, 1988. Originally published unabridged as *Folie et déraison: Histoire de la folie à l'âge classique*. Paris: Plon, 1961.

————. *The Order of Things: An Archaeology of the Human Sciences*. Translated by Alan Sheridan. New York: Pantheon Books, 1971. Originally published as *Les mots et les choses: une archéologie des sciences humaines*. Paris: Gallimard, 1966.

————. *The Archaeology of Knowledge*. Translated by Alan Sheridan. New York: Pantheon, 1972. Originally published as *L'archéologie du savoir*. Paris: Gallimard, 1969.

————. *The Birth of the Clinic*. Translated by Alan Sheridan. New York: Vintage, 1973. Originally published as *Naissance de la clinique: une archéologie du regard médical*. Paris: PUF, 1963.

————. *Discipline and Punish*. Translated by Alan Sheridan. New York: Pantheon, 1977. Reprint. New York: Vintage Books, 1979. Originally published as *Surveiller et punir: naissance de la prison*. Paris: Gallimard, 1975.

————. "Revolutionary Action: 'Until Now.'" In *Language, Counter-Memory and Practice*. Edited by Donald F. Bouchard. Translated by Donald F. Bouchard and Sherry Simon. Ithaca: Cornell University Press, 1977.

————. "Interview with Lucette Finas." In *Michel Foucault: Power, Truth and Strategy*. Edited by Meaghan Morris and Paul Patton. Sydney: Feral Publications, 1979.

————. *Herculine Barbin: Being the Recently Discovered Memoirs of a Nineteenth-Century Hermaphrodite*. Translated by Richard McDougall. New York: Pantheon Books, 1980.

————. *The History of Sexuality: Vol. 1: An Introduction*. Translated by Robert Hurley. New York: Vintage Books, 1980. Originally published as *Histoire de la sexualité, Vol. 1: la Volonté de savoir*. Paris: Gallimard, 1976.

————. *Power/Knowledge: Selected Interviews and Other Writings 1972–1977*. Edited by Colin Gordon. Translated by Colin Gordon et al. New York: Pantheon Books, 1980.

————. "Powers and Strategies." In *Power/Knowledge: Selected Interviews and Other Writings 1972–1977*. Edited by Colin Gordon. Translated by Colin Gordon et al. New York: Pantheon Books, 1980.

————. "Body/Power." In *Power/Knowledge: Selected Interviews and Other Writings 1972–1977*. Edited by Colin Gordon. Translated by Colin Gordon et al. New York: Pantheon Books, 1980.

————. "Confessions of the Flesh." In *Power/Knowledge: Selected Interviews and Other Writings 1972–1977*. Edited by Colin Gordon. Translated by Colin Gordon et al. New York: Pantheon Books, 1980.

———. "Two Lectures." In *Power/Knowledge: Selected Interviews and Other Writings 1972–1977*. Edited by Colin Gordon. Translated by Colin Gordon et al. New York: Pantheon Books, 1980.

———. "The Eye of Power." In *Power/Knowledge: Selected Interviews and Other Writings 1972–1977*. Edited by Colin Gordon. Translated by Colin Gordon et al. New York: Pantheon Books, 1980.

———. Afterword—"On the Genealogy of Ethics: An Overview of Work in Progress." In *Beyond Structuralism and Hermeneutics*, by Hubert L. Dreyfus and Paul Rabinow. Chicago: University of Chicago Press, 1982.

———. Afterword—"The Subject and Power." In *Beyond Structuralism and Hermeneutics*, by Hubert L. Dreyfus and Paul Rabinow. Chicago: University of Chicago Press, 1982.

———. "What Is Enlightenment?" In *The Foucault Reader*. Edited by Paul Rabinow. New York: Pantheon, 1984.

———. "What Is an Author?" In *The Foucault Reade*. Edited by Paul Rabinow. New York: Pantheon, 1984.

———. "Politics and Ethics: An Interview." In *The Foucault Reader*. Edited by Paul Rabinow. New York: Pantheon, 1984.

———. "Polemics, Politics and Problematizations: An Interview with Michel Foucault." In *The Foucault Reader*. Edited by Paul Rabinow. New York: Pantheon Press, 1984.

———. "Truth and Power." In *The Foucault Reader*. Edited by Paul Rabinow. New York: Pantheon, 1984.

———. "Nietzsche, Genealogy, History." In *The Foucault Reader*. Edited by Paul Rabinow. New York: Pantheon Books, 1984.

———. *The History of Sexuality: Vol. 2: The Use of Pleasure*. Translated by Robert Hurley. New York: Pantheon, 1985. Reprint. New York: Vintage Books, 1990. Originally published as *L'usage des plaisirs: histoire de la sexualité, Vol. 2*. Paris: Gallimard, 1984.

———. *The History of Sexuality: Vol. 3: The Care of the Self*. Translated by Robert Hurley. New York: Pantheon, 1986. Originally published as *Le Souci de Soi: Histoire de la Sexualité, Vol. 3*. Paris: Gallimard, 1984.

———. "Final Interview." In *Raritan* 5:2 (1985): 1–13.

———. "Nietzsche, Freud, Marx." In *Critical Texts* 3:2 (1986).

———. "The Ethic of Care for the Self as a Practice of Freedom." Translated by J. D. Gauthier, S.J. In *The Final Foucault*. Edited by James Bernauer and David Rasmussen. Cambridge: MIT Press, 1988.

———. "Technologies of the Self." In *Technologies of the Self: A Seminar with Michel Foucault*. Edited by Luther H. Martin, Huck Gutman, and Patrick Hutton. Amherst: University of Massachusetts Press, 1988.

————. "The Political Technology of Individuals." In *Technologies of the Self: A Seminar with Michel Foucault*. Edited by Luther H. Martin, Huck Gutman, and Patrick Hutton. Amherst: University of Massachusetts Press, 1988.

————. *Foucault Live: Collected Interviews, 1961–1984*. Edited by Sylvere Lotringer. Translated by Lysa Hochroth and John Johnston. New York: Semiotext(e), 1989.

————. "Clarifications on the Question of Power." In *Foucault Live: Collected Interviews, 1961–1984*. Edited by Sylvere Lotringer. Translated by Lysa Hochroth and John Johnston. NewYork: Semiotext(e), 1989.

————. "The Return of Morality." In *Foucault Live: Collected Interviews, 1961–1984*. Edited by Sylvere Lotringer. Translated by Lysa Hochroth and John Johnston. New York: Semiotext(e), 1989.

————. "Intellectuals and Power." In *Foucault Live: Collected Interviews, 1961–1984*. Edited by Sylvere Lotringer. Translated by Lysa Hochroth and John Johnston. New York: Semiotext(e), 1989.

————. "Power Affects the Body." In *Foucault Live: Collected Interviews, 1961–1984*. Edited by Sylvere Lotringer. Translated by Lysa Hochroth and John Johnston. New York: Semiotext(e), 1989.

————. "Governmentality." In *The Foucault Effect: Studies in Governmentality*. Edited by Graham Burchell, Colin Gordon, and Peter Miller. Chicago: University of Chicago Press, 1991.

————. "What Our Present Is." In *The Foucault Effect: Studies in Governmentality*. Edited by Graham Burchell, Colin Gordon, and Peter Miller. Chicago: University of Chicago Press, 1991.

————. "Politics and the Study of Discourse." In *The Foucault Effect: Studies in Governmentality*. Edited by Graham Burchell, Colin Gordon, and Peter Miller. Chicago: University of Chicago Press, 1991.

————. "Subjectivity and Truth." In *The Politics of Truth*. Edited by Sylvere Lotringer and Lysa Hochroth. New York: Semiotext(e), 1997. Originally published in *Political Theory* 21:2 (1993).

————. [Maurice Florence, pseud.], "Foucault, Michel 1926–." In *The Cambridge Companion to Foucault*. Edited by Gary Gutting. Cambridge: Cambridge University Press, 1994.

————. *The Essential Works of Foucault 1954–1984: Vol. 1: Ethics, Subjectivity and Truth*. Edited by Paul Rabinow. New York: New Press, 1997.

————. "Sexual Choice, Sexual Act." In *The Essential Works of Foucault: Vol. 1: Ethics, Subjectivity and Truth*. Edited by Paul Rabinow. New York: New Press, 1997.

————. "Sex, Power and the Politics of Identity." In *The Essential Works of Foucault: Vol. 1: Ethics, Subjectivity and Truth*. Edited by Paul Rabinow. New York: New Press, 1997.

————. "Subjectivity and Truth." In *The Essential Works of Foucault: Vol. 1: Ethics, Subjectivity and Truth*. Edited by Paul Rabinow. New York: New Press, 1997.

————. "Self Writing." In *The Essential Works of Foucault: Vol. 1: Ethics, Subjectivity and Truth*. Edited by Paul Rabinow. New York: New Press, 1997.

————. "The Ethics of the Concern for Self as a Practice of Freedom." In *The Essential Works of Foucault: Vol. 1: Ethics, Subjectivity and Truth*. Edited by Paul Rabinow. New York: New Press, 1997.

————. "Sexuality and Solitude." In *The Essential Works of Foucault: Vol. 1: Ethics, Subjectivity and Truth*. Edited by Paul Rabinow. New York: New Press, 1997.

————. "The Hermeneutic of the Subject." In *The Essential Works of Foucault: Vol. 1: Ethics, Subjectivity and Truth*. Edited by Paul Rabinow. New York: New Press, 1997.

————. "The Masked Philosopher." In *The Essential Works of Foucault: Vol. 1: Ethics, Subjectivity and Truth*. Edited by Paul Rabinow. New York: New Press, 1997.

————. "Social Triumph of the Sexual Will." In *The Essential Works of Foucault: Vol. 1: Ethics, Subjectivity and Truth*. Edited by Paul Rabinow. New York: New Press, 1997.

————. "The Third Thing Is that This Work on the Self." Manuscript. Berkeley Lecture. Paris: Foucault Archives, n.d.

————. "Le gouvernement de soi et des autres." Cours du 12/1/83 et 19/2/83 au Collège de France. Cassette 68 (03). Paris: Foucault Archives.

Fraser, Nancy. "Foucault on Modern Power: Empirical Insights and Normative Confusions." Originally in *Praxis International* 1:23 (October 1981): 272–87.

————. "Foucault's Body Language: A Posthumanist Political Rhetoric?" Originally in *Salmagundi* 61 (Fall 1983): 55–73.

————. "Michel Foucault, A 'Young Conservative?'" Originally in *Ethics* 96:1 (1985): 165–84.

————. *Unruly Practices: Power, Discourse and Gender in Contemporary Social Theory*. Minneapolis: University of Minnesota Press, 1989.

Fraser, Nancy, and Linda Nicholson. "Social Criticism Without Philosophy: An Encounter between Feminism and Postmodernism." In *Feminism/Postmodernism*. Edited by Linda Nicholson. New York: Routledge, 1990.

Freedman, Jill, and Gene Combs. *Narrative Therapy: The Social Construction of Preferred Realities*. New York: W.W. Norton, 1996.

Freeman, Jane, and Marge Piercy. *Getting Together: How to Start a Women's Liberation Group*. Boston: New England Free Press, n.d. In Femina Collection, Northwestern University Library.

Freud, Sigmund. "Three Essays on Sexuality." In *The Complete Psychological Works of Sigmund Freud, Vol. VII*. London: Hogarth Press, 1953.

————. *Introductory Lectures on Psychoanalysis*. Edited and translated by James Strachey. New York: W.W. Norton, 1966.

Frye, Marilyn. "Sexism." In *The Politics of Reality: Essays in Feminist Theory*. New York: Crossing Press, 1983.

———. "To See and Be Seen." In *The Politics of Reality: Essays in Feminist Theory*. New York: Crossing Press, 1983.

———. "Lesbian 'Sex.'" In *Willful Virgin: Essays in Feminism*. Freedom, CA: Crossing Press, 1992.

Fuss, Diana. *Essentially Speaking: Feminisim, Nature and Difference*. New York: Routledge, 1989.

Garber, Marjorie. *Vice Versa: Bisexuality and the Eroticism of Everyday Life*. New York: Simon and Schuster, 1995.

Gatens, Moira. *Imaginary Bodies: Ethics, Power and Corporeality*. New York: Routledge, 1996.

Giddings, Paula. *When and Where I Enter: The Impact of Black Women on Race and Sex in America*. New York: Bantam Books, 1984.

Gilligan, Carol. *In a Different Voice: Psychological Theory and Women's Development*. Cambridge: Harvard University Press, 1982.

Goujon, E. "Étude d'un cas d'hermaphrodisme bisexuel imparfait chez l'homme." In *Journal de l'anatomie et de la physiologie de l'homme (*1869): 599–616.

Griffiths, Morwenna. *Feminisms and the Self: The Web of Identity*. New York: Routledge, 1995.

Grimshaw, Jean. "Practices of Freedom." In *Up Against Foucault: Explorations of Some Tensions between Foucault and Feminism*. Edited by Caroline Ramazanoglu. New York: Routledge, 1993.

Grosz, Elizabeth. *Volatile Bodies: Toward A Corporeal Feminism*. Bloomington: Indiana University Press, 1994.

Gutman, Amy, ed. *Multiculturalism*. Princeton: Princeton University Press, 1994.

Gutting, Gary. "Foucault and the History of Madness." In *The Cambridge Companion to Foucault*. Edited by Gary Gutting. Cambridge: Cambridge University Press, 1994.

———, ed. *The Cambridge Companion to Foucault*. Cambridge: Cambridge University Press, 1994.

Haber, Honi Fern. "Foucault Pumped: Body Politics and the Muscled Woman." In *Feminist Interpretations of Michel Foucault*. Edited by Susan Hekman. University Park: Pennsylvania State University Press, 1996.

Habermas, Jürgen. "Taking Aim at the Heart of the Present." In *Foucault: A Critical Reader*. Edited by David Couzens Hoy. Oxford: Basil Blackwell, 1986.

———. *The Philosophical Discourse of Modernity*. Translated by Frederick G. Lawrence. Cambridge: MIT Press, 1987.

Hacking, Ian. *The Social Construction of What?* Cambridge: Harvard University Press, 1999.

Halperin, David. *One Hundred Years of Homosexuality and Other Essays on Greek Love*. New York: Routledge, 1990.

————. *Saint=Foucault: Towards a Gay Hagiography*. Oxford: Oxford University Press, 1995.

Haraway, Donna. "Situated Knowledges: The Science Question in Feminism and the Privilege of Partial Perspective." In *Feminist Studies* 14:3 (1988): 575–99.

Harding, Sandra. *The Science Question in Feminism*. Ithaca: Cornell University Press, 1986.

Hartmann, Heidi. "The Unhappy Marriage of Marxism and Feminism: Towards a More Progressive Union." In *Feminist Frameworks*. Edited by Alison Jaggar and Paula Rothenberg. New York: McGraw-Hill, 1993.

Hartsock, Nancy. "Foucault on Power: A Theory for Women?" In *Feminism/Postmodernism*. Edited by Linda Nicholson. New York: Routledge, 1990.

————. "Postmodernism and Political Change: Issues for Feminist Theory." In *Feminist Interpretations of Michel Foucault*. Edited by Susan Hekman. University Park: Pennsylvania State University Press, 1996.

————. "Postmodernism and Political Change." In *The Feminist Standpoint Revisited and Other Essays*. Boulder: Westview Press, 1998.

————. *The Feminist Standpoint Revisited and Other Essays*. Boulder: Westview Press, 1998.

————. "The Feminist Standpoint: Developing the Ground for a Specifically Feminist Historical Materialism." In *The Feminist Standpoint Revisited and Other Essays*. Boulder: Westview Press, 1998. Originally in *Discovering Reality: Feminist Perspectives on Epistemology, Metaphysics, Methodology and Philosophy of Science*. Edited by Sandra Harding and Merrill B. Hintikka. Dordrecht, Holland: D. Reidel Publishing, 1983.

Hechter, Michael, and Karl-Deiter Opp. "Introduction." In *Social Norms*. Edited by Michael Hechter and Karl-Deiter Opp. New York: Russell Sage Foundation, 2001.

Hekman, Susan. *Gender and Knowledge: Elements of a Postmodern Feminism*. Boston: Northeastern University Press, 1990.

————, ed. *Feminist Interpretations of Michel Foucault*. University Park: Pennsylvania State University Press, 1996.

Hirsch, Marianne, and Evelyn Fox Keller, eds. *Conflicts in Feminism*. New York: Routledge, 1990.

Hoagland, Sarah Lucia. *Lesbian Ethics: Toward New Value*. Palo Alto, CA: Institute of Lesbian Studies, 1988.

————. "Femininity, Resistance and Sabotage." In *Women and Values: Readings in Recent Feminist Philosophy*. Edited by Marilyn Pearsall. Belmont, CA: Wadsworth Publishing Co., 1993.

Hochschild, Arlie Russell. *The Managed Heart: The Commercialization of Human Feeling*. Berkeley: University of California Press, 1983.

Hoy, David Couzens, ed. *Foucault: A Critical Reader*. Oxford: Basil Blackwell, 1986.

Hunt, Lynn. "Foucault's Subject in the History of Sexuality." In *Discourses of Sexuality: From Aristotle to AIDS*. Edited by Domna C. Stanton. Ann Arbor: University of Michigan Press, 1992.

Hutchins, Loraine, and Lani Ka'ahumanu, eds. *Bi Any Other Name: Bisexual People Speak Out*. Boston: Alyson Publications, 1991.

Jaggar, Alison. "Feminist Ethics: Projects, Problems, Prospects." In *Feminist Ethics*. Edited by Claudia Card. Lawrence: University of Kansas Press, 1991.

Jaggar, Alison, and Susan Bordo, eds. *Gender/Body/Knowledge: Feminist Reconstructions of Being and Knowing*. New Brunswick: Rutgers University Press, 1989.

Jaggar, Alison, and Paula Rothenberg, eds. *Feminist Frameworks*. New York: McGraw-Hill, 1993.

Ka'ahumanu, Lani. "It Ain't Over 'Til the Bisexual Speaks." In *Bisexual Politics: Theories, Queries and Visions*. Edited by Naomi Tucker. New York: Harrington Park Press, 1995.

Kaplan, Rebecca. "Your Fence Is Sitting on Me: The Hazards of Binary Thinking." In *Bisexual Politics: Theories, Queries and Visions*. Edited by Naomi Tucker. New York: Harrington Park Press, 1995.

Katz, Jonathan. *The Invention of Heterosexuality*. New York: Penguin Books, 1995.

Kelly, Michael, ed. *Critique and Power: Recasting the Foucault/Habermas Debate*. Cambridge: MIT Press, 1994.

Keohane, Nannerl O. et al., eds. *Feminist Theory: A Critique of Ideology*. Chicago: University of Chicago Press, 1982.

Kerber, Linda. "Some Cautionary Words for Historians." In *An Ethic of Care: Feminist and Interdisciplinary Perspectives*. Edited by Mary Jeanne Larrabee. New York: Routledge, 1993.

Kittay, Eva Feder, and Diana T. Meyers, eds. *Women and Moral Theory*. Totowa, NJ: Rowman and Littlefield Publishers, 1987.

Koedt, Anne, Ellen Levine, and Anita Rapone, eds. *Radical Feminism*. New York: Quadrangle Press, 1973.

Koedt, Anne. "The Myth of the Vaginal Orgasm." In *Radical Feminism: A Documentary Reader*. Edited by Barbara A. Crow. New York: New York University Press, 2000.

L.A. NOW C-R Committee. "Consciousness-Raising Handbook" (Los Angeles: L.A. NOW C-R Committee, 1974). Pamphlet in Femina Collection. Northwestern University Library.

Larrabee, Mary Jeanne, ed. *An Ethic of Care: Feminist and Interdisciplinary Perspectives*. New York: Routledge, 1993.

Levin, David Michael. "The Body Politic: The Embodiment of Praxis in Foucault and Habermas." *Praxis International* 9:1/2 (1989).

Lloyd, Genevieve. *Man of Reason*. London: Methuen, 1984.

MacKinnon, Catherine. *Feminism Unmodified: Discourses on Life and the Law*. Cambridge: Harvard University Press, 1977.

——. "Feminism, Marxism, Method and the State: Toward Feminist Jurisprudence." *Signs: Journal of Women in Culture and Society* 8:4 (1983): 635–58.

Martin, Emily. *The Woman in the Body: A Cultural Analysis of Reproduction*. Boston: Beacon Press, 1989.

Martin, Luther H., Huck Gutman, and Patrick Hutton, eds. *Technologies of the Self: A Seminar with Michel Foucault*. Amherst: University of Massachusetts Press, 1988.

May, Todd. *Between Genealogy and Epistemology: Psychology, Politics, and Knowledge in the Thought of Michel Foucault*. University Park: Pennsylvania State University Press, 1993.

McLaren, Margaret. "Foucault and the Subject of Feminism." *Social Theory and Practice* 23:1 (1997): 109–28.

McNay, Lois. "The Foucauldian Body and the Exclusion of Experience." *Hypatia* 6 (1991): 125–37.

——. *Foucault & Feminism: Power, Gender and the Self*. Boston: Northeastern University Press, 1993.

McWhorter, Ladelle. *Bodies & Pleasures: Foucault and the Politics of Sexual Normalization*. Bloomington: Indiana University Press, 1999.

Meyers, Diana T. "The Socialized Individual and Individual Autonomy: An Intersection between Philosophy and Psychology." In *Women and Moral Theory*. Edited by Eva Feder Kittay and Diana T. Meyers. Totowa, NJ: Rowman & Littlefield Publishers, 1987.

——. *Subjection and Subjectivity: Psychoanalytic Feminism and Moral Philosophy*. New York: Routledge, 1994.

Minson, Jeffrey. *Genealogies of Morals: Nietzsche, Foucault, Donzelot and the Eccentricity of Ethics*. New York: St. Martin's Press, 1985.

Moi, Toril. "Power, Sex and Subjectivity: Feminist Reflections on Foucault." *Paragraph: The Journal of the Modern Critical Theory Group* 5 (1985): 95–102.

Moraga, Cherrie, and Gloria Anzaldua, eds. *This Bridge Called My Back: Writings by Radical Women of Color*. New York: Kitchen Table Press, 1981.

Morgan, Kathryn Pauly. "Women and the Knife: Cosmetic Surgery and the Colonization of Women's Bodies." *Hypatia* 6:3 (1991).

Morgan, Robin, ed. *Sisterhood Is Powerful: An Anthology of Writings from the Women's Liberation Movement*. New York: Vintage Books, 1970.

Morris, Meaghan, and Paul Patton, eds. *Michel Foucault: Power, Truth and Strategy*. Sydney: Feral Publications, 1979.

Morris, Meaghan. "The Pirate's Fiancée: Feminists and Philosophers, or Maybe Tonight It'll Happen." In *Feminism and Foucault: Reflections on Resistance*. Edited by Irene Diamond and Lee Quinby. Boston: Northeastern University Press, 1988.

Nichols, Michael P., and Richard C. Schwartz. *Family Therapy: Concepts and Methods.* Needham Hts., MA: Allyn and Bacon, 1998.

Nicholson, Linda, ed. *Feminism/Postmodernism.* New York: Routledge, 1990.

Nietzsche, Friedrich. *The Gay Science.* Translated by Walter Kaufmann. New York: Vintage Books, 1974.

Nussbaum, Martha C. "The Professor of Parody: The Hip Defeatism of Judith Butler." *New Republic* (February 1999): 37–45.

Okin, Susan Moller. *Justice, Gender and the Family.* New York: Basic Books, 1989.

Panizza, Oscar. "A Scandal at the Convent." In Michel Foucault, *Herculine Barbin: Being the Recently Discovered Memoirs of a Nineteenth-Century Hermaphrodite.* Translated by Richard McDougall. New York: Pantheon Books, 1980.

Pateman, Carole, and Elizabeth Gross, eds. *Feminist Challenges: Social and Political Theory.* Boston: Northeastern University Press, 1987.

Pearsall, Marilyn, ed. *Women and Values: Readings in Recent Feminist Philosophy.* Belmont, CA: Wadsworth Publishing, 1993.

Perl, Harriett, and Gay Abarbanell. *Guidelines to Feminist Consciousness-Raising.* Pamphlet self published, 1979. In Femina Collection, Northwestern University.

Pharr, Suzanne. *Homophobia: A Weapon of Sexism.* Little Rock, AR: Chardon Press, 1988.

Phelan, Shane. *Identity Politics: Lesbian Feminism and the Limits of Community.* Philadelphia: Temple University Press, 1989.

Porter, Elizabeth J. *Women and Moral Identity.* North Sydney: Allen and Unwin, 1991.

Puka, Bill. "The Liberation of Caring: A Different Voice for Gilligan's 'Different Voice.'" In *An Ethic of Care: Feminist and Interdisciplinary Perspectives.* Edited by Mary Jeanne Larrabee. New York: Routledge, 1993.

Queen, Carol A. "The Queer in Me." In *Bi Any Other Name: Bisexual People Speak Out.* Edited by Loraine Hutchins and Lani Ka'ahumanu. Boston: Alyson Publications, 1991.

Ramazanoglu, Caroline, ed. *Up Against Foucault: Explorations of Some Tensions Between Foucault and Feminism.* New York: Routledge, 1993.

Redstockings. "Redstockings Manifesto." In *Sisterhood Is Powerful: An Anthology of Writings from the Women's Liberation Movement.* Edited by Robin Morgan. New York: Vintage Books, 1970.

Reed, Evelyn. "Women: Caste, Class or Oppressed Sex?" In *Feminist Frameworks.* Edited by Alison Jaggar and Paula Rothenberg. New York: McGraw-Hill, 1993.

Rich, Adrienne. *On Lies, Secrets and Silence: Selected Prose, 1966–1978.* New York: W.W. Norton, 1979.

———. "Compulsory Heterosexuality and Lesbian Existence." In *The Signs Reader.* Edited by Elizabeth Abel and Emily K. Abel, 139–68. Chicago: University of Chicago Press, 1983.

Riley, Denise. *"Am I That Name?" Feminism and the Category of 'Women' in History*. Minneapolis: University of Minnesota Press, 1988.

Rorty, Richard. "Foucault and Epistemology." In *Foucault: A Critical Reader*. Edited by David Couzens Hoy. Oxford: Basil Blackwell, 1986.

Sawicki, Jana. *Disciplining Foucault: Feminism, Power and the Body*. New York: Routledge, 1991.

————. "Feminism, Foucault, and 'Subjects' of Power and Freedom." In *Feminist Interpretations of Michel Foucault*. Edited by Susan Hekman. University Park: Pennsylvania State University Press, 1996.

Scott, Joan W. "Deconstructing Equality-versus-Difference: Or, the Uses of Poststructuralist Theory for Feminism." In *Conflicts in Feminism*. Edited by Marianne Hirsch and Evelyn Fox Keller. New York: Routledge, 1990.

Seidman, Steven. "Identity and Politics in a 'Postmodern' Gay Culture: Some Historical and Conceptual Notes." In *Fear of a Queer Planet: Queer Politics and Social Theory*. Edited by Michael Warner. Minneapolis: University of Minnesota Press, 1993.

Shanley, Mary Lyndon, and Carole Pateman, eds. *Feminist Interpretations and Political Theory*. University Park: Pennsylvania State University Press, 1991.

Silverman, Hugh J., ed. *Writing the Politics of Difference*. Albany: State University of New York Press, 1991.

Soper, Kate. "Productive Contradictions." In *Up Against Foucault: Explorations of Some Tensions between Foucault and Feminism*. Edited by Caroline Ramazanoglu. New York: Routledge, 1993.

Spelman, Elizabeth. "Woman as Body: Ancient and Contemporary Views." In *Feminist Studies* 8:1 (1982).

————. *Inessential Woman: Problems of Exclusion in Feminist Thought*. Boston: Beacon Press, 1988.

Spender, Dale. *Man Made Language*. Boston: Routledge and Kegan Paul, 1980.

Stack, Carol. "The Culture of Gender: Women and Men of Color." In *An Ethic of Care: Feminist and Interdisciplinary Perspectives*. Edited by Mary Jeanne Larrabee. New York: Routledge, 1993.

Stanton, Domna C., ed. *Discourses of Sexuality: From Aristotle to AIDS*. Ann Arbor: University of Michigan Press, 1992.

Tardieu, A. "Mémoire sur la question médico-légale de l'identité." *Annales d'hygiène publique et de médecine légale*. (1872): 149–69 and 384–408.

Taylor, Charles. "Foucault on Freedom and Truth." In *Foucault: A Critical Reader*. Edited by David Couzens Hoy. Oxford: Basil Blackwell, 1986.

————. *Sources of the Self: The Making of Modern Identity*. Cambridge: Harvard University Press, 1989.

————. "The Politics of Recognition." In *Multiculturalism*. Edited by Amy Gutman. Princeton: Princeton University Press, 1994.

Tong, Rosemary. *Feminist Thought: A Comprehensive Introduction*. Boulder: Westview Press, 1989.

Tucker, Naomi, ed. *Bisexual Politics: Theories, Queries and Visions*. New York: Harrington Park Press, 1995.

Visker, Rudi. "Can Genealogy Be Critical? A Somewhat Unromantic Look at Nietzsche and Foucault." *Man and World* 23 (1990): 441–52.

————. "From Foucault to Heidegger: A One Way Ticket?" *Research in Phenomenology* XXI (1991): 116–40.

Walzer, Michael. "Foucault on Freedom and Truth." In *Foucault: A Critical Reader*. Edited by David Couzens Hoy. Oxford: Basil Blackwell, 1986.

Warner, Michael. "Introduction." In *Fear of a Queer Planet: Queer Politics and Social Theory*. Edited by Michael Warner. Minneapolis: University of Minnesota Press, 1993.

Weedon, Chris. *Feminist Practice & Poststructuralist Theory*. Oxford: Blackwell, 1987.

Weise, Elizabeth Reba, ed. *Closer to Home: Bisexuality and Feminism*. Seattle: Seal Press, 1992.

Weiss, Gail. *Body Images: Embodiment as Intercorporeality*. New York: Routledge, 1999.

Welton, Donn, ed. *The Body*. Oxford: Blackwell Publishers, 1999.

Wilchins, Riki Anne. *Read My Lips: Sexual Subversion and the End of Gender*. Ithaca, NY: Firebrand Books, 1997.

Young, Iris Marion. "Socialist Feminism and the Limits of Dual System s Theory." *Socialist Review* 50–51 (1980): 169–88.

————. "Throwing Like a Girl: A Phenomenology of Feminine Bodily Comportment, Motility and Spatiality." In *Throwing Like a Girl and Other Essays in Feminist Philosophy and Social Theory*. Bloomington: Indiana University Press, 1990. Originally in *Human Studies* 3 (1980): 137–56.

INDEX